Acclaim for *Optimal Th...*

Optimal Thinking

How to Be Your Best Self

Rosalene Glickman, Ph.D.

An Imprint of

Manjul Books Pvt. Ltd.

In memory of my beloved parents,
Sarah and Joe Glickman.
Thank you for your unconditional love and support.

First published in India by Anthem,
An imprint of:

Manjul Books Pvt. Ltd.
10, Nishat Colony, Bhopal - 462 003 INDIA
Phone : 91-755-5240340, Fax : 91-755-2736919
E-mail : manjul@manjulindia.com
Website : www.manjulindia.com

First published - 2005

This publication is designed to provide accurate and authoritative
information in regard to the subject matter covered. It is sold with the
understanding that the publisher is not engaged in rendering professional
services. If professional advice or other expert assistance is required, the
services of a competent professional person should be sought.

Cover design by Manjul Creative Team

ISBN - 81 - 89631 - 00 - 4

Printed & bound in India by
Gopsons Papers Ltd., Noida, INDIA

Contents

Acknowledgments

It is my greatest pleasure to acknowledge my agent, Lynn Franklin, for her commitment and professionalism. The first time I spoke with Lynn, I knew she was the right person to represent Optimal Thinking. She has validated that decision all along the way!

When I met Tom Miller at Wiley, I felt privileged to have the ear of the consummate professional. Thank you Tom for pinpointing the issues and leading me in the right direction.

Howard Baller, thank you for everything.

My dear friend Halina Margan has lovingly supported me through life's challenges for thirty years. Thank you Halina.

To Marvin Wolf, my mentor and friend, thank you for your personal and professional guidance.

Bill Hughes deserves the highest praise for cutting through to the heart of issues and for his timely support during the toughest times.

I am also most appreciative of the encouragement and feedback I have received from Daniall and Julie Wong, Patricia Rust, and Eilleen Steinberg.

To Fred Plotke, Iris Weithorn, MFT, Howard Baller, Ph.D., Halina Margan, Ph.D., Elliot Goldstein, and James Buckley, thank you for your contributions to the manuscript.

My corporate clients, seminar participants, and personal clients deserve my gratitude. Without you, Optimal Thinking would not have been tried, tested, and proven.

Optimal Principles

Every thought is creative.

Make the choice to be your highest and best self,
regardless of the circumstances.

The language of your highest and best self is
Optimal Thinking.

Accept what is out of your control, and optimize what
is within your control.

Ask the best questions to invite the best answers.

Choose the best, then put the issue to rest.

Optimal thinking is the basis of Optimal results
(sense of completion).

Function at your peak by thinking Optimally.

Create your best life with Optimal Thinking.

PART ONE

Help Yourself to Optimal Thinking

"The highest first."
—Maharishi Mahesh Yogi

Rate Your Level of Thinking

The following questionnaire will help you identify your dominant level of thinking. You may choose to write your answers in the book itself. If you'd rather write your answers on a separate piece of paper, this may be the perfect time to start your Optimal Journal. You might like to view this book and your journal entries as a private conversation between you and me. As you read through *Optimal Thinking*, you will optimize your thinking and behavior. You can record your Optimal Action Steps, design your best life, and monitor your progress in your Optimal Journal.

For each statement below, circle the number that best describes your thoughts about yourself, about others, and about your current situation. Then add your score.

3 = *Always*   1 = *Reasonably or sometimes*

2 = *Usually or often*   0 = *Rarely or never*

1. I am responsible for making the most of my life.	0	1	2	3
2. I am in control of my life.	0	1	2	3
3. I like myself.	0	1	2	3
4. I get along well with people.	0	1	2	3
5. I deserve to have what I want.	0	1	2	3
6. I deserve the best in life.	0	1	2	3
7. I can have the best in life.	0	1	2	3
8. I am comfortable with success.	0	1	2	3
9. I view failure as a learning opportunity.	0	1	2	3
10. I accept what is out of my control, and optimize what is in my control.	0	1	2	3
11. I can handle rejection.	0	1	2	3
12. I can handle pain.	0	1	2	3
13. I am happy to be alive.	0	1	2	3
14. I do my best. I give life my best shot.	0	1	2	3
15. I embrace negativity as a natural part of life.	0	1	2	3
16. I have realistic expectations of myself, of others, and of life.	0	1	2	3
17. I bring out the best in others.	0	1	2	3

18. I handle conflict effectively.   0 1 2 3
19. I accomplish my most important goals.   0 1 2 3
20. I am comfortable with all my feelings.   0 1 2 3
21. I am happy about my career prospects.   0 1 2 3
22. My financial situation satisfies my needs.   0 1 2 3
23. I consider the worst event scenario and the best contingency plan when evaluating risks.   0 1 2 3
24. I make the most of whatever crosses my path.   0 1 2 3
25. I am where I need to be in my life right now.   0 1 2 3

If your score is 70–75, you are already using Optimal Thinking consistently. This book will validate your thinking and provide you with many new ways to optimize your thinking and your life.

If your score is 46–70, your thinking is extraordinary, but not in your best interest. Optimal Thinking will empower you to maximize your talents, resources, and time. You will acquire the mental software to be your best in every situation.

If your score is 16–45, your dominant thinking level is mediocre. You think in moderate, middle-of-the-road terms. With Optimal Thinking, you will gain the mental tool to support your best interests. You will then be equipped to make the wisest choices in every situation, and make the most of your life.

If your score is 0–15, your dominant thinking level is negative. You are probably feeling distressed right now and may be wondering if it is possible to get your life on track. I often see people like you in my practice. I want to assure you that this book will provide you with the mental tool to be your best and empower you to create your best life. Optimal Thinking is simple, immediately applicable, and does not require a leap of faith. You are on the right path.

CHAPTER 1

Optimal Thinking: The Next Step Beyond Positive Thinking

Do you enjoy the best life has to offer or are you stuck with a life of compromise and substitutes?

Optimal Thinking is for all who want to be their best and enjoy the best in life. If you are willing to optimize your life by making the most of your thinking, Optimal Thinking is for you!

Many people would love to experience the ultimate relationship but find themselves settling for second best. Some people want to make the most of their professional lives, but are making only limited progress. They dream of all the rewards of financial success, yet are restricted by tight budgets. Others are overworked, trapped in the wrong jobs, and unfulfilled at home.

Optimal Thinking is not just another self-improvement book. It is your definitive guide for self-optimization—a quantum leap! This book does not make assumptions about what is important to you, but instead offers an approach to empower you to discover your highest priorities and create your own best solutions. You'll learn how to ask yourself and others the best questions to make the most of everyday situations. You'll learn a style of thinking that provides the best chance of creating anything and everything you will ever want.

So where do we start? Let's explore the various levels of sub-optimal thinking and then compare the results with those you can experience with Optimal Thinking.

Suboptimal Thinking

You have, I'm sure, practiced a wide variety of thinking before you decided to read this book. You may have noticed that your thinking is not always in your own best interest. Are you aware of your current thought mix? How much do you identify with the following thinking styles?

Negative Thinking

Do you sometimes find yourself thinking negatively about yourself, about others, or about circumstances? Is your focus on what's wrong, on limitations, or on destructive viewpoints? Although negative thinking is often detrimental and scorned by many in society today, *it is valuable*. Negative thinking enables us to define and express our vulnerability, integrate trauma, and grieve the meaningful losses in our lives. It also warns us of imminent danger. Negative thinking cautions us against investing our hard-earned money in fraudulent get-rich-quick schemes, or against diving into deep water when we don't know how to swim. It is necessary in any design process to anticipate flaws in products, services, and projects so that they can be rectified.

We all think negatively from time to time. Do you experience worry, depression, or blame? Do you complain, criticize, or use words like "can't" and "won't"? Are you ever unreasonable? Do you direct your anger at people who have nothing to do with its cause or solution? Negative thinking can be very *destructive*. Negative thinkers often waste valuable ideas and opportunities for success by dwelling on why things can't be done. They anticipate failure in their endeavors and use their losses to validate their pessimistic perspective. They see life as a series of problems, focus on what they don't have, and are usually unhappy.

All of us experience varying degrees of negativity. Sometimes we have a few doubts about the workability of a situation, while at other times we are convinced that it *can't* work—under any circumstances. When we believe that what we want is unattainable or that whatever we do won't make any difference, we feel helpless. Here are some examples:

Craig, a real estate agent, has been divorced twice. During each marriage he created havoc because he couldn't control his temper. Now, lonely and disillusioned, he is afraid of intimacy and sabotages relationships with women. He doesn't believe that he can make a committed relationship work.

Miles sold his chiropractic practice after he broke his arm. He then invested in several unsuccessful business ventures where he was misguided and defrauded. He now feels hopeless, and believes that the grass will turn brown even where he waters it.

Some people have a slightly negative disposition whereas others are extraordinarily negative. How much of *your* time is spent thinking negatively? _____%

Positive Thinking

Are you a positive thinker? Are you confident and self-assured? Is your thinking constructive and productive? When evaluating a situation, do you focus on the bright side? Do you think in terms of victory and success? Positive thinkers see themselves as good, loving, productive, competent, and worthy of life's favorable offerings. They concentrate on the value in themselves, in others, and in the world. They focus on how things *can* be done—and make them happen. They approach life with a "can do" and "will do" attitude, believing that the grass will turn green where they water it.

Consider Heather, a positive thinker. As an aspiring actress in her early forties, Heather believed that her age would help rather than hinder her. She took acting lessons from well-regarded teachers and zealously refined her craft. She approached each day enthusiastically and auditioned for roles whenever she could. For Heather, each audition provided an opportunity to display her talent. Believing that success would soon be hers, she persisted through numerous temporary setbacks and developed confidence as an actress. One day she was offered an important role in a high-budget film. She excelled in that role and went on to become a successful actress.

We all know that positive thinking can motivate us to be productive, efficient, and successful. But there are varying shades of positive thinking. Let's examine some of them.

Mediocre Thinking

You may be a positive thinker, yet your thinking could, in fact, be mediocre. Do you think you're quite good at your job? Are you a pretty good family person, friend, or athlete? Is your thinking rarely unusual? Do you feel comfortable being one of the crowd? American business writer Lou Vickery believes: "Nothing average ever stood as a monument to progress. When progress is looking for a partner it doesn't turn to those who believe that they are only average. It turns instead to those who are forever searching and striving to become the best they possibly can. If we seek the average level, we cannot hope to achieve a higher level of success. Our only hope is to avoid being a failure."

Here is a typical example of such a mediocre thinker:

Mary, a good-hearted woman, owns a modest home, drives an ordinary car, and lives a reasonably comfortable life. She doesn't aspire to the best things in life because she doesn't believe she could ever have them. Although she has some worthwhile goals, she is not excited about achieving them. She gets along quite well with others because she avoids conflict and does not make waves. Mary's mediocre thinking began early in life because, sadly, her parents constantly denigrated her intellect, behavior, and aspirations. She was continually told that she couldn't have what she wanted and that she must compromise. To this day Mary avoids taking actions that might evoke disapproval from others. Having settled for second best all her life, at forty-four she has not overcome her early restrictive conditioning.

Are you a mediocre thinker? When people ask you how you are, do you automatically respond with "not bad," "okay," or "pretty good"? Many people are in the habit of responding in mediocre terms instead of considering their options and figuring out a reply that is in their best interest. Best-selling author Stephen Covey suggests: "You have to decide what your highest priorities are and have the courage—pleasantly, smilingly, non-apologetically—to say 'no' to other things. And the way you do that is by having a bigger 'yes' burning inside. The enemy of the 'best' is often the 'good.'"

Mediocre thinkers are regular people who feel comfortable being considered average in their thinking and actions. Their style of thinking is generally moderate and conservative. American actor and critic Uta Hagen believes: "We must overcome the notion that we must be regular. It robs us of the chance to be extraordinary and leads us to the mediocre."

Most people are committed to this middle-of-the-road form of thinking. Others simply tinker with it. How much of your time do you devote to mediocre thinking? _____%

Extraordinary Thinking

Does extraordinary thinking describe you? Do you think in terms of being more than ordinary, unusually great, exceptional? Do you prefer to think beyond the realms of mediocrity? Do you like to challenge the limited thinking of most people? Do words like "remarkable," "brilliant," "outstanding," "great," and "high achiever" describe you?

Extraordinary thinkers achieve exceptional results in all walks of life because they don't settle for the ordinary. Former NASA astronaut Dr. Mae Jemison was the first African American woman to venture into space. She admits: "My mission is to make unique contributions." Well-known real estate developer Donald Trump claims: "As long as you're going to be thinking anyway, think big." According to former Soviet and Russian political leader Boris Yeltsin, "It is especially important to encourage unorthodox thinking when the situation is critical: At such moments every new word and fresh thought is more precious than gold."

By listening carefully, you can identify extraordinary thinkers. Recently the chief executive officer of a large and successful oil corporation came to my office for a business consultation. His response to the question "What is the primary purpose of your company?" was "to create *exceptionally high* returns for our shareholders" as part of his overall statement. He was an extraordinary thinker.

Many extraordinary thinkers refuse to give in to seemingly insurmountable limitations and obstacles. Thomas Edison invented the electric lightbulb when everyone believed it wasn't possible. He succeeded after ten thousand attempts. When the world believed it couldn't be done, Roger Bannister ran the mile in four minutes. We don't know exactly how these people achieved their successes, but we do know that they courageously challenged and surpassed the conventional thinking of their time. Their extraordinary thinking may or may not have produced the best possible outcome, but it certainly provided the mental foundation for exceptional results.

Does this describe you? How much of your time is invested in extraordinary thinking? _____ %

By now, you are probably wondering how positive thinking differs from Optimal Thinking. Read on to learn that when you compare the levels of positive thinking—even extraordinary thinking—to Optimal Thinking, positive thinking is suboptimal!

What Is Optimal Thinking?

"Wisdom denotes the pursuit of the best ends by the best means."
—Francis Hutcheson

Have any of these thoughts ever crossed your mind?

- I deserve the best in life.
- How can I make the most of this situation?

- What's the best solution?
- I'm taking the smartest actions toward my most important goal.
- I'm doing my best.
- I'm maximizing my options.
- What's the most constructive use of my time right now?

If you entertain such thoughts, please welcome yourself into the Optimal Thinking community.

Optimal Thinking is the language of your highest self. It empowers you to be your best and stops you from settling for second best. With Optimal Thinking, your highest self takes charge. You focus on the best or most constructive thought at all times. You choose your best option in any given moment and experience the results of your own best thoughts. When thinking Optimally, you are not concerned with others' concepts of "the best." You are not in competition with anyone. You are concerned with what "the best" means to you and you attach your own value to it. Of course, "the best" has a different meaning for each of us. When considering the purchase of a gift for a loved one or coworker, one Optimal Thinker may think that the best choice is the highest quality available, and isn't concerned with price. Another may choose the gift that offers the most value relative to price.

When you use this superlative form of thinking, you are aligned with your highest level of creativity—and creation. You can choose the best actions to accomplish what's most important to you. You automatically use words like "best," "wisest," "greatest," "most productive," "supreme," and "maximize." Here is the quantum leap!

Suboptimal Positive Thinking	Optimal Thinking
good, better	best
great	greatest
high, higher	highest, peak, top
smart, smarter	smartest
important	most important
enjoyable	most enjoyable
profitable	most profitable
effective	most effective
improve, manage, increase	maximize, optimize, make the most of
outstanding	most outstanding

You can employ Optimal Thinking to instantly make the most of your life by asking questions like:

- What is most important to me?
- What's my major objective?
- Which resources will be most beneficial in helping me to achieve it?
- What are my greatest talents and abilities?
- How can I make the best use of them?
- What is the most constructive action I can take right now?
- Who are the right people with whom to share my goals and dreams?
- How can I optimize my gratitude for life?

With Optimal Thinking, you can also bring out the best in others. Just focus on the best ways to help them achieve what's most important to them. In Optimal interactions, when someone is off track, ask the "best" questions to help them find the best resolution. For example:

- What's the best way to handle this?
- What's the best solution?
- What's your highest priority right now?
- What's the best opportunity you can act upon right now?

If you run a business, you can maximize its success using Optimal Thinking. You will need to define your business in terms of its strengths, weaknesses, opportunities, threats, values, objectives, and plans by answering Optimal questions like:

- What are the greatest strengths of this company?
- Who are our most valuable employees?
- Who are our best customers?
- What are their most important needs?
- What are our most beneficial products/services?
- What are our most profitable products/services?
- How can we make the most of these strengths?
- What are our greatest weaknesses?
- What's the best way to minimize them?

Who Thinks Optimally?

We are all Optimal Thinkers. Some of us use Optimal Thinking from time to time, others use it more frequently, but most of us don't use it consistently. Until now, this peak form of thinking has not been acknowledged or structured. That's why I coined the term Optimal Thinking. We all know that green is a color that is seen frequently in nature. Once we know that green is created when blue and yellow are combined, it's easy to reproduce it consistently. Similarly, once we identify Optimal Thinking as a specific form of thinking and understand its structure, we can use it consistently.

What's most exciting about Optimal Thinking is that you can use it at any time and in any place. You don't have to be a rocket scientist to be an Optimal Thinker. It doesn't matter what stage of life you are in, or in what circumstance you find yourself. You can use Optimal Thinking to *instantly make the most of your life*.

Consider Brian and Lynn, both physicians and Optimal Thinkers, who have been happily married for twenty years. When asked about the success of their relationship, Lynn said, "We take complete responsibility for our own feelings and behavior, and do our best to make the relationship the best it can be. Our favorite phrases are, 'What's our highest priority? What is best for both of us?'" Brian explained, "Whenever we have an argument, we embrace the present moment, observe our inner reactions, and explore what we are doing to cause them. We then figure out the best solution for both of us."

Optimal Thinking can be used to make the most of any situation. A perfect example is Gerry, a football player and Optimal Thinker, who was suffering from a severe knee injury. His doctor told him that he would risk further injury if he didn't take sufficient time to recover. To make the right decision, Gerry asked himself the following Optimal questions: "What's in my best interest? What's best for the team? What's the best solution?"

When the chief executive officer of a leading telecommunications company described the primary purpose of his company, he said: "To *maximize* returns to our shareholders." I knew he was an Optimal Thinker.

Do You Recognize These Optimal Thinkers?

History books are crammed with Optimal Thinkers from every walk of life. Albert Einstein encouraged us to live according to an Optimal standard. He said: "We have to do the best we can. This is our sacred human responsibility." American industrialist Harvey Samuel Firestone held an Optimal human relations perspective. He believed: "You get the best out of others when you give the best of yourself." Jordan's King Hussein I understood his highest priorities. He wrote: "Above all, I believe in God. I believe also, that I must live with myself. I must be able to face myself each morning and say: 'I did my best yesterday. I will do my best again today.'" Benjamin Franklin put Optimal Thinking to work when he said, "An investment in knowledge pays the best interest." And after eight years of unprecedented economic expansion in the United States, Federal Reserve chairman Alan Greenspan restated his main objective, "to achieve maximum sustainable economic growth."

Optimal Thinkers are everywhere. Below is a selection of Optimal Thinking from well-known people and businesses.

American Political Leaders

"In any moment of decision, the best thing you can do is the right thing. The worst thing you can do is nothing."
—*Theodore Roosevelt*

"I come to the office each morning and stay for long hours doing what has to be done to the best of my ability. And when you've done the best you can you can't do any better."
—*Harry S. Truman*

"To those people in the huts and villages of half the globe struggling to break the bonds of mass misery, we pledge our best efforts to help them help themselves, for whatever period is required."
—*John F. Kennedy*

"I will do my best. That is all I can do. I ask for your help—and God's." —*Lyndon B. Johnson*

"Never be satisfied with less than your very best effort. If you strive for the top and miss, you'll still 'beat the pack.'" —*Gerald Ford*

"I am not a perfect servant. I am a public servant doing my best against the odds. As I develop and serve, be patient. God is not finished with me yet." —*Jesse Louis Jackson*

Performers and Sports People

"Living your best life is your most important journey in life."

"Doing the best at this moment puts you in the best place for the next moment." —*Oprah Winfrey*

"A problem is a chance for you to do your best." —*Duke Ellington*

"Things turn out best for the people who make the best out of the way things turn out." —*Art Linkletter*

"Go in there and do the best you can. That's all you can do."
—*Tiger Woods*

"When she (my mother) passed away, I kind of understood the commitment that she made to make sure that I could stay in skating. And I wanted to live up to whatever I could. Not so much win everything, but just to be the best that I could possibly be, to honor her memory and everything she went through to make sure that I was given the opportunities to be the best that I can be. Not to be a world champion or an Olympic gold medalist, but to be the best that I could be. And that was the most important thing that ever happened in my career."   —*Scott Hamilton*

Corporations

Many well-known companies use Optimal slogans to publicize Optimal standards.

Air New Zealand—The world's warmest welcome

Amazon.com—Earth's biggest selection

Barclays Bank—The best bankers in business

BMW—The ultimate driving machine

CNBC—The world leader in business news

Gillette—The best a man can get

Kelloggs—The simple things in life are often the best

Sharp—Simply the best

Do you think like this? If so, how much of your time is invested in Optimal Thinking?_____%

Take the Quantum Leap!

"We are shaped by our thoughts. We become what we think."
—**Buddha**

One of the most exciting aspects of Optimal Thinking is that at this very moment and at any time in the future, you can optimize your thinking. Just as you can choose to think suboptimally—positively or negatively—you can choose to think Optimally. You can easily take the quantum leap!

Imagine you agree to meet a friend for dinner at an average restaurant. Your choice of dress is mediocre. The restaurant is moderately attractive and the chairs are reasonably comfortable. The food is somewhat ordinary, nothing to write home about. The background music is okay. Your friend is basically a suboptimal thinker. She talks about her husband for most of the evening. She tells you that he is giving her a hard time and that she's fed up. She even cracks some pretty good jokes at his expense. You listen and agree that he's a jerk. You don't attempt to find a solution. Let's tune in on part of the conversation:

> *Suboptimal Thinker:* My husband is really getting me down. He treats me well sometimes, but he's emotionally abusive. I'm tired of walking on eggshells around him. When it comes to our relationship, he always gives his full thirty-four percent!
>
> *Suboptimal You:* He's a jerk. Why do you put up with him?
>
> *Suboptimal Thinker:* I'm afraid of being alone, and I don't believe I'll find anyone better.
>
> *Suboptimal You:* If that's how you feel, I guess you're just going to have to grin and bear it.

How do you both feel now?

Now imagine yourself as an Optimal Thinker. You arrange to meet the same friend for dinner at your favorite restaurant. You are looking your best. The ambience is just right and the seating is entirely comfortable. You agree that the food couldn't be better. The resident pianist even plays your favorite music.

Your friend shares her problem. You direct the conversation toward discovering the best solution and the most effective actions to implement. You assist your friend in minimizing her weaknesses and maximizing her strengths and opportunities. You focus on her finest attributes, favorite activities, and the best means of achieving her most important goals. You bring out the best in her! Let's tune in now to your Optimal responses to your friend's comments:

> *Suboptimal Thinker:* My husband is really getting me down. He treats me well sometimes, but he's emotionally abusive. I'm tired of walking on eggshells around him. When it comes to our relationship, he always gives his full thirty-four percent!
>
> *Optimal You:* It sounds like you're having a really hard time. I have three questions for you. Why are you tolerating his bad behavior? What are your options? What do you think is the best way to resolve this?
>
> *Suboptimal Thinker:* I'm scared he'll leave me, and I'm afraid of being alone. I guess I have three options. I can put up with

his lousy behavior, stand up to him, or leave. I really need to overcome my fear of being alone, and show him that I won't tolerate his nasty behavior.

Optimal You: That sounds like a good place to start. What's the most constructive way to approach this so that you can achieve what's best for both of you?

Suboptimal Thinker: Good question. I need to explore why I am so afraid of being alone, and then figure out how to overcome my fear. I also need to stand up for myself. The next time my husband is emotionally abusive, I'll say: "I love you, but this behavior is no longer acceptable to me. I can't be available for this. When you're ready to treat me respectfully, please let me know." If he continues to treat me badly, I will remove myself from his presence.

How do you both feel now? How does it feel to be your best and bring out the best in others? This is what Optimal Thinking is all about! With practice, Optimal Thinking will become second nature to you.

Why Positive Thinking Falls Short

For decades, the motto of the productive world has been "Think positive!" Meanwhile, the divorce rate has increased, highly intelligent people are unhappy, and our leaders' morals and ethics are often considered dubious. It's time to acknowledge that *positive thinking is not enough.*

Let's look at five reasons why positive thinking falls short and how Optimal Thinking resolves these shortcomings.

1. Positive Thinking Is Often Used to Suppress Negativity

Many positive thinkers often judge, suppress, and ignore negativity. They want to hear the good news only and alienate themselves from any negative thoughts or feelings. Such positive thinkers may have many concerns about their financial situation but choose to ignore them. You have probably heard these people say, "I don't want to hear any negativity!" They do not want to face the truth. By alienating themselves from negativity, they sacrifice authenticity, vulnerability, wholeness, and intimacy.

Recently, a business executive informed me that two years ago he told his family that he was tired of listening to their negative thinking. Subsequently, whenever he walked into the living room, dead silence prevailed. His family had stopped sharing their problems and concerns with him, and he became an outsider.

Some years ago, I had a similar experience within a well-known international company. The vice president repeatedly said, "Stay away from negative people. If you want to fly with eagles, don't mix with turkeys!" The employees were expected to show enthusiasm at all times. Whenever anyone expressed thoughts or feelings of doubt, anxiety, or unhappiness, they were labeled "negative," and were denigrated and disregarded.

Negative thoughts and feelings are not resolved when we suppress, deny, or devalue them. We just function with layers of unresolved problems, which affects our morale, stress level, productivity, and teamwork. It's like putting a coat of fresh paint over rust. Sooner or later, the paint peels off and the rust resurfaces. *Suppressing negativity with positive thinking can be very harmful.* Many positive thinkers experience severe emotional and financial distress because they ignore negative warning signals.

Consider Betty, an executive I recently counseled through a painful situation. Betty married Kevin even though she knew he had cheated on his two previous wives. She believed that she was prettier, smarter, and better suited to him and that he would never jeopardize their relationship by repeating his old pattern. Six months later, she discovered that he was seeing an old girlfriend. By sweeping the problem under the rug instead of dealing with it, Betty had set herself up for disaster.

Here's another conversation in which, in dealing with an undesirable reality, Betty uses positive thinking to suppress unwanted information.

Ellen: I don't have enough money to cover my bills this month.

Betty: Just be positive and it will all work out fine.

Let's experience the difference when Optimal Thinkers embrace the same problem and seek the best solution:

Jack: I don't have enough money to cover my bills this month. What is the best thing I can do?

Ralph: What is causing the problem? What are your options? What do you think is the best solution?

The use of Optimal Thinking eliminates the suppression of negativity and lack of resolution that often occur with suboptimal positive thinking. *Optimal Thinkers acknowledge and respect negativity as an authentic expression of reality.* When we notice ourselves finding fault and worrying, we accept our negative viewpoints, seek to understand them, and immediately *ask the most constructive questions in order to find the best solution.* This is the simple path we travel to become fully realized beings. We acknowledge the rust, treat it, and then apply the best paint! We embrace all there is, and call on our best self to produce our greatest accomplishments.

Embrace the Negative, then Optimize!

This concept can be most effective in resolving emotional pain from the past. Unfortunately, many of us were emotionally wounded while growing up. Some of us were abused, betrayed, or abandoned by those who were most important to us. Until we acknowledge and deal with these wounds, we continue to be affected by them. With Optimal Thinking, we gain access to our best or highest self. When we are ready to deal with our childhood wounds, to acknowledge the pain and begin the healing process, this part of ourselves can serve as our greatest source of strength and nurturing. Our highest self discovers the best solution to all the problems we encounter. Here's an example.

Tony, a divorcé I coached, had never been in a healthy intimate relationship. He longed for a good relationship but spent most of his time alone. Tony's childhood had been miserable. His parents fought continuously, and his mother was verbally and physically abusive. He was terrified of her and dreamed of being left alone. When Tony left home, he tried to put his past behind him. He married a sweet woman but couldn't bring himself to be warm to her. After his divorce, he became involved in a number of superficial short-term relationships with unstable women.

During our consultations, he recalled the pain of his childhood and his bad feelings toward his mother. He realized that he had been protecting himself from getting close to women because he was afraid they would be like his mother. He was achieving his childhood (and childish) wish of being left alone. Once he understood what he was doing, he used Optimal Thinking to explore the best ways to deal with the abusive situations he feared. His feelings of terror and helplessness subsided as he continued to anticipate the most constructive actions. Tony eventually met a lovely woman who was sensitive to his feelings, and for the first time in his life, he became involved in a healthy intimate relationship.

When Juan was twenty-six years old, he immigrated to America with his wife and daughter. Although he had enough money to purchase a home for his family, he thought the real estate market was overpriced. Juan decided to wait until the real estate market took a serious downturn. In the early 1990s, when the bottom had fallen out of the real estate market, Juan knew the time was right. He purchased his first home when his neighbors were most pessimistic and prices were rock bottom. Juan optimized a negative situation and within five years, his home had doubled in value.

Do you have a pen and notebook handy? If not, take a few moments to get them now. Think about a negative idea, feeling, or experience you have suppressed. Write it down. What are the best actions to resolve it? Jot them down. Now prioritize these actions and decide upon the best time frames to complete them. When you act in your best interest, you optimize your life.

2. Positive Thinking Is Often No More Than Wishful Thinking

In *The Power of Positive Thinking*, Norman Vincent Peale stated: "Expect the best at all times. Never think of the worst. Drop it out of your thought, relegate it. Let there be no thought in your mind that the worst will happen. You can overcome any obstacle. You can achieve the most tremendous things by faith power."

Many positive thinkers believe that their dreams will be realized by a magical, divine process that is triggered by the intensity of their hopes, wishes, and faith. They approach life with a false sense of security, and are ill prepared for negative consequences. Their positive thinking is often no more than wishful thinking and can be extremely dangerous.

Consider Betty, who told me about her last experience with wishful thinking. She actually quit her job and sold her house in Los Angeles, convinced that if she were steadfast in her faith, she would secure a job with a well-known company in San Diego. When Betty discovered that someone else got the job, she was devastated. Her wishful thinking put her out in the cold.

Do you experience feelings of disappointment because you entertain unrealistic expectations? Many optimistic thinkers expect the best from others, and pay a big price for it. Peter, a small-business owner, told me that kind of story. When he met Jodi at his local church, she told him that she had twenty years of sales experience in his industry and was responsible for tripling sales at her last job. Peter assumed that she was telling the truth and hired her on the spot. Every day, Jodi informed Peter about meetings with top executives that would soon result in large contracts, and Peter believed her. When Peter did not see any concrete results after three months, he concluded that he should have more faith in her. After six months of listening to Jodi's stories and paying her salary, Peter asked if he could see her list of contacts. In six months, she had made contact with only two potential clients. The rest of her time had been spent at Chamber of Commerce meetings, networking with people who had no decision-making authority or interest in his business. When Peter asked her why she had not sought out qualified prospects, Jodi answered, "I guess I haven't been asking the right questions. I am willing!" Peter's desire to see the best in Jodi had thwarted his good judgment.

During the flurry of excitement over the emerging dot-com phenomenon, many investors practiced wishful thinking. These optimistic thinkers convinced themselves that Internet stocks could be evaluated with unrealistic criteria. They assumed that stock prices could be bid up to any level investors were willing to pay, and would stay there. Their illusions were permanently shattered when their stocks lost 50 to 100 percent of their value. Here is a conversation I overheard where positive thinking had become wishful thinking.

Ellen: I am having sleepless nights. I'm worried about leaving my money in the stock market.

Betty: Trust the universe. Just stay positive and everything will fall into place.

"You have to accept whatever comes and the only important thing is that you meet it with the best you have to give."
—Eleanor Roosevelt

Let's experience the difference when two Optimal Thinkers seek the best solution to the same situation.

Jack: I am having sleepless nights. I'm worried about leaving my money in the stock market. What is the best thing I can do?

Ralph: What's the worst thing that could happen? What do you think is your best strategy if the worst occurred? How can you minimize your risk? What are the most constructive actions you can take under the current circumstances?

When Ralph realized that Jack was facing considerable danger, he asked questions to help his friend determine the best contingency plan.

> *Optimal Thinking Is Optimal Realism—*
> *It Is Not Optimism!*

In *Learned Optimism*, Dr. Martin Seligman states: "If the cost of failure is high, optimism is the wrong strategy. Sometimes we need to cut our losses and invest elsewhere rather than find reasons to hold on." *Optimal Thinkers eliminate unnecessary disappointment, because they entertain realistic expectations and focus on optimizing situations within their control.* They realize that even with the best intent, some people are more capable than others. They exercise a realistic appraisal of others' strengths, weaknesses, capabilities, and limitations. Optimal Thinkers ask the best questions to invite the best responses from others, but recognize that they are ultimately powerless over others' decisions and actions. They simply explore their options and make the Optimal choice from realistic alternatives. Optimal Thinkers embrace reality and ask: *What's the best thing I can do under the circumstances?* When the stakes are high, they employ an Optimal contingency plan against the worst-event scenario to minimize danger and negative consequences.

Here is an example: Most businesses understand that data loss caused by computer hardware failure is costly and can even be catastrophic. The probability of such failures is also considerable. As the cost of duplicating records is not prohibitive, it is common practice for companies to establish backup systems. The most prudent companies back up their records and house them in external facilities in case of fire, flood, or earthquake. In such instances, where employees are unable to gain access to the company's premises, damages are significantly reduced. *When evaluating risk, we must weigh the probability and cost of failure (including the ability to cope with the consequences) against the cost and benefits of prevention.*

Immediately following the devastating attacks on the World Trade Center on September 11, 2001, where thousands of innocent lives were lost, Deutsche Bank was able to safely evacuate approximately five thousand people from its four downtown Manhattan locations. These employees were relocated to other Deutsche Bank facilities. The bank successfully transferred its systems and data to backup facilities according to existing contingency plans. All critical applications were up and running. When the American equity markets reopened, the bank settled all equity trades successfully and was an active market participant. Deutsche Bank's risk management systems functioned as designed and enabled the company to successfully continue operating.

It isn't always possible to protect against detrimental outcomes. We take calculated risks throughout our lives. Recently I met with two representatives who were interested in producing Optimal Thinking products. During our initial conversation, the first executive said: "It's going to be a great day today. Did you know that Mercury is no longer in retrograde?" I wondered how much of his attention was invested in forces and events outside of his control. The other executive immediately asked: "What is the difference between optimism and Optimal Thinking?" I responded with, "I like your question. What you're really asking is what's the difference between hoping for the best, and asking: "What's the best thing I can do under the circumstances?" She smiled, and we were off to the right start!

Take some time now to consider the role of wishful thinking in your life. In your notebook, write down your greatest wish. Are you hoping that your wish will manifest miraculously or effortlessly? How realistic is this? Are you willing to use Optimal Thinking to give yourself the best chance of making your wish come true? Underneath your wish, write down: *What's the best thing I can do under the circumstances?* Listen carefully to the response and decide upon the best time to take your first Optimal action step. Put your best foot forward!

3. There Are Varying Shades of Positive Thinking

Communication between positive thinkers on different levels is often problematic. Conversation between them does not provide the best outcome because they are not on the same wavelength. For example, the mediocre positive thinker acts as a "wet blanket" to the extraordinarily positive thinker, who is the "energizer." The different levels of positive thinking are not harmonious. Here is a typical conversation:

Extraordinary Ed: Your home is in a fantastic location. You're close to the shops and your view is sensational.

Mediocre Mary: Yes, it is quite good.

Extraordinary Ed: You should be very happy with it. Your home is a great investment.

Mediocre Mary: I suppose it's okay.

Unfortunately, Mary and Ed often experience the disparity and frustration that prevail among the various levels of positive thinkers. In our world of infinite diversity, some people want to be good and others want to be great. Here's a scenario involving a married couple.

John, a mediocre positive thinker, makes a good living and is quite happy with the status quo. He has no desire to achieve extraordinary results. Susan is an extraordinarily positive thinker. She envisages herself as a multimillionaire with highly successful businesses throughout the world. John believes that Susan is a wishful thinker. Susan perceives John as mediocre and limiting. They are in continual conflict because their different levels of positive thinking are not in harmony.

No doubt you have experienced different levels of positive thinking. Often family members exhibit a mixture of thinking—most are suboptimal and on different wavelengths. Let's listen in on a conversation at AnyFamily:

Mediocre Mary: We need to plan our next vacation. John is a good travel agent and could give us a good price.

Extraordinary Ed: John is good, but I think Steven would do an outstanding job. He's terrific at finding unusual deals at great prices.

Mediocre Max: I hear what you say, but I think John will do a pretty good job. He's a regular guy who finds good deals for regular folks like us.

Now imagine the same problem being discussed at OptiFamily. The family members have all been exposed to Optimal Thinking and do their best to use it consistently. Optimal Thinking provides the thinking that empowers the family members to focus on the most desirable outcomes—and to contribute their best. Here is the difference:

Ralph: We need to plan our next vacation. Who's the best travel agent around?

Cheryl: Jim, Peter, and Jack would all be great, but Jack is the most appropriate person. He has the right contacts, the best track record, and the best deals at the best price.

Brian: You're right. He's also the most reliable. What's the best way to approach him about it?

> *Optimal Thinking Is the Common Form of Thinking That Empowers Us to Be Our Best and Communicate at Our Peak.*

Now let's listen to another conversation between two Optimal Thinkers during a recent *Optimal Thinking for Communicators* seminar. Brian and Lynn are on the same wavelength. Their communication demonstrates their ability to create and experience their Optimal relationship.

Brian: What is your vision of the Optimal relationship?

Lynn: An honest relationship where we care about each other's feelings as much as our own. We support each other to be the best we can be. When conflict arises, we face it and work out the best solution for both of us. What do you think?

Brian: I agree with you. I also think that discussing our plans on a daily basis is in our best interest. How do you feel about allocating time to do our favorite activities together?

Lynn: That makes sense. Can we keep Sundays open for tennis?

Brian: That sounds perfect. Are you ready for a game of tennis followed by a candlelight dinner?

Lynn: Definitely. What can I do to make sure it is most enjoyable for both of us?

Are you ready to let your best self take charge in your dealings with others? In your notebook make a list of all the people who are important to you, and write down the level of thinking you believe they are most comfortable with. Now jot down one Optimal question or statement you would like to use when you next speak with each person. Here is a sample listing to help you formulate your own:

Name	Dominant Thinking Level	Optimal Question or Statement
Elana	mediocre positive	You deserve the best in life!
Jimmy	extraordinarily positive	How can you optimize your schedule?
Craig	negative	What's the best thing you can do about it?

Name	Dominant Thinking Level	Optimal Question or Statement
Ralph	Optimal	Who's the right person to speak to about this issue?
Susan	extraordinarily positive	How can you make the most of your relationship?
Lionel	mediocre positive	What's most important to you?
Brian	Optimal	What's the best way to achieve your objective?
Mary	mediocre positive	What's in your best interest?
Cheryl	Optimal	I want to support you in being your best.

4. Suboptimal Thinking Is Not the Mental Basis of Peak Performance

You may ask: What is peak performance? Many professionals claim that if we think positively; display courage, persistence, and self-reliance; and use their suggested techniques for setting goals, managing time, and relating to others, then we will achieve peak performance. Such qualities and techniques are certainly constructive ingredients for success, but what is *essential* for peak performance is peak or Optimal Thinking. *We cannot function at our peak when we think in suboptimal terms.* Whenever we think suboptimally, it costs us time, energy, joy, and money. Our performance is always compromised if we think in only mediocre or even extraordinary terms.

Many people pay a heavy price for their suboptimal thinking. Mary, the homeowner and mediocre positive thinker, was such a person. When she needed a building contractor to remodel her home, she chose Michael because his price was reasonable and she thought he would do an adequate job. Mary didn't check his references because she was afraid of making waves. Michael agreed to start work on Mary's home immediately, took a deposit from her, but didn't do anything for three months. When Michael told Mary that he was working on a more important job, she got angry. She realized that he had a contract with a large building firm and had no intention of fulfilling his contract with her. Mary eventually took him to court. Sadly, Michael lied during the hearing and Mary lost the case. Mary had wasted time and money because she did not ask the best questions or take the most productive actions to ensure that her needs were met.

Many of us have been told that if we want to experience peak performance, we must copy the thinking and actions of highly successful people. The following scenario illustrates why this philosophy is sometimes ineffective. Rowland, an Emmy Award–winning writer, had made a very comfortable living for the past twenty years, even though he didn't put his best efforts into his work. He actually hated writing and wanted to be a producer. When Pamela, an aspiring writer, met him at an industry function, she invited him to have lunch with her and asked him: "What do you think makes you so successful? What makes you different from the rest?" Rowland responded, "I don't have any pretensions as to what I do. It's not all that important. I write for a living. I don't write because I like it. I am successful at what I do because I don't get emotionally involved." Pamela knew she needed to be passionate about a project in order to give it her best shot. Duplicating Rowland's success formula could not motivate her to function at her peak!

Let's listen to a suboptimal positive thinking mother's complacency about her ten-year-old daughter's mediocre academic performance: "My daughter's grades are pretty good. She's quite motivated to succeed."

Now let's tune in to an Optimal Thinking mother's thoughts on how to encourage her daughter to do her best: "My daughter's grades are pretty good. Now how can I encourage her to put her best foot forward? What are her strengths? How can I inspire her to make the most of them? What are her weaknesses? How can I help her to minimize them? How can I guide her to achieve the best possible results?"

When my client Lynn joined a large sales organization, she discovered that some of the top achievers were using a sales script to deliver their sales presentations. Lynn was uneasy with the hard-sell tactics in the script. Nevertheless, she used it during numerous sales calls, but without success. Lynn was determined to make the most of her sales career. She studied the strengths and weaknesses of her product range, and gained the knowledge she required to accurately resolve her customers' concerns. She then modified her sales presentation to focus on their best interests. In her own unique way, she continually put her best foot forward. After three months, Lynn not only achieved the success she desired, but also became the company's top salesperson—without any hard-sell tactics!

> *Optimal Thinking Is the Mental Basis of Peak Performance.*

We can employ the most productive action at any given moment, and function at our peak when we think in peak or Optimal terms! Optimal Thinking truly empowers our best self to take charge so that we experience peak performance—a blinding flash of the obvious! Here again is the quantum leap:

Suboptimal positive thinkers achieve good and great results. Optimal Thinkers achieve the best and greatest results. Suboptimal positive thinkers are interested in being productive. Optimal Thinkers make sure they are most productive. Suboptimal positive thinkers take a smart approach to achieve an important goal. Optimal Thinkers take the smartest approach to achieve their most important goal. Suboptimal positive thinkers manage their resources and improve their performance. Optimal Thinkers maximize their resources and their performance.

The following conversations provide an opportunity for you to make an instant Optimal choice. If your spouse had a similar problem, which friend would you consult? Let's listen to a conversation with Bill and his friend:

Bill: My wife has been cranky ever since her father died.

Suboptimal Friend: You'll have to put up with it if you want to stay married.

Now let's listen to some Optimal Thinkers discuss the same problem:

Ralph: My wife has been cranky ever since her father died. What's my best strategy for dealing with this?

Optimal Friend: That's the right question! What is the most productive attitude you can adopt during her time of grief? What are the best actions you can take to support her through this? How can you take the best possible care of yourself emotionally at the same time?

There are infinite ways an Optimal Thinker can experience peak performance and inspire it in others. Consider Sam, a single father and business consultant, who had been in the habit of promising his clients the world, taking shortcuts, and doing just enough to get by. For over fifteen years he went from job to job, covering up his mistakes whenever he could. After discovering Optimal Thinking, he wrote to me on two occasions.

On the first occasion, Sam told me about an incident with his ten-year-old son. When presented with mediocre homework, instead of accepting it as he had always done, Sam asked, "Is this the best you can do?" His son quickly admitted that he had better options. Sam then inspired his son's peak performance when he said, "Give this project your best shot and then show it to me tomorrow."

On the second occasion, Sam explained how Optimal Thinking empowered him to make the most of a shaky business situation. Prior to attending a meeting with his clients, he was painfully aware of how he had let them down and of everything that had gone wrong. He was afraid of facing them with the truth. This is when he decided to employ Optimal Thinking. He accepted his fear, and asked: "What's in my best interest here? What's in the best interest of the project?" He then proceeded to sort through his options. Armed with the most profitable solutions to the best and worst scenarios, he was able to go to the meeting with purpose, contribute his best, and gain maximum benefit from the meeting. His clients immediately hired him to do additional work.

Are you willing to give life your best shot? Write down one behavior that reflects suboptimal thinking and performance you are ready to change. For example, you might notice that your exercise regimen is suboptimal, or that you are not making the best use of your time when dealing with a friend or acquaintance. Optimize your thinking by asking: *What's the best thing I can do about this?* Write down your answer. Now decide upon the time frame that will work best for you to optimize your performance. You are now on the Optimal path. Doing your best is the best you can do!

5. If We Don't Maximize a Situation, We Don't Complete It

Many positive thinkers constantly seek to improve their situation. They want better relationships, more satisfying work, and higher living standards. If the current solution is better than a previous solution, it's good enough. Such thinkers rarely experience complete satisfaction because the unexplored alternatives continue to haunt them. They are often regretful because they focus on what *could* have happened, *should* have happened, and *would* have happened, if only—. Here is an example:

For years Jenny, a pretty television producer, had a busy social life. During her twenties and thirties, she dated lots of men who wanted to have children, but she invariably found fault with them. She was always looking for someone better. When she was in her late thirties, she met a good man and married him. Jenny assumed her husband wanted children but soon learned that this was not the case. At forty, although Jenny was happier than when she was single, she was plagued with regret. She asked: "Why didn't I make the most of my situation when I was in my thirties? Why didn't I ask the right questions before I married? Why didn't I marry a man who wanted children? Why was I so frivolous when I had men in my life who wanted children?"

Do you constantly strive to better your life but rarely feel satisfied? These days many people are self-improvement junkies. They read the latest books, listen to cassette tapes, and attend copious seminars on personal and professional development. They hunger for any piece of information that will improve their lives. They savor what they find, and digest their valuable insights. Many wisdom seekers are surprised when their appetites return; some are discouraged or even desperate. Something is missing and incomplete. They never seem to have enough.

Whenever you think suboptimally and seek to improve—rather than *maximize*—your current situation, the quality of your life is compromised. Consider Harry, a seventy-two-year-old extraordinarily positive thinker who attended a series of Optimal Thinking seminars. At the end of the first day, he shared with the participants that over the past thirty years he had purchased hundreds of books and attended countless self-help seminars. He had gained a lot from them but always felt that there was something missing. He was dissatisfied and looking for more.

Optimal Thinking provided Harry with the solution to his problem. Harry learned how to choose the best in every circumstance. He became peaceful and got into the habit of making the most of his life. His daughter recently shared with me that he had stopped telling her how things "should" be done. He simply asked, "Is this the best we can do?" At seventy-two years of age, Harry was a new man. He felt whole and complete.

> *Choose the Best, Then Put It to Rest.*

Optimal Thinkers do more than improve attitudes, skills, relationships, and lifestyles. We maximize them. *We accept what we can't control* (like the weather, interest rates, and others' choices) *and maximize what we can control.* We embrace the present moment, trust our intuition, investigate the alternatives for solving our challenges, weigh their advantages and disadvantages, and determine the best solution within the given time constraints. We choose the best and then put it to rest. Having surrendered our best contribution, we can peacefully move on to the next supremely important issue. Let's look at how this simple concept enabled Sam to buy the right home.

Sam had been looking for a new home for six months. The market was tight and nothing remotely close to what he wanted had become available. His realtor had just located two homes in Sam's price range. The first was an improvement on his current home but it didn't have everything he wanted. The second home had everything on his checklist but was much more expensive than the first one. Sam told me how he used Optimal Thinking to purchase the right home. He simply posed one question: "Which is the best home in my price range?" The answer was obvious. He purchased the second home and laid the issue to rest.

Ten years ago, I conducted a series of *Optimal Thinking* seminars at a large bank. The bank had been downsizing, and most of the employees were afraid of losing their jobs. The training director was an Optimal Thinker. He knew that many of the participants would be out of work shortly and he wanted them to learn to apply Optimal Thinking in the toughest of circumstances. "What's the best thing I can do under the circumstances?" was displayed on a chalkboard throughout the seminar. The participants learned how to apply Optimal Thinking to their own specific circumstances. At the end of the seminar, those expecting to be laid off said, "We can relax now. We have the tools to make the most of our lives!" When I asked them how they felt, they answered, "On top of the world!"

Last year, I was invited to do another *Optimal Thinking* seminar at the same bank. I was on top of the world when I saw a large plaque in the entrance hall. It read: "What's the best thing I can do under the circumstances?"

It's your turn now. *Optimal Thinking is easily learned, instantly applied, and does not require a leap of faith!* So, what's the best thing *you* can do under the circumstances?

Optimal Questions

1. When am I most likely to think Optimally?
2. Am I embracing suboptimal thinking and behavior and optimizing it?
3. What is the best thing I can do under the circumstances?

4. Am I accepting what is out of my control and optimizing what is within my control?
5. Am I choosing the best and then putting my issues to rest?

Optimal Action Steps

1. As soon as you notice yourself thinking negatively, embrace this vulnerable part of yourself without judgment. Then ask: "What's causing this? What is the best thing I can do about it? What's the best solution?"
2. Notice when someone you know is thinking negatively. Instead of avoiding that person, determine if he or she is open to input. You might say: "I'm sorry this is a problem for you. Can I help you resolve it? What do you think is the best thing you can do about it? What are your options? What's the best solution?" If the person is too angry to be reasonable or is intent on maintaining a negative perspective, you could say: "I understand you are upset at the moment. When you are open to finding the best solution to this issue, I will be happy to give you my most constructive input."
3. Share a meal with a family member or friend. Consciously choose to use Optimal Thinking, and optimize, optimize, optimize!

CHAPTER 2

What Does "Optimal" Mean to You?

"The history of free men is never really written by chance but by choice—their choice."
—Dwight D. Eisenhower

Use Your Whole Brain

In the upper part of your brain are two lobes, or hemispheres, commonly known as the right and left cerebral hemispheres. Research on brain dominance indicates that each hemisphere has distinctly different functions, processes different kinds of information, and is involved with different types of activities. The left brain is the logical, linear side. It is used for reasoning, analysis, and calculation. It is mathematical, verbal, sequential, and pragmatic. Your left brain is concrete and time-ordered and is responsible for language and for processing facts. It is the rational side of the brain. The right hemisphere is imaginative and thinks in pictures. It is intuitive and is used for synthesis (the combination of parts to form a whole). The right hemisphere is holistic and embraces all aspects of a concept or situation simultaneously. It is the artistic, creative, and musical side of your brain.

We live in a predominantly left-brain-oriented world, where words and logic are revered and the creative, intuitive, artistic right brain is often subjugated. Many people even have difficulty performing right-brain activities.

Although we all use both sides of our brains, one side—either left or right—tends to be dominant in each person. Left- and right-brain people process life in different ways. In *Free Flight: Celebrating Your Right Brain*, right-brained Barbara Meister Vitale discusses her life with her left-brained husband. She says, "When my husband and I recognized our differences, we stopped trying to change each other. We learned to accept and enjoy each other. After all, together we make a whole brain."

Make Optimal Choices

Every moment, regardless of your brain orientation, you are given an opportunity to consciously choose how you will live your life. Whenever you make a choice, consequences are created, whether you are ready to accept them or not. You are then faced with more choices, one of which is the Optimal choice. It is in your best interest to use both hemispheres to consciously choose what "Optimal" means to you.

Left-Brain Decisions

Following are two predominantly left-brain approaches to help you determine the Optimal solution to your problems and challenges. The first approach is most effective for less complex decisions.

How to Optimize Simple Decisions

Here is a predominantly left-brain Optimal approach for making simple decisions. Remember Betty, the optimist who gave up her job and sold her house, believing that she would get a new job, which never transpired? Betty used the following seven-step formula to work out her best solution.

Step 1. *Define the problem.*

Step 2. *Define the time frame in which the decision must be made.*

Step 3. *Explore options for resolving the problem.*

Step 4. *Eliminate the options that are unrealistic.*

Step 5. *Examine the consequences of each option.*
Write down the advantages and disadvantages (pros and cons). Take responsibility for the consequences of each option.

Step 6. *Rate or "weigh" the pros and cons on a scale from 1 to 10* (1 = least important, 10 = most important).

Step 7. *Determine which option is in your best interest.*
Sometimes several options are highly advantageous. In such a case, the best solution may be to employ two or more of your options.

Here's how Betty defined her biggest problem, evaluated her options, and decided upon the best solution.

Problem: I don't have a roof over my head. I need a place to live.

Deadline for Decision: 6 P.M. today.

Question: What are my options for resolving this problem?

Answer: Option 1. Stay with my mother until I rent or buy a home.
Option 2. Stay with my friend Jane until I rent or buy a home.
Option 3. Move into a hotel until I rent or buy a home.

Question: What is the rating for each option?

Option 1
Stay with my mother until I rent or buy a home.

Advantages (Pros)	Value	Disadvantages (Cons)	Value
Can move in today	10	Mom can annoy me	6
Won't have to pay rent	5	My bedroom is very small	6
Will be welcome there	8		
Can stay as long as I like	9		
Can store belongings	3		
Home is well located	9		
Moral support from Mom	7		
TOTAL	51	TOTAL	12

Value of *Option 1:* +39 (51 – 12)

Option 2
Stay with my friend Jane until I rent or buy a home.

Advantages (Pros)	Value	Disadvantages (Cons)	Value
Roof over my head	10	Home is not well located	9
Won't have to pay rent	5	Can't store belongings	3
Jane is lots of fun	9	Can stay for only 3 weeks	9
Moral support from Jane	7	Can't move in until Friday	10
Will be welcome there	8		
TOTAL	39	TOTAL	31

Value of *Option 2:* +8 (39 – 31)

Option 3

Move into a hotel until I rent or buy a home.

Advantages (Pros)	Value	Disadvantages (Cons)	Value
Can move in today	10	Very expensive	10
Will be welcome there	8	Can't store belongings	3
Can stay as long as I like	9	Small living space	9
		Will feel lonely	9
		Don't know which hotel	7
TOTAL	27	TOTAL	38

Value of *Option 3:* –11 (27 – 38)

Optimal Question: Which option is in my best interest?

Optimal Answer: Option 1.

By using this seven-step process, you prepare yourself for the consequences of your Optimal choice. Invest about 15 percent of your time in accurately defining the problem and 85 percent of your time in exploring the options and determining the best solution.

How to Optimize Complex Decisions

Here is a predominantly left-brain Optimal approach for complex decisions. When you are faced with life-changing decisions such as buying a home, changing careers, or having children, the following nine-step formula can assist you in making the Optimal choice.

Step 1.   *Decide upon what you most want to achieve.*

Step 2.   *Define the time frame in which the decision must be made.*

Step 3.   *Make a list of the most important factors (criteria) that will influence your decision.*
       Criteria are the yardsticks by which you measure/evaluate your options.

Step 4.   *Rate your criteria.*
       Since not all criteria are equally important, you must give them a rating or weight. Rate each factor according to its importance on a scale from 1 to 10.

Step 5.   *Rate how well your first option meets your criteria.*

Step 6.   Multiply the ratings for your criteria (Step 4) by the ratings for how your first option meets the criteria (Step 5).
Step 7.   Determine the total score.
Step 8.   Complete Steps 6 and 7 for your other options.
Step 9.   Decide on your best option based on the highest score.

John had earned a six-figure annual income with a well-known network marketing company until it went out of business. He wasn't sure which career move would be in his best interest. John decided to use this nine-step process. He wrote down the factors that would influence his decision and then rated his criteria. Let's take a look at his list:

Criterion	Rating
Job satisfaction	10
Industry growth prospects	10
Income	9
Stable business structure	9
Personal status	8
Freedom to travel	7
Flexible hours	6
Location	5

Below is the list of options that John believed were worthy of serious consideration:

Option 1.   Join another network marketing company in the same industry.
Option 2.   Join the fastest-growing network marketing company in the country.
Option 3.   Start my own business.
Option 4.   Join a direct sales company in the same industry.

John rated his first option on a scale from 1 to 10 against his eight criteria. He then multiplied the scores in both columns to obtain his total score. Here's how he completed Steps 5 and 6 for *Option 1:*

Criterion	Rating	× Option 1	= Value
Job satisfaction	10	8	80
Industry growth prospects	10	3	30
Income	9	6	54
Stable business structure	9	2	18
Personal status	8	10	80
Freedom to travel	7	9	63
Flexible hours	6	9	54
Location	5	7	<u>35</u>
		Total score for *Option 1:*	414

John then calculated the scores for his other options and compared them. It became clear that *Option 2* was his Optimal choice.

Total score for Option 1: 414

Total score for Option 2: 462

Total score for Option 3: 382

Total score for Option 4: 402

Right-Brain Decisions

In *Peak Performance*, Dr. Charles Garfield shares his research on the world's top athletes and several successful businesspeople. His findings show that nearly all use their right brains to visualize desired end results. They see, feel, and experience every detail of what they want before they take action. You can use your right brain to get in touch with what "the best" means to you. Try the following visualization:

Picture yourself involved in an activity in which you feel totally resourceful, capable, and confident. You may wish to direct your attention toward the simple process of breathing.

Relax into the feeling of total mastery. Now visualize everything in your life that encourages you to feel completely competent and confident. Now focus on your greatest blessings. Reflect on what you like most about yourself, your environment, and your life. You can choose to surround yourself with your favorite people and enjoy your favorite music. Decide what you want to see, hear, think, and feel. Now imagine you are receiving your greatest desire! *You can use Optimal Thinking whenever you want!*

Sometimes you intuitively know what's best for you. It just feels right. You sense that it is in your best interest. When your brain wave activity is reduced with techniques such as hypnosis and meditation, or when you take a nap, the left brain shuts down and you gain access to the right brain, which houses your intuition. Your right brain also becomes dominant when you are highly aroused. Activities such as jogging and brisk walking can provide you with the necessary brain wave activity to experience your greatest flashes of insight.

Right-Brain Optimizers

"Trust your hunches. They're usually based on facts filed away just below the conscious level."

—Dr. Joyce Brothers

Many entrepreneurs, businesspeople, entertainers, and professionals rely upon intuition to guide them to the best solutions to challenges. Their decisions born from keen intuition are often superior to those based on careful, analytical thinking

Conrad Hilton was such a person; he was convinced that his hotel empire succeeded because of his intuition. A prime example of the success of his hunches was his purchase of the Stevens Corporation, which owned the Stevens Hotel in Chicago. After he had submitted his offer for $165,000, he claimed that "somehow that didn't seem right to me." He said, "Another figure kept coming, $180,000. It satisfied me. It seemed fair. It felt right. I changed my bid to the larger figure on that hunch. When they were opened, the closest bid to mine was $179,800. I got the Stevens Corporation by a narrow margin of $200. Eventually, those assets returned me $2 million."

Albert Einstein attributed his theory of relativity to a flash of insight, not to the cold rationalism of the objective, data-oriented researcher in the laboratory. True, his mind had been prepared by much study and thought, but as he said later, "The really valuable factor is intuition."

In a recent television interview, Gloria Estefan described her singing career. She said, "I'm fortunate that I am able to do what I love to do. It still feels right."

What Does "Optimal" Really Mean?

You are now ready to learn more about what "Optimal" means to you. As you complete the following sentences, do not be influenced by anyone else's concept of "the best." Your answers will reflect your own brand of Optimal uniqueness. Be sure to jot down how you arrive at your decisions in your notebook. Recording your insights in writing will help you get the most out of this Optimal Thinking exercise.

My favorite color is .....

My most attractive physical feature is .....

I look my best when .....

My favorite artist is .....

The sounds of nature I appreciate most are .....

My favorite music is .....

The funniest comedian I have heard is .....

The singer who has the most pleasing voice is .....

The most cheerful person I know is .....

The most comfortable chair in my home is .....

I feel my best when .....

The most enjoyable vacation I can recall is .....

My favorite food is .....

When it comes to friendship, my most positive attribute is .....

What I like most about my best friend is .....

I can maximize my relationship with my partner by .....

My greatest fantasy is .....

I can maximize my income this year by .....

The best career move for me this year is .....

The best action I can take today toward my most important goal is .....

By using this sentence-completion process, you can discover what "the best" means to you in whichever context you choose. Simply complete the Optimal sentence, "What I value most about ..... is" repeatedly until you are completely satisfied with your response. You can then look at your answers and decide what you value above all else. Here is an example:

What I value most about friendship is .....
Answer: Trust

What I value most about trust is . . . . .

Answer: I can share my innermost thoughts and feelings.

What I value most about sharing my innermost thoughts and feelings is . . . . .

Answer: I feel accepted for who I really am.

What I value most about feeling accepted for who I really am is . . . . .

Answer: When I feel accepted, I feel loved.

What I value most about feeling loved is . . . . .

Answer: I feel valuable.

The above example can guide you to discover your highest values. Try it yourself. In your notebook, jot down the following statements and determine what is most important to you. Feel free to add your own unique Optimal statements to assess your highest priorities.

What I value most about my home is . . . . .

What I value most about my partner/best friend is . . . . .

What I value most about my career is . . . . .

What I value most about my spiritual life is . . . . .

What I value most about my body is . . . . .

What I value most about mind is . . . . .

What I value most about life is . . . . .

What I value most about being in nature is . . . . .

What I value most about summer/winter/spring/fall is . . . . .

The Key to the Optimal Answer Is the Optimal Question

"Always favor the person who is tolerant enough to understand that there are no absolute answers, but there are absolute questions."

—Elie Wiesel

Consider the importance of questions in your life. The quality of the questions you ask determines the quality of your life. When faced with disappointment, do you ask questions like "What's the use?" or "Why does this always happen to me?" or "How could I have been so stupid?" When you ask negative questions, you invite negative solutions.

Many people destroy their lives by ruminating on questions that render them powerless. Carolyn was miserable for three years because she fixated her thoughts on one negative question. She had been in a relationship with Fred, a seemingly generous and loving man, for over two years. When Fred asked Carolyn to marry him, she refused. She just couldn't bring herself to make the commitment. Shortly after that, Carolyn discovered that she had breast cancer. Fred was unsympathetic, showed no interest in helping her through the crisis, and even got involved with another woman. Carolyn felt devastated and constantly asked herself, "How could he do this to me?" Because she ruminated on this question for three years, she was unable to forgive Fred, release the pain, and move on.

When Carolyn learned about the value of Optimal questions, she asked, "What can I learn from this experience so that I can make the right choice in the future? What are the most nurturing actions I can take for myself? How can I make the most of my life? What's the best thing I can do to meet a loving life partner?" She decided that it was in her best interest to forgive Fred and release the hurt. Six months later, she was in her most fulfilling relationship ever, with a first-rate man.

When you ask the best questions of yourself and others, you invite the best answers. You can discover what "the best" means in whichever context you choose. You can even create the best path to your most desired outcomes.

To obtain the most enjoyable path to your goal, you simply ask *most enjoyable questions:*

- What are my most enjoyable activities?
- How can I maximize my enjoyment of these activities?
- What's the most enjoyable use of my time right now?
- What will make this most enjoyable?

You can ask *most profitable questions* to obtain the most profitable path to your goal:

- What's my most profitable activity?
- How can I maximize the profitability of this activity?
- What's the most profitable use of my time right now?

Ask *most loving questions* to create the most loving path:

- What's the most loving way to handle this?
- What's the most loving action I can take?

You can face and resolve simple challenges by asking: *What's the best thing I can do about this?* For more complex challenges, ask: *What are my options for resolving this? What are the best actions I can take?* Confront your most difficult challenges by asking: *What's causing this problem? What are my options for resolving this? What's my best strategy? What are the most constructive/productive actions I can take?*

Design Your Optimal Life

Imagine that this is the first day of your Optimal life. You are free to design it however you want. Here are some Optimal questions to ask yourself and others. I recommend that you arrange them in your own order of priority before answering them—the highest first!

Optimal What Questions

What do I like/admire most about myself?

What is my greatest asset/talent/ability?

What are my favorite activities?

What is my most important goal right now?

What is the best action I can take toward it now?

What will make each task today most pleasurable?

What is the best opportunity I can act upon right now?

What is the most empowering question I can ask right now?

What is the best solution to my problems/concerns?

What is the best use of my time now/next week?

What can I do to bring out the best in myself/you/others?

What are my/your best suggestions?

Optimal Why Questions

Why is this my greatest asset?

Why is this my most important goal?

Why is this my best opportunity right now?

Why is this our most profitable product?

Why is this our most popular product?

Why is this the best solution?

Optimal How Questions

How do I identify the best?

How can I bring out the best in myself and others?

How can I best utilize my greatest talents and abilities?

How can I most easily attain/maintain peak health and fitness?

How can I reach my goal in the shortest time possible?

How can I make the best use of my strengths?

How can we be of greatest service to our customers?

How can we maximize profits?

How can we make the most of this situation?

Optimal Who Questions

Who is the most important person in my life?

Who can I count on most?

Who do I admire most?

Who do I most prefer to be with?

Who do I most want to work with?

Who are my best customers?

Who can benefit most from what I have to offer?

Who is the best person to speak to about this?

Optimal When Questions

When is the best time to take this action?

When is the best time to start this task/project?

When is the best time to complete this project?

When am I most productive?

When am I at my best?

When is the best time to talk with you?

Optimal Where Questions

Where is your favorite city/beach/ski resort/location?

Where is the best place for us to talk privately?

Where is the best restaurant in this city?

Where will I find the best people?

Where can I most easily relax?

Where is the best place for me to fulfill my most important goals?

Where is my best source of inspiration?

Where is the best location to work?

Five Optimal Questions to Start Your Day

Imagine yourself starting each day with five Optimal questions, such as:

1. What is supremely important to me?
2. What are my most important goals today?
3. Which actions will be most beneficial for my self-confidence and self-respect today?
4. What will make each task today most profitable/beneficial/enjoyable?
5. What is the most constructive use of my time right now?

Now, write down five Optimal questions to answer every morning. The answers will stimulate you to make the most of your life!

1. _____
2. _____
3. _____
4. _____
5. _____

Optimal Action Steps

1. Place your five Optimal questions to start your day where you are most likely to see them in the morning. Make sure you answer them each and every morning.
2. Determine the Optimal solution to a simple problem using the seven-step left-brain Optimal decision-making procedure.
3. Determine the Optimal solution to a complex problem using the nine-step left-brain Optimal decision-making procedure.
4. Determine the Optimal solution to a problem using the right-brain Optimal decision-making procedure. Allow your intuition to provide you with the information you need. It will feel right when it comes.

CHAPTER 3

How to Use Optimal Thinking Consistently

"Consciously choose to think Optimally at every given moment, monitor your progress, and overcome your limiting core beliefs!"
—Optimal Thinker

By now, you probably see that Optimal Thinking is simple. It *is* simple to think in Optimal terms. You have probably employed Optimal Thinking, but not consistently. Why is this so? Why aren't you continually employing the thinking that brings you the best of life? Simply because you haven't been shown how. You entered life with the best computer you could wish for—your brain—but without an instruction manual that shows you how to use the mental software to be your best: Optimal Thinking.

Using Optimal Thinking Consistently Is a Process

"Practice is the best of all instructors."
—Publilius Syrus

Is it possible to think Optimally continuously? In my view, it is unrealistic to expect to think Optimally all the time, simply because we're human, and we get off track. However, it is in your best interest to use Optimal Thinking as often as possible. What is the process? I like to use the analogy of learning to drive a car. Initially you are unaware of what you don't know. When you sit next to your driving instructor for the first time, you become aware of your incompetence. As you learn to drive and practice driving, however, you become aware of your increasing competence. Ultimately, you find yourself choosing the correct responses on the road automatically. Below is a summary of the stages involved:

Stage 1.   *Unawareness of incompetence*
Stage 2.   *Awareness of incompetence*
Stage 3.   *Awareness of competence*
Stage 4.   *Unawareness of competence*

Before Lorraine attended the *Optimal Thinking* seminar series, she had always responded to the question "How are you?" with "Not bad" or "Pretty good." She had no idea that she was a mediocre thinker. During the seminar series, she became acutely aware of her mediocre thinking and resolved to optimize her thinking. She decided to respond to this particular question with, "I'm doing my best" or "First class, thank you!" Her Optimal response would reinforce her decision to optimize her thinking. When the seminar ended, every time someone asked, "How are you?" Lorraine consciously chose one of her two responses. Initially she felt awkward but after a while, her Optimal response became automatic. With practice, Optimal Thinking had become second nature to her.

You can employ Optimal Thinking more frequently and overcome the obstacles that prevent you from accessing the full power of your mind. To become consistent in your use of Optimal Thinking:

1.   Consciously choose Optimal Thinking.
2.   Monitor yourself.
3.   Overcome your limiting core beliefs.

Consciously Choose Optimal Thinking

In *Anatomy of the Spirit*, Caroline Myss states: "Managing the power of choice, with all its creative and spiritual implications, is the essence of the human experience. . . . Choice is the process of creation itself."

In any given moment, you can become conscious of your highest self by choosing who you most want to be. On a moment-by-moment basis, *consciously choose your best self and think at peak level. Ask the best questions to invite the best answers.* When you notice yourself thinking suboptimally, simply accept and honor this as an authentic expression of your reality. Then use Optimal Thinking to get back on your best track with minimum time loss. Remember to ask yourself and others: What's in my/our best interest? Is this the best I/we can do? Your Optimal questions can provide you with delightful answers. For example, if your response to "What is in my best interest?" is "Take a nap," then do it! You can choose to snooze knowing it is in your best interest.

Monitor Yourself

Optimal Thinkers choose to be the right person, in the best place, at the best time, engaged in the most important activity in the best way. You can monitor your effectiveness as an Optimal Thinker by asking yourself: *Am I the right person in the best place at the best time, involved in the most important activity in the best way?* When you notice that you're not in the right place, for example, you can ask, *Where is the best place for me now?* and go there. If you decide that it is not the best time to undertake your current activity, choose the right time. If you're not involved with the most important activity, simply ask, *What is the most important activity I can involve myself with now?* and then do it.

At the end of each day, week, and month you can ask, *What percentage of today (or this week or this month) was I the right or best person in the best place at the best time involved in the most important activity in the best way?* Here's how three people used this monitoring procedure.

James, an extraordinary thinker and real estate salesman, felt very pleased with his progress. He was doing exceptionally well at work. He had recently moved into a new home that was almost ideally suited to his needs. He had lots of fine friends and hobbies and nearly always had something interesting to do. He evaluated his effectiveness as an Optimal Thinker as follows:

	Percentage of Day as Optimal Thinker	Percentage of Week as Optimal Thinker
Right person	90	90
Best place	90	90
Best time	90	80
Most important activity	85	90
Best way	85	75

As a result, James became more aware of his thinking and committed himself to continually optimize his thoughts. He engaged a top interior decorator to help him furnish his home and used the extra time to maximize his skills at work.

Lionel, a mediocre thinker, was reasonably happy with his life but things could have been better. He had a secure but unstimulating job. He would have liked to live in a nicer home but didn't have the means. He evaluated his effectiveness as an Optimal Thinker as follows:

	Percentage of Day as Optimal Thinker	Percentage of Week as Optimal Thinker
Right person	65	65
Best place	55	60
Best time	60	60
Most important activity	40	40
Best way	65	65

Lionel felt obliged to consider his options. He loved animals and decided to work in his friend's pet store on the weekends. When the timing was right, he would purchase his own store. Eventually, he would be able to afford the home he really wanted.

Ellen, a secretary and negative thinker, felt trapped. She didn't like city living in general, but wasn't sure where she wanted to be. She resented having to work, didn't like her job, and complained constantly. Ellen evaluated her effectiveness as an Optimal Thinker like this:

	Percentage of Day as Optimal Thinker	Percentage of Week as Optimal Thinker
Right person	25	25
Best place	5	5
Best time	0	0
Most important activity	0	0
Best way	25	25

Ellen realized that negative thinking was preventing her from enjoying life. She wrote down five Optimal questions and answered them every morning. She even decided to make the most of her job while she was deciding where she wanted to be.

You can start monitoring your progress right now. In the chart below, make your own evaluation based on the same questions. Then schedule the best time to do this on a regular basis.

	Percentage of Day as Optimal Thinker	Percentage of Week as Optimal Thinker
Right person	_____	_____
Best place	_____	_____
Best time	_____	_____
Most important activity	_____	_____
Best way	_____	_____

When you use Optimal Thinking consistently, you will enjoy the best that life has to offer.

Overcome Your Limiting Core Beliefs

"Our beliefs are invisible ingredients in all our activities."
—Dr. Wayne W. Dyer

Henry Ford said, "If you believe that you can do a thing, or if you believe you cannot, in either case, you are right." Most of us don't consciously choose our beliefs; they are often based on interpretations of past experiences and information we've received from respected sources. Our beliefs vary in intensity and have the power to make us or break us. Consider these questions.

Why do some people enjoy the best in life while others settle for second best?

Why do we sabotage our success?

Why do we compromise, accept substitutes, and live mediocre lives?

Why do we repeat self-defeating behavior?

Many people have been conditioned to want and expect less than the best. You may have opposing beliefs about your ability and worthiness to experience life's greatest offerings. You may not believe that it is possible for you to enjoy the best that life has to offer. You *can* uncover and overcome the core beliefs that prevent you from using Optimal Thinking consistently. You can maximize the power of the beliefs that strengthen you and neutralize those that weaken you.

Some years ago I created a series of Optimal seminars and personal consultations to discover the most prevalent core beliefs that inhibit us from enjoying the best in life. The Optimal program was designed to uncover, confront, and overcome our most damaging mental conditioning. I discovered the following six major culprits.

1. I Am Not Responsible for My Life

"People are always blaming their circumstances for what they are. I don't believe in circumstances. The people who get on in this world are the people who get up and look for the circumstances they want, and, if they can't find them, make them."
—George Bernard Shaw

Many people did not receive the love and acceptance they needed as children. They feel inadequate, defective, unimportant, unlovable, powerless, empty, lonely, bad, and even worthless. Instead of facing their painful feelings and healing their wounds, they block them out with defensive behavior. Many wounded people misplace their angry feelings and take on the victim posture, perceiving themselves as emotional prey for others. The victim focuses on blaming others to redirect the anger, or on changing others to diminish the anger, instead of using the anger to protect and assert their needs. Do you attempt to control others with anger, criticism, praise, or withdrawal? Do you please others in order to gain their approval? If you hold on to the illusion that you have control over others, you will inevitably be disappointed and feel powerless.

Unfortunately, many people choose addictions to medicate their feelings of powerlessness, emptiness, loneliness, and despair. They embrace substances, material possessions, people, or activities, and then feel controlled by them. Consider Doug, a forty-nine-year-old business executive who felt hopeless about his love life. When the pain was overwhelming, instead of putting his best foot forward and resolving it, he turned to crack cocaine for relief. After a three-day binge, he felt even more demoralized. He repeated this vicious cycle for five years and continued to feel victimized.

Are you taking full responsibility for your life or do you turn over this responsibility to substances or to others? Many people hand over the role of affirming their value and lovability to other people, and then feel wounded and rejected when these others fail to make them feel valuable and lovable. When they don't receive the approval they need, they blame others for their feelings of jealousy, resentment, hurt, loneliness, or disappointment. By allowing others to define us, we give away our power to them and then are dependent on their choices. Some people were brought up to believe that their role in life is to support others and that their personal goals and desires are secondary. They feel selfish when they consider themselves first. You may believe that you can only be happy when you are in a loving relationship. When your sense of wholeness depends upon being in a loving relationship, you are in a victim state. Making your happiness dependent upon others gives them the power to make or break you.

Consider Barry, a business owner who is miserable when he isn't in a committed relationship. By centering his thoughts and activities on his girlfriend, he avoids facing his pain and healing himself. Barry focuses on his girlfriend's feelings but ignores his own. He makes her responsible for affirming his value and lovability, and for making his life meaningful. However, when he doesn't get the attention and approval he needs, he feels cheated and angry. He blames his girlfriend for abandoning him, even though he is actually abandoning himself. When the relationship ends, he compulsively repeats the cycle with another woman.

Whenever we attribute our pain to any external source, we are choosing to be irresponsible. Sadly, many of us choose the victim role by believing that life happens to us. If it hadn't been for this, that, or the other, we would be doing very well now. Blame is the name of the victim's game. We blame others for our pain because we don't want to take responsibility for the source of our distress: our own thoughts, feelings, and actions. By volunteering for the victim role, we avoid personal responsibility for our choices and their consequences. As long as we believe we are victims, we don't have to take responsibility for healing our pain. Until we accept the truth that our wounded feelings come from our choices and that we are responsible for the thoughts, beliefs, and actions that create our feelings, we will continue to feel powerless. It is not others' behavior that is the source of our anguish, but our interpretation of their behavior and our responses.

Are you willing to give up your need for approval from others? Start by observing your victimizing thoughts and emotions without judging them, and consider how to best deal with them. Avoid the temptation of having others define you by asking yourself such questions as, *What do I want from others that I am not giving to myself?* Whenever you are angry with someone, ask yourself, *What am I doing to myself that I am blaming others for doing to me?* As soon as you realize what you're doing to hurt yourself, you can take the best corrective actions. By taking full responsibility for defining yourself, you claim your personal power.

Here's how Richard, a chiropractor, found himself. He had lost control of his business during a stressful divorce and was forced to sell it five years ago. He had been unemployed since that time and in a dead-end relationship. When he came to my office for private consultations, he was depressed and without direction. Here is a small part of our conversation.

Rosalene: What do you want above all else?

Richard: I want people to look up to me.

Rosalene: Richard, do you look up to yourself?

Richard: I don't know what that means. I am lost. I don't know who I am.

Rosalene: So your main purpose in life is to obtain approval from others?

Richard: Yes. I need people to like me. I tell them what they want to hear.

Rosalene: Richard, when you are untrue to yourself and give your power away to get their approval, how does that feel?

Richard: Lousy. I don't have any respect for myself.

Rosalene: So it feels bad. Richard, in order to respect yourself you need to figure out what you stand for, and be true to yourself. You have to be prepared to lose everyone in life other than yourself. Would you be willing to do that? Would that be in your best interest?

Richard: Wow. I guess I have to make some serious changes. What I've been doing certainly isn't working. I am miserable.

Rosalene: I understand that it's been difficult for you. Richard, if you respected yourself, what kind of person would you be?

Richard: I would take care of my health, be true to myself, follow the Ten Commandments, contribute to the lives of others with meaningful work, be financially successful, and take calculated risks to move ahead.

Rosalene: If you did this, would you respect yourself? Is this all you would need in order to look up to yourself?

Richard: Yes, definitely.

Do you have doubts about your right to take complete responsibility for creating your path in life? Many people experience conflict with their religious beliefs when challenged to take full responsibility for their life's direction. You may believe that people are here to follow divine direction. If you are guided by religious beliefs or astrological influences, are they sufficient to empower you to achieve all you want? Do you need to take more control of your life?

Some people who feel inadequate and powerless live from day to day wondering what will happen to them. They say things like: "Something has got to change. Things can't stay the way they are!" These people confront life day after day, hoping that their desires will be fulfilled. They invariably focus on what is out of their control, use external sources for instant gratification, and neglect to evaluate the consequences of their choices and actions. They make irresponsible choices and then feel victimized by the consequences. They set themselves up to be victims of their circumstances.

You can take full responsibility for your choices. You can evaluate the consequences of your choices and accept full responsibility for them. You can also explore your relationship with victim thinking and Optimal Thinking by answering the following Optimal questions:

- Do I focus excessively on what is out of my control?
- Am I willing to take full responsibility for optimizing my thoughts, feelings, actions, and life?
- Is my greatest desire to learn how to take care of myself or do I want someone or something to do this for me?
- What do I need from an external source that I am not giving myself?
- What is the wisest way of dealing with this?

Here's how Ted, an engineer, optimized his perspective and his life. For four years, he had felt stuck in a job he absolutely detested. Ted talked continually about changing his career but did nothing about it. He was convinced that he was a victim of circumstance. How could he possibly change careers at forty-seven years of age? It was too late. Employers were interested in young blood; if only he had done something about it when he was younger. By dwelling on issues outside of his control and assuming the victim role, Ted did not have to take responsibility for his misery, or face the risk of rejection in a new career search.

When Ted stopped playing the victim, he took control of his life. He decided to invest six hours every week looking into job possibilities. He scoured the Sunday classified ads, submitted his résumé when it felt right, and attended job interviews during his lunch breaks. Within four months he found a new job that he thoroughly enjoys. He stopped being a victim and chose to become a victor.

2. Something Is Wrong (with Me, You, or the World)

"Tolerance is the first principle of community; it is the spirit which conserves the best that all men think."

—Helen Keller

Unfortunately, when our parents are wounded and do not know how to love us, we are powerless to do anything about it as children. Because accepting that we are powerless would be life-threatening and intolerable, most of us choose to deny the truth. Rather than blame our parents, we blame ourselves. We falsely conclude that by modifying our behavior we can control getting the love and acceptance we need from them. When changing our behavior does not bring us the approval we seek, instead of thinking "I did something wrong," we shame and condemn ourselves with "They don't love me because something is wrong with me!"

Many people who feel defective use criticism of others and of circumstances to avoid their own feelings of inadequacy and powerlessness. Although criticism and judgment have been hailed by our society as intelligent applications of an analytical mind, they are entertained mostly by the wounded for negative purposes. *Criticism serves the best interests of those involved only when it precedes the search for the best solution to a problem or defect.* When we are preoccupied with criticism and judgment, we cut off compassion and are unaware of what's in our best interest. We enter a negative spiral and discount our best self.

Do you attack yourself with statements like: "I'm not good/ smart/rich/young/attractive enough"? Do you judge others and the world with comments like: "How can you be so stupid?" or "I can't trust anyone" or "This place is full of phonies"? If you continue to believe "something's wrong with me, you, or the world," you will sabotage your experiences, friendships, and plans by finding fault with them. You will see injustice and misery everywhere.

Now consider what could happen if you committed yourself to

focusing on what is right with yourself, others, and the world. You could experience yourself as the right person in the right place at the right time, with the right people, doing the right thing the right way. Imagine that! You probably recognize elements of truth in both points of view, but *what is most important is which core belief is in your best interest*. When you believe that something's right with you, others, and the world, you have a foundation from which to be your best.

How can you divest yourself of a primary belief that something is wrong? Embrace your inner critic with compassion, and weigh the advantages and disadvantages of this negative core belief. When you decide that a belief is not in your best interest, the door of new possibilities can open for you. Try the same procedure that Joan, a homemaker, used to weigh the advantages and disadvantages of believing that something was wrong with her.

Core belief

Something is wrong with me.

Advantages (Pros)	Value	Disadvantages (Cons)	Value
I am aware of my weaknesses and can improve them	10	I let people abuse me	10
		I can't be my best	10
		I feel pessimistic	10
		I feel like a victim	9
		I feel inadequate	10
		I feel self-conscious	10
		I feel like a bad mother	10
		I give in even when I'm right	7
		I overeat	9
TOTAL	10	TOTAL	85

Value of this core belief: − 75 (10 − 85)

Joan immediately concluded that it was far from her best interest to remain committed to the core belief that something is wrong with her. She then decided to weigh the advantages and disadvantages of believing that there is something right about her. Here is her first draft:

New belief

Something is right with me.

Advantages (Pros)	Value	Disadvantages (Cons)	Value
Good for self-esteem	9	May overlook what's	7
Feel happier	10	wrong	
Stand up for myself	8		
Feel more comfortable with people	9		
Stop being a victim	10		
Stop blaming myself when things go wrong	10		
TOTAL	56	TOTAL	7

Value of new belief: + 49 (56 - 7)

When Joan looked at the figures, she realized it was in her best interest to adopt the belief, "something is right about me." However, she was used to focusing on what was wrong with her. Here are some of her reasons:

Belief	Reasons I Believe It
Something's wrong with me	Parents have always criticized me
	I am overweight.
	My sister got more love and attention.
	I got average grades at school.
	I have a poor memory.
	I drink too much.
	I am physically unattractive.
	My husband doesn't respect my ideas.
	My kids don't listen to me.

Here is a sample of how Joan resolved these reasons, and changed her negative view of herself. You can overcome feelings of inadequacy and shame when you identify the reasons you believe you are defective and resolve them. Try it for yourself!

- *Reason for believing negative core belief*
  Parents have always criticized me.
- *What are my options for resolving this?*

  > *Option 1.* Be aware that's their point of view—I don't have to believe what they say.
  >
  > *Option 2.* Keep adding to my list of what is right about me to change my perspective.
  >
  > *Option 3.* If there really is something wrong and I can do something about it, take the best actions to fix it.
  >
  > *Option 4.* Mix with people who treat me nicely and validate me.
  >
  > *Option 5.* Don't allow my family to put me down.

- *What is the best solution?*
  A combination of options 1, 2, 3, 4, and 5.

There are many critics who concentrate on denigrating the success of others. Don't let them destroy you. When confronted with a committed critic, respond with your warmest, softening statement. You can say, "I appreciate your feedback." Follow up with questions like: "Can you give me your most constructive ideas on how to resolve this issue?" or "I'm also interested in your most constructive feedback. Would you please share it with me?" When you know your critic's statements are incorrect, you can respectfully acknowledge their point of view, share what you believe is best under the circumstances, and then ask for their most constructive input. Always encourage a critic to suggest their best alternative instead of dwelling on finding fault.

Several years ago, a tough critic watched one of my first television shows. I had worn what I considered to be a suitable, elegant red dress. When I asked for his comments, he informed me that I looked like a "madam" in my red dress. Stunned by his cutting remark, I acknowledged his opinion, and then asked him what he thought would be most appropriate. I also requested his most constructive feedback on the interview. He immediately rattled off a list of helpful remarks. Later he shared with me that our verbal exchange had made him realize that it's far more rewarding to acknowledge and make the most of what's good and of value than it is to criticize.

Take some time now to write down what's right with you, others, and the world. Use the following charts to guide you. Believe me, it is in your best interest!

Belief	Reasons I Believe in It/Evidence
Something is right about me.	_____
	_____
	_____
	_____
	_____
	_____
	_____

Belief	Most Beneficial Effects
Something is right about me.	_____
	_____
	_____
	_____
	_____
	_____
	_____

3. I Don't Deserve the Best in Life

"The best is good enough. Your best is good enough!"
—Optimal Thinker

Many of us would love to travel the world first class, pampered all the way—accommodated in the finest places, chauffeur-driven in limousines, never having to pick up a piece of luggage, accompanied by our favorite people. Do you deserve this? Why do so few of us experience this? Why are so few of us doing whatever is necessary to accumulate the required financial resources?

Many of us don't give ourselves what we really want because we feel unworthy. Whatever we do, it's never good enough. As a child, you might have been led to believe that your best wasn't good enough. Your parents, teachers, and peers may have undermined your confidence because they lacked confidence in themselves. They may have convinced you that you were inadequate and didn't deserve to have what you wanted. You learned to compromise, accept substitutes, and settle for second best. Perhaps you still have a problem giving yourself what you really want because of such early experiences. If you continue to believe in your unworthiness, you are voluntarily absolving yourself of responsibility for creating your best life. You are choosing to be a victim and setting yourself up to receive what you don't want. You are sabotaging your most desirable lifestyle.

In order to become a consistent Optimal Thinker and live your best life, you must accept that you deserve the best that life has to offer. You must accept that you are entitled to it. Perhaps a part of you already believes this, but you sometimes think in lesser terms when confronted with life's more challenging experiences.

Many people achieve what they want but feel unworthy. Bill, a science teacher, was promoted to chair of the science department. When he gathered his staff together to discuss the syllabus, he was afraid to make eye contact. He was so nervous that he mistakenly referred to irrelevant material, and even called several staff members by the wrong name.

Patricia had always been attracted to Jim. When he asked her out to dinner, she felt overwhelmed. She worried that her clothes weren't suitable and that she wasn't smart enough to hold his attention. The day before the dinner, she came down with the flu.

Gary, a small-business owner, was married to Anne, a pretty, classy, upbeat woman. He knew Anne was the best thing that could have happened to him. Whenever their relationship was going smoothly, he would become obnoxious and push her away.

Are you in touch with the discomfort you experience because you believe you're not worthy of the best in life? Until you eliminate your belief in your lack of worthiness, you will sabotage your plans by creating tiredness, accidents, sickness, and other obstacles.

To check where you now stand in relation to the best that life has to offer, take out your notebook. On the left-hand side of a page, repeatedly write *I deserve the best in life*. On the right-hand side, record the responses that come to mind. Notice your supportive reactions and take time to appreciate them. You may also notice mediocre and conflicting thoughts, feelings, and experiences that stop you from experiencing the best in life. Explore the responses that deserve serious consideration by answering these questions:

- What has caused this problem?
- What am I thinking or doing to feel this way?
- What are my options for resolving it?
- What is the best solution?
- What's the best action I can take to overcome this?

Consider Joan's example:

Optimal Alternative	Response	Supportive	Unsupportive
I deserve the best in life.	I feel angry.		YES
I deserve the best in life.	I never have the best in life.		YES
I deserve the best in life.	Rich people have the best.		YES
I deserve the best in life.	That's true.	YES	
I deserve the best in life.	Then why don't I have it?		YES
I deserve the best in life.	Why is life so tough?		YES
I deserve the best in life.	My kids don't think so.		YES
I deserve the best in life.	Life isn't fair.		YES
I deserve the best in life.	I'm good— I deserve it.	YES	
I deserve the best in life.	It's really true.	YES	

Now let's look at Joan's suboptimal responses that deserve serious consideration.

Suboptimal Reactions	Worthy of Serious Consideration	Unworthy of Serious Consideration
I feel angry.	YES	
I never have the best in life.		YES
Rich people have the best.	YES	
Then why don't I have it?	YES	
Why is life so tough?	YES	
My kids don't think so.	YES	
Life isn't fair.		YES

Let's explore how Joan resolved an unsupportive response.

- *Unsupportive response*
  I feel angry.
- *What has caused this?*
  I am upset because I keep settling for second best. My husband believes that we are average folks and should not expect too much from life. I'm afraid he'll think I'm crazy.
- *What are my options for resolving this problem?*

  > Option 1. Accept that I do deserve the best in life and tell my husband that I want to have it. Believe in myself!
  >
  > Option 2. Work out what "the best" means to me, and put together an action plan to achieve it.
  >
  > Option 3. Get some counseling from a professional.

- *What is the best solution?*
  Employ a combination of options 1 and 2 for six months. Monitor myself and seek professional help after six months if I need it.

Once you have resolved the unsupportive responses, you will become aware of thoughts and feelings related to having exactly what you want. You will become energetically connected and committed to the best that life can offer you. You can then visualize the best means to accomplish your most important goals and activate your plans. You *are* worthy of them!

Many people express their belief of being unworthy by creating shortages of what they consider most important to them. Are you short of money, career satisfaction, or love in your life? If you ever feel that there's not enough of something you need or want, think about why you believe that you don't deserve to have it. Consider the cost involved in holding on to this belief. Then imagine how you'll feel when you truly believe you deserve to have what you want. Note your reactions to believing that you are worthy. Take time to appreciate the supportive responses, then dispute and resolve the unsupportive ones. Invest fifteen to twenty minutes each day on this exercise until you're satisfied that you have dismantled this crippling core belief.

4. I Experience Fear

> *"As we are liberated from our own fear, our presence automatically liberates others."*
>
> —Nelson Mandela

If you knew that you could cope with every possible life situation, would you have anything to fear? The answer is obviously no. Fear is nature's way of preparing you to defend yourself against danger. You experience fear when you anticipate a loss or a wound. You fear what you believe should be feared. When you believe in your ability to cope with all situations, you automatically minimize fear. Your security lies not in what you have, but in the knowledge that you can cope with whatever crosses your path.

You can start to minimize your fears by facing them. Determine what you are afraid of and then take the best actions to resolve the threats that are causing the fear. Working through fear is far better than living with feelings of immobility and helplessness. Most accomplishments are achieved with some fear. You can acknowledge and deal with your greatest fear right now. What are the best actions you can take to overcome it? Empower yourself continually by answering questions like:

- What's the truth here?
- Am I risking more than I can afford to lose?
- What do I need to feel safe?
- What's the best way of handling this?
- How can I make the most of this?

The five major fears that sabotage your capacity to consistently use Optimal Thinking are fear of loss of self, fear of rejection, fear of failure, fear of success, and fear of pain.

Fear of Losing Self

Many of us become resistant when others try to control us and violate our personal domain. We are afraid of losing ourselves. As children, resistance was the only defense we could use to maintain our sense of self when faced with controlling, invasive parents or authority figures. When we resist others out of our fear of being controlled, we are unable to make choices that are in our best interest. By attempting to exert control over being controlled, we are actually controlled by our own resistance. Here is an example.

When Harry was growing up, his mother tried to control every detail of his life. Whenever he didn't conform to her wishes, she threw a tantrum or gave him the cold, silent treatment. In order to survive, Harry yielded to his mother's control and manipulation at the expense of his authentic self. Even though he did what was expected of him, a part of him refused to give in. He discovered ways to resist his mother, so that he was not completely engulfed by her. Harry asserted himself by letting her down when he could not be held fully responsible.

Harry's mother desperately wanted grandchildren, and never missed an opportunity to let him know about it. When Harry became an adult, he started a business, traveled the world, and dated lots of women. Even though he sincerely wanted to marry and have a family, he was only attracted to women who were unavailable. Whenever Harry met a woman who was interested in marriage, he would resist forming an attachment by finding fault with her. Sadly, getting even with his mother had become more important to him than being happy. Because of his mother's compulsion to dominate him, Harry was terrified of being controlled by anyone or anything. His desire for a mate and a family was being thwarted by his fear of being consumed by them. Ironically, his life was controlled by an inner power struggle. His resistance to being controlled was blocking him from creating what was in his best interest. Here is a snippet of his internal power struggle:

Controlling Voice: From now on I'm going out four nights a week to singles clubs. When I meet an attractive woman, I'm going to be punctual and optimistic. By the end of this year, I'll be married.

Resistant Voice: I have no energy for this. Most of the attractive women out there are gold diggers, and I really don't want to be their meal ticket. I can't stand the idea of having to put up with their demands and tantrums. I've had enough of nagging women to last me a lifetime!

Sometimes your fear of being controlled can be so great that it actually becomes your identity, your basic way of relating to the world. Any attempt to violate your identity is then perceived as deadly. So how can you overcome resistance? As resistance was the primary way you protected yourself from feeling powerless when you were invaded and violated as a child, it became a habit. Giving up a habit that is protecting you from feeling your pain can feel like opening death's door. You can start by noticing the resistant part of you without judging it. Notice how you feel when someone is trying to get something from you, and consider the consequences of your resistance. You will see that your feelings result from your fear of being controlled, and not from what other people are saying and doing.

You cannot control others' attempts to control you. You can prevent invasion from others, however, by communicating your personal limits or boundaries to them with comments like, "I would love to be able to help you with this, but it doesn't feel right for me."

"I am flattered that you want my help, but I am overwhelmed at the moment. I can't help you today." Or "I know this is important to you and I really want you to get the right help, but I'm not comfortable with it. Forgive me!"

Keep your focus on what is going on inside of you, and take responsibility for your own safety. Ask yourself, *Am I resisting what is in my best interest because someone else wants this for me?* When protecting yourself from being controlled becomes less important than choosing what is in your best interest, you will no longer be stuck. You can maintain your sense of self by making choices that are in your best interest, and not from the fear of losing yourself. You can give generously because it feels right—without the feeling of sacrificing yourself.

When you are feeling stuck or notice a self-defeating pattern of behavior, observe your internal power struggle. Is an authoritarian part of you attempting to run your life? Does a part of you ignore your feelings in an attempt to control you? Is this generating a power struggle with the resistant part of you that refuses to be controlled? Even though your controlling and resistant selves are trying to keep you safe, you will invariably recognize an impasse between them. Fearing invasion and annihilation, your resistant self repeatedly sabotages your controlling self. As soon as you watch yourself choosing to resist, you are no longer functioning unconsciously. Conscious choice is now available to you. You can choose what is in your best interest instead of resisting control.

Fear of Rejection

Some people were abused and abandoned by their parents, and are carrying thick scars of emotional deprivation. Some suffered intolerable rejection when they did not comply with their parents' wishes. If you didn't learn that you are essentially valuable and lovable, you may still depend on others to define your value. Fear of rejection is a direct consequence of not defining your own value and lovability. By seeking external definition, you are at tremendous risk of further rejection. When you experience rejection from others, you are personally affected in direct proportion to your self-esteem.

You may refrain from pursuing your goals for fear of the scorn, anger, or jealousy that you could receive from others. In an effort to please others and be acceptable to them, you may even violate your principles by acting in ways that are at cross purposes with your authentic needs. You are afraid of being lonely and feeling unlovable.

You can overcome your fear of being unlovable by observing

how you reject yourself. By compassionately embracing your inner rejecter, you will learn about its needs and purpose. You can then formulate your most constructive strategy to get these needs met. By accepting all aspects of yourself—particularly the most wounded, ugly parts—and taking the best actions to take care of them, you will reduce your dependency on others to do this for you. Once you take responsibility for loving yourself, you can view rejection from others as your teacher. The more rejections you experience, the more knowledge you will accumulate. When you look upon rejection as your best opportunity to learn and optimize, you will be empowered to approach people you find attractive, make the extra attempt to sell your product, interview for a job you have always wanted, or set a loving boundary to avoid violating yourself. Ask yourself: *What would I do right now if I wasn't afraid of what other people would think about me?* Then put your best foot forward. The most successful people are those who face the most rejection. They learn how to handle rejection by subjecting themselves to many rejections. The fear of rejection does not stop them from moving forward.

Many famous actors were rejected on numerous occasions before they became successful. The production studios in Hollywood repeatedly rejected the film *Crocodile Dundee*. They thought it had little box office appeal. Nevertheless, actor Paul Hogan and manager John Cornell persisted. *Crocodile Dundee* was a major international success and broke box office records in the United States.

Eighteen publishers rejected Richard Bach's best-selling book *Jonathan Livingston Seagull*. It was finally published in 1970. By 1975, more than seven million copies had been sold in the United States, and millions more throughout the world.

Actually, there is no such thing as rejection—only a mismatch of agendas. It is not unreasonable to expect that people won't want the same things at the same time. Don't take it personally if others don't want you in their lives. You are just as good as the best of them. Focus on accepting yourself unconditionally, thinking Optimally, feeling as good as possible, and doing what's in your best interest.

Fear of Failure

"You must never give up. You must remember that you have to take risks in order to achieve anything and sometimes you will suffer defeat. But the mark of any individual is to recover from defeat and disappointment and go on and give it his best shot."
—Richard Milhous Nixon

All of us have experienced the disappointment of broken dreams. We feel bad when we think of goals we didn't achieve. Most of us have experienced a broken relationship, lost money in a business venture, or failed to achieve the results we wanted in an important project. Many people who haven't affirmed their intrinsic value believe that their accomplishments define their worth. This erroneous belief creates performance anxiety and fear of failure.

Do you fear the hurt and disappointment often associated with failure? Do you choose to play it safe rather than risk failure? As a baby, you made numerous attempts to walk before you accomplished the task successfully. Failure is an educational aspect of progress. *Your greatest failures provide you with your most valuable learning opportunities.* Each learning experience arms you with knowledge and insight to use *next time.*

The following is an inventory of a life history of failures. This man

at age 22, failed in business;

at age 23, was defeated in a legislative race;

at age 25, failed in business again;

at age 26, experienced the death of a loved one;

at age 27, experienced a nervous breakdown;

at age 29, was defeated in an election;

at age 34, was defeated in a congressional race;

at age 37, was defeated in a congressional race;

at age 39, was defeated in a congressional race;

at age 46, was defeated in a senatorial race;

at age 47, failed to become vice president;

at age 49, was defeated in a senatorial race;

at age 51, was elected the president of the United States.

His name was Abraham Lincoln.

Do you appreciate the value of adversity? Are you aware that adversity shows you what you're made of? It actually inspires personal optimization. You need not be concerned with how low you fall. How you respond to adversity—how quickly you optimize— and how high you rise above it are what count. Simply call forth your highest self. A pilot continually corrects his flight course before reaching the chosen destination. He simply notices the deviations and takes the best actions to rectify them. Similarly, Optimal Thinkers confront obstacles and undesired outcomes by accepting them, learning from them, and then taking the best actions to overcome them. They minimize time loss by asking: *Which action(s) will express my best self?*, *What's the best action I can take to overcome this?*, *What's the best solution?* When suboptimal thinkers experience the same obstacles, they stay off track for longer periods and don't bounce back to their Optimal level.

When faced with obstacles, negative thinkers often give up on their goals. They scold themselves with statements like: "If only I had tried this" or "Every time I make a little headway, something bad gets in the way." The price they have to pay seems overwhelming and the rewards do not appear to justify the means. They label their lack of persistence as failure. By concentrating on unwanted outcomes, negative thinkers experience fear and program themselves for failure.

You can maximize your motivation to accomplish goals by constantly reminding yourself of what you will lose by not achieving them and of all the benefits you will enjoy once you reach them. Visualize your goals as already achieved and trust in your ability to meet your own needs. Right now, what would you attempt if you knew there was no chance of failure? Would you act differently? Has fear of failure been holding you back?

Fear of Success

Many people fear the changes that can accompany success. They fear that their success will be gained at someone else's expense or that they might grow away from family and friends and end up alone. They may fear public scrutiny, disapproval, and jealousy. They may be terrified of the unknown. Some people fill their environment with clutter or become ill in an attempt to thwart their own success.

Recently I chatted with a business owner who told me that he was reluctant to have his personal name associated with any of his company's projects. He was afraid that if his name was linked to the pinnacle of success, his life would go downhill. He said, "What goes up must come down."

Last year, I presented an *Optimal Thinking for Sales Success* seminar to forty sales executives of a medium-size company. During the seminar, I talked about salespeople who experienced intolerable anxiety as they approached success. After the seminar, Angela came to my office for some private consultations. She had a history of moving from job to job. As soon as her sales were above quota, Angela experienced excruciating anxiety and was unable to work. She would distract herself with unimportant tasks, find fault with her job, and soon thereafter quit.

I inquired about her relationship with her parents, and how she felt as a young girl when she experienced success. She confessed that her parents rarely paid attention to her when she was growing up. The only time she received attention from them was when she was sick. She recalled how lonely and hurt she felt when she landed the lead role in her school play and her parents didn't bother to show up. After that painful experience, she never auditioned for an acting role. I responded with, "Is it possible that you are afraid of losing your parents if you become successful?" Angela's face crunched up and she began to sob. After about ten minutes, she told me that whenever she quit a job, her parents were there for her. However, when she was doing well, she didn't hear from them. I asked: "Is it more important to have your parents' attention, or to do your best and achieve your full potential?" She beamed and said: "I now understand what has been blocking my success. I am ready to be my best!" The following week, Angela entered my office grinning from ear to ear. "My sales are skyrocketing!" she gloated.

In order to associate feelings of safety and comfort with success, think about how your fear of success weakens you. Weigh the destructive impact of this core belief against the advantages you are experiencing. Now consider why it is in your best interest to be successful. Think about all the times you've experienced success and were relaxed and comfortable. Gather as much evidence as you can that you are comfortable with success. Embrace success as your birthright. You were born to create a successful life, and to enjoy all the benefits. To overcome your fears, ask Optimal questions such as:

- What am I thinking or doing that is causing me to feel unsafe?
- What am I thinking or doing that is preventing me from being all I can be?
- What are the best actions I can take to overcome this?
- What must I think and do to feel completely comfortable with success?
- How can I enjoy making the most of my life?

Make friends with your fears. They are an integral part of you and there are reasons for them. Face them mercifully, seek to understand them, and commit yourself to resolving them. Entertain thoughts of safety, and visualize yourself enjoying success at every opportune moment.

Fear of Pain

"Give the world the best you have and you may get hurt. Give the world your best anyway."

—Mother Teresa

Most parents do their best to shield their young children against pain. Sometimes, however, they protect themselves from their own pain by stopping the children from expressing theirs. We grow up afraid of pain and develop defenses to protect us from experiencing it. Have you ever been hurt and then stopped risking because you were afraid of more pain? You cannot eliminate pain in life, but you can minimize it by learning what hurts most and by understanding the source of the pain. Your fear of pain can then motivate you to solve your problems without delay.

Many people are hindered by their fear of physical pain. Sandy was such a person. Sandy's back had been troubling her for over a year but she had done nothing about it. When her boyfriend invited her to Aspen, she refused because she was afraid of the pain she might experience if she lost her balance on the ski slopes. When Sandy realized what she was missing out on, she became motivated to resolve her pain and took the best actions to find relief.

Most people fear emotional pain. Consider Wendy, a woman who had been emotionally hurt in several relationships. Her last boyfriend knew about it and was attentive to her every need. He was reliable and called her several times a day. He romanced her with thoughtful cards and candlelit dinners, introduced her to his family, helped her resolve her problems, and bought her gifts. He told Wendy that he loved her and that she was his ideal woman. He then asked her to stop seeing other men.

After several months, Wendy committed herself to him. One week later, he began to boast about his previous conquests with other women. He stopped attending to her emotional needs and didn't call when he said he would. He also began to shower her with a variety of expensive gifts. Baffled by his behavior, Wendy asked him if he was seeing another woman. He swore to her that there was no one else. Then Wendy received several phone calls from his ex-girlfriend—who told Wendy that she was in a triangle—and when her boyfriend refused to see her that Saturday night, she knew she had to end the relationship.

Wendy felt betrayed and shattered. A year later she was still afraid of trusting another man and of risking more pain. During an *Optimal Thinking for Relationships* seminar, Wendy admitted that she had been aware of her boyfriend's dishonesty early on, but that her need for a relationship had taken precedence over her good judgment. She took complete responsibility for the hurt she had created and for her life in general. She then committed her best efforts to finding a trustworthy man.

Has fear of pain been holding you back? If so, take some time to identify the pain you are most afraid of. Now consider the actions you can take to overcome your fear. Write them down. Choose the best so that you can put this to rest!

5. I Can't Have What I Want

"When you want what you can have, you can have what you want."
—Optimal Thinker

When you believe you can't have what you want, you can become fearful of even thinking about what you want, because you "know" you can't have it. How can you eliminate this disabling belief? Think about how this belief originated. You may have been denied what you wanted from an early age. Perhaps you were labeled selfish for even wanting something for yourself. Perhaps your aspirations were ridiculed. You may have felt uncomfortable sharing your dreams and goals. You may have been frustrated because you didn't have what you wanted.

As a child, Collette had big dreams. Many people thought she had delusions of grandeur. She was even told that what she wanted didn't exist. As an adult, Collette made a list of her most important goals. She was tired of feeling frustrated and wanted to believe that she could have what she wanted. She was ready to stop limiting herself and to free her mind of restrictions. She knew that if she continued to believe she couldn't have what she wanted, that's what would happen. Whenever she lost track of her goals, she told herself, *I can have exactly what I want.* She then confronted and resolved her unsupportive responses.

If you committed yourself to designing your most desirable lifestyle, what would it look like? How would it empower you? You can experience it right now. During the seminar mentioned previously, participants listen to an audiotape. "I can have exactly what I want" is gently repeated while soothing background music plays. Some participants experience no mental chatter and feel inspired and invigorated. Others actually visualize having what they want. Many, however, experience obstructing thoughts, feelings, visions, childhood memories, and recent experiences requiring resolution.

If you are strongly committed to the belief that you can't have what you want, start thinking about all the damage this belief has caused you in the past and the pain you will experience if you hold on to it. Once you have decided that holding on to this belief is not in your best interest, note your reactions to the following declarations:

- I'm willing to believe I can have what I want.
- I'm willing to have what I want.
- I can have exactly what I want.

Be sure to seek the best resolution of any unsupportive thoughts or feelings rather than denying and suppressing them.

To integrate the belief of having what you want, keep your mind on what you want, the benefits you will gain, and the reasons why you can have it. Written Optimal declarations strategically placed in the most appropriate locations will assist you in staying focused. Place your declarations in your diary or wallet, on the bathroom mirror, refrigerator door, or car dashboard. The best places to display them are where you are most likely to see them. You may even be inspired to compose a poem. The most compelling visual representations of your greatest desires combined with the Optimal question *What's the best action I can take toward my goal right now?* will keep you steadily on the best track.

If you are predominantly auditory, you can record your most important goals as declarations on an endless cassette. Create pauses between statements so that you can tune in to your responses. You might want to include soothing background music to maximize the integration process. You can also record your Optimal thoughts on a cassette tape as lyrics to your favorite tune. Create your own Optimal song! Listen to it and sing it with full fervor as often as possible. Make it your theme song!

Here's how it worked for Sandra, a social worker who had always been unproductive at the beginning of the day—she just wasn't a morning person. Sandra recorded her Optimal declarations to song and played the tape on her way to work. By the time she arrived, she was on top of the world. Make a tape for yourself and sing yourself into your Optimal state of being. When you are in this state of being, you will attract more of it around you. You can create your ultimate daily life!

If you are predominantly feelings-oriented, consider which feelings you associate with Optimal experiences. Meditate on feeling calm, relaxed, and peaceful as you imagine yourself having exactly what you want.

6. Life Is a Struggle

Many people did not have an easy home life. Their parents may have been very difficult to please. They may have had to compete with brothers or sisters and struggled desperately to be their siblings' equal in areas that did not utilize their greatest talents. Their parents may have struggled to make ends meet financially. They got the message that life is a struggle.

Many people who have experienced life as a struggle truly believe that this is the way it's meant to be. Even the former prime minister of Australia, Malcolm Fraser, shared this belief. Some years ago, he declared to the Australian nation that "Life wasn't meant to be easy!" Here are some more examples:

Martin lost his father at an early age. His mother was forced to work very hard to support her three children and was rarely at home. From that time on, Martin believed that life was a struggle. He worked extremely hard, eventually becoming a real estate developer. His days were fraught with worry and indecisiveness. His nights were often sleepless. Even when he became highly successful, he couldn't enjoy his money. He felt depressed and purposeless. His life continues to be a struggle.

Helen finds it very difficult to keep her body in shape. Even though she feels guilty when she binges on large quantities of junk food, she can't stop herself. She knows she should exercise, but keeps putting it off. The battle of the bulge feels like an endless struggle that is mostly out of her control.

Many people create struggle by refusing to accept "what is" in the present moment. The intensity of your struggle is directly related to your degree of resistance. *The present moment is all there is, all you have, and all you will ever have, so it is senseless to resist it.* By resisting the eternal present, you are resisting life itself. By disidentifying with your resistance and observing it, you discover your innermost power. You access the full might of your own conscious presence. Instead of judging and resisting the present moment, just allow it to be. Accept it as if it were your own choice. This will give you an experience of freedom from external circumstances, and authentic inner peace. Once you accept the present moment and work with it rather than against it, life starts working for you rather than against you. You can resolve unacceptable external situations by accepting them completely, optimizing them, or removing yourself from their influence. Just take the most discerning actions and observe what happens. If necessary, you can call upon the past and future to optimize the present moment.

Are you creating internal battles because you believe in hardship and struggle? You can weaken your belief in struggle by questioning your reasons for accepting it. Be sure to answer the Optimal question *What is the easiest path to ensure my success in life?* Take some time to acknowledge the ease with which you accomplish daily activities such as getting dressed, preparing breakfast, and reading the newspaper. Choose goals that are clearly attainable, then take the easiest path toward them by answering Optimal questions like:

- What's the easiest way to reach this goal?
- What's the easiest action I can take?
- What's the path of least resistance?

Now, in your notebook, make a list of all the things you have accomplished with ease, and review it every day.

Norma's Story

Here's an example of how life can change when you get rid of self-limiting core beliefs.

When Norma's mother abandoned her at five years of age, she decided that there must be something wrong with her. She then spent six happy years in a foster home before her mother took her back—against Norma's wishes. As a result, Norma concluded that she couldn't have what she wanted.

Her mother struggled to make ends meet and often told Norma that "aspiring for the best things in life will only lead to disappointment." Norma adopted her mother's belief of not being worthy of the best in life and developed a fear of success. Because she associated success with disappointment, she felt hopeless and experienced life as a struggle. Norma married a man she didn't love because she thought no one else would want her. Even when she knew she was right, she didn't stand up for herself. After her divorce, she had several painful relationships with men who abused her physically and emotionally.

When Norma heard me on a radio interview, she called my office. Although now a successful marketing executive, she was unhappy in her job. She wanted to start her own business but was afraid to make a move. She felt bad because she had not been in a relationship for six years and was overweight. During our private consultations, Norma's self-limiting core beliefs were uncovered and dismantled. She became consistent in her use of Optimal Thinking and began to make the most of her strengths and opportunities. She doubled her sales output and her division became the best in her region. She lost the excess weight and entered into a relationship with a fine man. She even started a part-time home-based business with a group of friends. She gained full control of her life.

Some time later, Norma came to an *Optimal Thinking for Self-Esteem* seminar. She radiated ultimate self-confidence and self-respect. When the participants were tested for negative core beliefs and saw that Norma was free of them, they asked her what it was like. She replied, "I am taking full responsibility for my life. I can truly say that I am making the most of it."

When you consciously choose to use Optimal Thinking at every opportune moment, monitor your progress, and commit to dismantling your limiting core beliefs, your life will reflect the best of you.

Optimal Questions

1. What is most important to me?
2. Which beliefs do I need to achieve what is most important to me?
3. How can I be sure that these beliefs are in my best interest?
4. What is the best way to overcome any obstacles that do not support these beliefs?
5. How much of my activity validated these beliefs today/this week?

Optimal Action Steps

1. Think about the last time that you felt victimized by another person. What did you want from that person that you were not giving yourself? If you haven't done so already, decide upon the best actions to provide this for yourself.
2. Decide upon a unique Optimal statement for responding to criticism. Write it down and practice using it in situations where you anticipate admonition. When you are face to face with a critic, employ your Optimal response. Initially you may feel

awkward, but with practice, your Optimal response will become second nature.

3. In your notebook, complete the sentence "If I wasn't afraid, I would _____" until you have exhausted everything that comes to mind. Now ask: *What am I thinking or doing to create this fear?* Finally, ask: *What are the best actions I can take to overcome my fear?*

PART TWO

Optimize Yourself

"Your thought is the parent that gives birth to all things."
—Neale Donald Walsch

Rate Your Self-Esteem, Purpose, and Goals

The following questionnaire will enable you to assess your self-esteem, purpose, and goals. Simply circle the number that best describes your thoughts about yourself and your current situation. Then add your score.

3 = *Always*   1 = *Reasonably or sometimes*
2 = *Usually or often*   0 = *Rarely or never*

1. I am confident that I can enjoy the best in life.   0   1   2   3
2. I feel competent to deal with my life.   0   1   2   3
3. I accept all parts of my personality.   0   1   2   3
4. I am comfortable expressing my thoughts, needs, and wants.   0   1   2   3
5. I believe in myself.   0   1   2   3
6. I accept my body completely.   0   1   2   3
7. I can rely on myself to make the wisest decisions.   0   1   2   3
8. I put my best self in charge.   0   1   2   3
9. I am aware of my purpose in life.   0   1   2   3
10. I know what is supremely important to me.   0   1   2   3
11. I am committed to living life with purpose.   0   1   2   3
12. I know the best way to achieve my most important goal.   0   1   2   3
13. I make the best use of my time.   0   1   2   3
14. I deserve to be happy.   0   1   2   3
15. I forgive myself for making mistakes.   0   1   2   3
16. I make the best use of a daily calendar.   0   1   2   3
17. My decisions are consistent with my highest values and principles.   0   1   2   3
18. I am a compassionate person.   0   1   2   3
19. I am comfortable when I am alone and with others.   0   1   2   3
20. I am grateful for all the good in my life.   0   1   2   3
21. I deal with my feelings as soon as I notice them.   0   1   2   3

22. I listen to the messages my painful feelings
    give me.   0   1   2   3

23. I give love without expectation of anything
    in return.   0   1   2   3

24. I can handle myself when I am emotionally hurt. 0   1   2   3

25. I trust myself to behave appropriately.   0   1   2   3

If your score is 70–75, you are already employing Optimal Thinking consistently. This section of *Optimal Thinking* will reinforce your thinking and provide you with additional ways to optimize your self-esteem, purpose, and goals.

If your score is 46–70, your self-esteem, purpose, and goals are extraordinary; however, you have not accomplished what might still be possible or in your best interest. This section of *Optimal Thinking* will empower you to take the best actions to make the *most* of yourself and your life. When you choose the best and do not settle for second best, you experience a sense of completion in your life.

If your score is 16–45, your self-esteem, purpose, and goals are mediocre. You doubt your capabilities and are not making the most of your talents and life. In this section of *Optimal Thinking*, you will gain knowledge, skills, and confidence to support your best interests. You will embrace your uniqueness, and learn how to make the most of yourself and your life.

If your score is 0–15, your self-esteem, purpose, and goals are negative. You are probably feeling disheartened right now. You may believe that you don't have what it takes to create a life that supports your best interests. Many people feel like that. In this section of *Optimal Thinking*, you will gain knowledge, skills, and confidence to optimize your self-esteem, purpose, and goals. Just take as much time as you need to complete the exercises. You will create a SUPREME plan to make the most of your life. You can then take actions that are in your best interests. Go for it!

CHAPTER 4

Achieve Optimal Self-Esteem

"If you are doing all that you can to the fullest of your ability as well as you can, there is nothing else that is asked of a soul."
—Gary Zukav

Self-Esteem: What's It All About?

"I have trouble forming a healthy intimate relationship because deep down I don't feel good about myself."

"When everything is going right, this little voice inside me says this is too good to be true, and sure enough, something goes wrong. I can't seem to win!"

"I feel guilty whenever I argue with anyone, even when I know I'm right."

When you were growing up, your parents and other important people gave you many signals about the kind of person you were. Some of their signals were encouraging, loving, and validating. They may have said such things as "I love you," "You are my pride and joy," "You're a clever kid," "You can succeed at anything when you put your mind to it." Other messages from these authorities were far from Optimal and certainly not affirmative. You may have heard: "Why did you do a dumb thing like that?," "You never do anything right," "You're a bad child." What you thought about yourself and how you felt when receiving those messages formed the basis of your self-esteem. Your level of self-esteem today is based on the thoughts and feelings you have accumulated about yourself since that time.

In *The Six Pillars of Self-Esteem*, Dr. Nathaniel Branden, commonly known as "the father of the self-esteem movement," offers this definition: "Self-esteem is the disposition to experience oneself as competent to cope with the challenges of life and as deserving of happiness." At the First International Conference on Self-Esteem in Oslo in 1990, Dr. Branden said: "We have reached a moment in history when self-esteem, which has always been a supremely important psychological need, has also become a supremely important economic need—the attribute imperative for adaptiveness to an increasingly complex, challenging, and competitive world. . . ."

The way you think and feel about yourself affects every aspect of your life. When you love, accept, respect, and approve of yourself, you validate your existence. Do you feel worthy of life's greatest offerings? Are you confident that you can experience the best in life? You can maximize your self-esteem. You will achieve your highest level of self-esteem when you can rely upon yourself to accurately assess your reality, make the best choices to deal with your challenges, and make the most of life. You will be comfortable expressing your thoughts, needs, and wants, and will feel entitled to enjoy the results of your best efforts. You will feel worthy of happiness and of life's best offerings.

In an article entitled "Hey, I'm Terrific!" in the February 17, 1992, issue of *Newsweek*, the following information was revealed. "Although only one in 10 Americans believes he personally suffers from low self-esteem, according to a *Newsweek* Gallup Poll, more than 50 percent diagnose the condition in someone else in their families."

Unfortunately, many people don't like or respect themselves. People with low self-esteem feel there is something wrong with them. They are self-critical and feel bad about themselves. They lack self-confidence and self-respect. They consider themselves incompetent and unworthy of the best in life. Do you identify with this description? If so, you can learn how to minimize those thoughts and feelings.

Some people experience great success but feel empty inside. Although admired by their spouses, business associates, and friends, they feel unworthy. Others are honored for their actions with awards, yet deep down regard themselves as incompetent. They lack confidence in their ability to handle life's problems and challenges. Marilyn Monroe, superstar actress, was such a person. Even though she was crowned as a sensational beauty, adored by the masses, and pursued by the most powerful men of her day, Marilyn often felt bad about herself.

Perhaps you fluctuate between liking and disliking yourself. People with average self-esteem fluctuate between feeling good and bad, right and wrong, worthy and undeserving. At times they are confident, and at other times uncertain. Does this describe you?

Our Internal Voices

"Words are a lens to focus one's mind."

—Ayn Rand

Self-esteem is an internal experience. It implies a sense of personal confidence, worthiness, and competence. When we are compassionate toward our weaknesses and forgive ourselves for making mistakes, we embrace our vulnerability and humanity. When we validate ourselves and trust our internal voices, we esteem ourselves. We all hear internal chatter. Represented below are some inner voices. Which do you identify with most often?

Optimal Voice—Your Highest Voice!

The Optimal voice expresses mastery, completion, and everything superlative: the most constructive, the best, the highest, the wisest, the most valuable; what is right, impeccable, supreme, peak, maximum, optimum, uppermost, ultimate, paramount, unsurpassed, unparalleled—Optimal!

It maximizes, masters, epitomizes, perfects, corrects, solves, completes, fulfills, fills, wins, tops, triumphs, accomplishes, succeeds, heads, accepts, appreciates, leads, takes the best path, loves unconditionally—optimizes!

Listen to these Optimal voices speak:

- I accept myself, warts and all. I deserve the best life has to offer.
- I am doing the best I can!
- I'm making the most of my situation.
- I completed every design project on budget and on time last year.

To make the best use of your Optimal voice, start by affirming your right to be exactly as you are without justification or judgment. Accept, approve, and love yourself unconditionally. You are doing your best according to your awareness at this time!

Suboptimal Voices

The *negative suboptimal voice* is heard in criticism, judgment, attack, slander, harm, hurt, disadvantage, frustration, failure, fault-finding, destruction, tragedy, inferiority, weakness, loss, hopelessness, injury, aggravation. It criticizes, demeans, slanders, blames, sabotages, undermines, depreciates, hurts, rejects, disapproves, doubts, worries, fears, discourages, condemns, destroys, weakens.

The *positive suboptimal voice* focuses on the certain, beneficial, sound, confident, assured, wise, constructive, affirmative, accepted, valuable. It assures, encourages, inspires, validates, empowers, affirms, confirms, supports, uplifts, respects, appreciates, esteems, enjoys, strengthens.

The *mediocre suboptimal voice*, which can be negative, neutral, or positive, talks about the ordinary, fair, good, common, commonplace, average, insignificant, customary, usual, conventional, run-of-the-mill, unnoticeable, moderate. It compromises, averages, takes the middle path.

Finally, the *extraordinary suboptimal voice*, which can be negative or positive, expresses the great, outstanding, remarkable, exceptional, stunning, sensational, astounding, fabulous, phenomenal, incredible, mammoth, uncommon, unusual. It surpasses, exceeds, stands out, stuns, distinguishes, impresses.

Optimize Your Suboptimal Voices

Do your suboptimal voices dominate your thinking process? You can accept them, learn from them, and optimize them. Acknowledging and resolving your destructive negative voice is necessary for a healthy self-concept. Embracing and optimizing your other suboptimal voices is your commitment to your highest level of self-esteem.

You can make the most of your internal talk by employing your Optimal voice at every opportune moment. When your suboptimal voices chatter, commission OptiSelf—your highest self, best friend, imaginary ultimate mentor, cosmic guide, unconditional lover—to talk to them. OptiSelf takes care of all your needs and expresses the best of you. OptiSelf understands that you are a multifaceted being with good, bad, and ugly voices like all humankind. OptiSelf always embraces and validates your suboptimal voices, then optimizes them. Let's tune in on some of OptiSelf's responses to negative voices.

Negative Voice: I should have eaten less. It's difficult to get rid of this extra weight!

OptiSelf: I know you're feeling guilty and overweight. What's the best thing you can do right now to stop feeling guilty and start losing weight?

Mediocre Negative Voice: I'm pretty lousy at resolving conflicts.

OptiSelf: You lack confidence in your ability to resolve conflicts. What's the most important thing that you can keep in mind to optimize your skills at resolving conflicts? What's the best thing you can do to optimize your self-confidence?

Extraordinarily Negative Voice: I feel deeply hurt right now.

OptiSelf: You're feeling very wounded. I'm here for you no matter how you feel. Are you willing to look at what are you thinking or doing to create this? What do you think is the best thing you can do about it?

Extraordinarily Negative Voice: I feel extremely inadequate. I'm trying very hard and am not getting what I want.

OptiSelf: I understand that you're feeling deficient. Just remember that I accept you unconditionally. Now, what's preventing you from achieving the results you want? What's the best way to overcome these obstacles? What's the best use of your time?

To optimize your suboptimal voices, start writing your Optimal responses on paper. Carry your notebook with you. Jot down each suboptimal message, then write OptiSelf's response. The more you practice, the more competent you will become. When the technique becomes second nature, you can do it mentally. Now let's listen to OptiSelf maximize other suboptimal voices.

Positive Voice: I produced the video and I'm pleased with it.

OptiSelf: You're feeling happy. What did you like most about it?

Mediocre Positive Voice: Some pretty good opportunities come my way from time to time.

OptiSelf: You sound reasonably optimistic. What's the best opportunity you can act upon right now?

Extraordinary Positive Voice: My business is flourishing. It is incredibly profitable.

OptiSelf: Your business is doing very well. What is your most profitable product? How can you maximize its profitability?

How Do You Value and Rate Yourself Now?

It's now time to do some personal stocktaking. Take your pen and notebook to a quiet place where you won't be disturbed. Be diligent in following the written instructions.

Assets

When we were growing up, our parents and teachers cautioned us against boasting. We were criticized for being braggarts when we talked expansively about ourselves. Many of us were told, "Actions speak louder than words." As a result, most of us feel uncomfortable talking openly about our strengths.

The six categories below have been chosen to assist you in accurately describing your assets. For each category, write down your favorable attributes. Note what you like about yourself. Be as specific as possible. After you have identified your strengths, arrange them in order of greatest benefit to you, starting with your greatest asset and then proceeding down your list with those assets of lesser benefit to you.

Here is how Anne, a successful public relations executive I counseled, defined her hierarchy of assets. Use the same format for your inventory.

1. Physical Assets

large blue eyes
well-proportioned body
well-shaped mouth, white teeth
good height
long blond hair
look good in fitted clothing
well-shaped calves

2. Mental and Spiritual Strengths

intuitive
mostly positive, sometimes Optimal
polished behavior with spontaneous wit
confident about mental capability
single-minded when necessary
belief in a supreme universal force
logical

good knowledge of world affairs
creative thinker

3. Personality Strengths

inspiring
extrovert
responsible
warm
open
fun
talkative
fairly even-tempered

4. Social Strengths

interested in others
communicate openly
sincere
generally positive
good listener, compassionate
warm, caring
tolerant of others' ideas

5. Career and/or Daily Task Strengths

punctual
excellent face-to-face presentation skills
generally keep my word
competent P.R. skills
well organized
establish good rapport with clients

6. Personal Achievements

offered a 20 percent salary increase
established supportive group of friends
top P.R. person in company this year
bought three-bedroom home
lost over 30 pounds last year
key speaker at P.R. Institute convention

7. *What I Like Most about Myself*

can be very positive and inspiring
I am tenacious
attractive appearance
I have a good sense of humor
warm, kind, and caring to family, friends, and others

Liabilities

Now, for each category, make a list of your negative traits. When addressing your weaknesses and limitations, avoid the use of disparaging terminology. Be specific and nonjudgmental. For example, instead of saying, "I have terrible skin," say, "At the moment there are two blemishes on my cheeks." Instead of "I'm a fat slob," substitute "I'm fifteen pounds overweight." After you have identified your weaknesses, rank them in order of priority, starting with your greatest liability and then proceeding down your list with those liabilities that are less of a problem to you.

Anne's liability inventory took the following form:

1. *Physical Liabilities*

poor muscle tone
nearly 6 pounds overweight
thighs 1 or 2 inches too large
wrinkles around eyes
freckles, liver spots, and scars on skin
cellulite on upper legs

2. *Mental and Spiritual Liabilities*

repeat self on occasion, repeat self on occasion, repeat self . . .
overly critical
too negative
perfectionist
don't accept conflicting religious beliefs graciously

3. *Personality Weaknesses*

argumentative at times
overly talkative
dogmatic on occasion
moody
compromise integrity on unimportant issues

4. Social Weaknesses

can be loud
easily upset by others' put-downs
overly critical of others
can be unforgiving
fluctuate in feelings toward people
sensitive, angry when contradicted

5. Career and/or Daily Task Weaknesses

wavering dedication and motivation
poor delegation skills
inconsistent

6. Personal Disappointments

My two marriages were disasters

7. What I Dislike Most about Myself

I am overly critical of myself and others
I can't cook
I feel like a failure when I am around couples with children
my two marriages were disasters, and I don't have a steady
   boyfriend now
I am overweight
my body is not sufficiently toned

When Anne completed her list of weaknesses she noticed the items mentioned were more specific than those on her strengths inventory. She realized that she had always focused more attention on her liabilities than on her assets.

Your Self-Esteem

How would you describe your self-esteem? Do you have low, average, high, or Optimal self-esteem? Take some time now to jot down your thoughts and feelings about yourself. When Anne wrote how she felt about herself in the paragraph below, she realized she wavered in her liking for herself.

Sometimes I like myself and feel good. At other times, I dislike myself and feel inadequate. I guess I have average self-esteem. I seem to have extraordinarily high self-esteem when it comes to my work and social life. In other areas, there is plenty of room for improvement. At times I feel like a failure because I haven't managed to find a life partner and have a family. I also hate myself when I compromise my principles over small issues. I don't know why I do that.

Your Best Self

"Making the best of ourselves is the reason we were born, but it requires patience and perseverance."
—Sarah Ban Breathnach

It is time to embrace your vision of your best self—and your highest level of self-esteem. You deserve to experience ultimate self-confidence and self-respect, and to see yourself as the person you want to be. To help you make your vision of your best self completely concrete, review the following Optimal techniques, suggestions, and questions.

Optimize Your Assets

Take out the notebook that lists your assets and liabilities and look at your list of assets. Now, under each asset, write the best actions you can take to appreciate, optimize, and enjoy the full benefit of it. It is in your best interest to accept what you can't change and optimize what you can! For example, you may think, "It would be terrific to be taller!" In this case, all you can do is accept your height, focus on all the advantages of being as tall as you are, and make the most of it. To optimize an asset, simply ask the Optimal question, *How can I make the most of this asset?* Take pride in all your assets by reminding yourself of all the benefits you enjoy because of them. You can do this at every opportune moment.

The following represents a selection from Anne's list.

1. Physical Assets
Large blue eyes. Optimize by appreciating this asset daily; investigate best makeup to make the most of size, color, and shape of eyes.

2. Mental and Spiritual Assets
Intuitive. Optimize by appreciating this asset daily; make sure to trust and follow my intuition at every opportune moment.

Mostly positive, sometimes Optimal. Optimize by appreciating this asset daily; place Optimal signs in strategic places to remind me to think Optimally.

3. Personality Strengths

Inspiring. Optimize by appreciating this asset daily; encourage Ray to finish his project.

Extrovert. Optimize by appreciating this asset daily; make sure I am in contact with at least two clients and one prospective client every day.

4. Social Strengths

Interested in others. Optimize by appreciating this asset daily; ask others about their greatest pleasures. Find out what I can do to bring out the best in them.

Communicate openly. Optimize by appreciating this asset daily; tell my friends that I wish to support their best endeavors and ask them to share with me how I can best do this.

5. Career and/or Daily Task Strengths

Punctual. Optimize by appreciating this asset daily.

Excellent face-to-face presentation skills. Optimize by appreciating this asset daily; schedule one hour each day to maximize presentations.

6. Personal Achievements

Offered a 20 percent salary increase. Optimize by appreciating this asset daily; book a vacation to Hawaii; buy a new dining room set.

Established supportive group of friends. Optimize by appreciating this asset daily; make sure I speak to each of them at least once a week. Invite friends over at least twice each month.

7. What I Like Most about Myself

Can be very positive and inspiring. Optimize by appreciating this asset daily; affirm "I am an Optimal Thinker. I am now optimizing my mental attractiveness. I am the most inspiring person I can possibly be."

When Anne wrote her list of action steps to optimize her assets, she identified, in order of priority, the actions that would have the most beneficial effect on her self-confidence and self-respect. She identified the specific actions necessary to experience herself at her best. Here is the first part of her prioritized list:

1. Place items from my list of Optimal assets on computer screen saver and bathroom mirror to remind me to think Optimally and follow my intuition. (this evening)
2. Tell Julie, Robin, Chris, Henry, and Ray that I wish to support their best endeavors and ask them to share with me how I can best do this. (make the calls tonight)
3. Ask Julie, Robin, Chris, Henry, and Ray about their greatest pleasures. Find out what I can do to bring out the best in them. (during calls tonight)
4. Schedule time to make contact with at least two clients and one prospective client every day. (every morning at 9 A.M.)
5. Schedule one hour each day to maximize presentations. (every day, from 10:30 A.M. to 11:30 A.M.)
6. Book a vacation to Hawaii next month. (call travel agent Friday)
7. Buy a new dining room set. (set aside next Saturday to look for furniture)
8. Affirm "I am an Optimal Thinker. I am now optimizing my mental and spiritual attractiveness. I am the most inspiring person I can possibly be." (every morning when I wake up and just before I go to bed)

Have you completed your lists of action steps? What did you discover about yourself when you wrote out your inventory of personal assets and the best actions to make the most of them? Make sure you give yourself enough time to complete your most constructive actions. It is best to transfer your list to your daily calendar to ensure that it gets done. Allow me to encourage you to DO IT NOW!

Minimize Your Liabilities

As you go through your list of weaknesses, decide to accept yourself unconditionally. By extending compassion toward your weaknesses, you are honoring your humanity. Simply accept the weaknesses that can't be changed and resolve to correct those that can be changed.

To minimize any weakness, simply answer the following Optimal questions:

- What are all the benefits I will gain by correcting this weakness?
- What are all the losses I will avoid by correcting this weakness?
- What's the best way to minimize this weakness?

- What's the best action I can take NOW to move toward what I want?

Anne felt terrific when she completed her list. Here is a selection.

1. Physical Liabilities

Poor muscle tone. Minimize by accepting this; carry photo in purse to remind myself how great I can look and feel. Schedule five mornings a week, from 6:30 to 7:30 A.M. to work out at gym. When I'm working out, stay focused on the end result. Reward myself each time by taking an extra half hour to do what I really enjoy.

2. Mental and Spiritual Liabilities

Repeat self on occasion, repeat self on occasion, repeat self . . . Minimize by accepting this; be more aware of it and stop whenever I notice myself doing it.

Overly critical. Minimize by accepting this; affirm: "I now focus on what's right with myself and others. I am an Optimal Thinker. Whenever I focus on a problem, it's only because I'm looking for the best solution."

3. Personality Weaknesses

Argumentative at times. Minimize by accepting this; ask: "Is this the best thing to do right now? How can I achieve what I want without arguing? How can I make the most of this situation?"

Overly talkative. Minimize by accepting this; ask: "What's the best use of my time right now?" Be aware of the time I waste by talking too much.

4. Social Weaknesses

Can be loud. Minimize by accepting this; make a concerted effort to speak softly.

Easily upset by others' put-downs. Minimize by accepting this; get back on track by affirming: "This will pass. What's the best action I can take to overcome this?" or "I am now choosing to focus on what gives me the best feelings about myself." Talk to the person who put me down.

5. Career and/or Daily Task Weaknesses

Wavering dedication and motivation. Minimize by accepting this; schedule time to clarify the purpose of my work and its priority in my life.

6. Personal Disappointments

My two marriages were disasters. Minimize by accepting each marriage as the right opportunity to learn and grow. I did the best I could with the knowledge I had at the time.

7. What I Dislike Most about Myself

I am overly critical of myself and others. Minimize by accepting this; affirm: "I now focus on what's right with myself and others. I criticize only when I am interested in finding the best solution to the problem."

I can't cook. Minimize by accepting this; start using every opportune moment in the kitchen to maximize my cooking skills. Take cooking lessons.

When Anne completed her list of actions to correct her weaknesses, she again noticed that her weaknesses were more specific than her strengths. She had always been interested in self-improvement: she suddenly realized that she had formed the habit of finding fault with herself and correcting her flaws to temporarily avoid feeling bad about herself. By neglecting to appreciate and make the most of her strengths, she had robbed herself of self-esteem.

When she finished making the most of her assets, she concentrated on minimizing her weaknesses. She prioritized her most important action steps by asking: *Which action will be most beneficial to my self-confidence and self-respect?* In this way, she was able to choose from her lists the best actions to maximize her self-esteem. Here is her prioritized list of action steps to minimize her weaknesses:

1. Place photo of myself with toned body in purse. (this afternoon)
2. Schedule five mornings a week, from 6:30 to 7:30 A.M., to work out at gym. (Monday to Friday)
3. Schedule half hour fun time to reward myself for working out in gym. (Friday 5 P.M.)
4. Place affirmations on bathroom mirror, refrigerator, and computer screen saver to remind me to be the best person I can be. (tomorrow night)
5. Schedule time to clarify the purpose of my work and its priority in my life. (Wednesday 8 P.M.)
6. Enroll in cooking class at local community college. (call tomorrow afternoon)

You've seen what Anne did. Now look at your list of liabilities, then write down, in order of priority, the actions you will take to minimize your weaknesses. Make sure you write down the best actions to minimize your liabilities and negative traits. Be sure to allocate enough time, and to place your prioritized list on your daily calendar.

Use Optimal Affirmations

Optimal affirmations are first-person, present-tense, Optimal statements you implant in your mind to affirm the best results. They are verbal "act as if . . ." creative statements. When you have decided which Optimal affirmations you wish to integrate, you can write them repeatedly in your notebook. Be sure to jot down and resolve your unsupportive responses. You can also create other visual reminders. You can meditate on them, sing them, or record them on a cassette tape to listen to whenever you want. Here are some Optimal affirmations you may wish to use.

Optimal Affirmations for Body
- I enjoy the best of health. It's my birthright.
- I accept my body completely. I am making the most of it.
- Everything I eat produces my Optimal health, beauty, and weight.
- My body is in peak condition.
- I am looking my best.

Optimal Affirmations for Mind and Spirit
- I am an Optimal Thinker. I place my best self in charge.
- I now resolve to be the best I can be.
- I am doing my best.
- I can rely on myself to make the wisest decisions.
- I am now enjoying the best life has to offer.
- I am making the most of this situation.
- I am one with all of nature.

Optimal Social Affirmations
- I associate with the right people.
- I bring out the best in others.
- I have all the friends I need.
- I ask for what I want.
- I choose to accept and love others as they are.

Visualize Your Best Self

"Your imagination is the preview to life's coming attractions."
—Albert Einstein

Our minds can't easily distinguish between what we visualize and what we actually experience. Many experiments support this. One well-known experiment by psychologists involved a number of men divided into three groups. One group practiced basketball every day, the second mentally visualized themselves practicing, and the third—the control group—did neither. The study found that the men who physically practiced and those who mentally practiced were equally good on the court. The control group lost to both groups.

Other experiments have shown that when people visualize themselves performing an action—running, for example—the muscles associated with that action contract in small but definite amounts. You can prove this to yourself by closing your eyes and imagining yourself sucking on a lemon. Your mouth will pucker and start to water.

Optimal visualization enables you to convey to your subconscious mind exactly what you want by using the best pictures and symbols and all of your senses. By giving yourself the Optimal preview, the desired result becomes real and concrete and you prepare yourself to experience the best. You start to adjust yourself toward having what you want by incorporating it physically, emotionally, and mentally. Optimal visualization prepares you to reach your most desired goals.

Following is an example you may use in its entirety or modify to suit your needs. You can record the most relevant sections on a cassette tape or have a friend read them to you. Be sure to find a comfortable place where you will not be disturbed.

Take a few deep breaths. Relax . . . There is nothing here to bother you, nothing to interrupt you. In your mind's eye, imagine yourself in the most beautiful place in nature, a place that is just yours. It may be somewhere you have been before, or it may be a place in your imagination—it doesn't matter. This is your ultimate sanctuary, a place of total safety and comfort at a time that is dedicated to you. You may be in a meadow, at the beach, in the desert, on a mountain, or on a grassy hillside. You feel the warm rays of the sun on your skin, and a cool breeze brushing against your face. Relax . . .

Now picture yourself involved in an activity in which you feel completely in control. You may wish to direct your attention toward the simple process of breathing. Breathe in to the count of four, then out to the count of four. Breathe in and out, in and out. Relax into the feeling of total mastery. Think about everything in your life that encourages you to feel completely competent and confident. Just let your mind melt into the nooks and crannies of your masterful self.

Now imagine you are a vessel of pure, unconditional love. You are full of compassion and joyfully accept every aspect of yourself. You embrace your wounded self with unbounded tenderness and take the most loving actions on its behalf. You cherish your suboptimal voices—always listening carefully to their needs and desires, so that you can do whatever it takes to understand and fulfill them. You provide the softest pillow for your frightened, hurt, angry, shamed, and helpless selves to rest and find renewal. They call on you whenever they need you. They are never alone. You feel blessed to have them in your life, to love them with all your heart, and to steer them to their greatest good.

Now imagine you are optimizing whatever comes your way. You feel completely confident in your ability to assess situations accurately and make the most constructive decisions. You resolve your challenges by allowing your highest self to ask the right questions. Imagine your Optimal mind-set. Concentrate now on your highest thought about yourself. Imagine living this thought for the rest of your life. Listen to your other viewpoints, embrace them all, and commit to those that empower you to create your best life. Happiness is your birthright and all your thoughts reflect your worthiness to create and enjoy everything you want.

Now see yourself accepting your body completely. Appreciate the infinite intelligence of the various functions of your body. Focus your attention on the blessings you experience by living in your body. Reflect on what you like most about it. Imagine yourself taking the best actions to experience your ultimate body. See and experience this in detail. You deserve to have the body you want.

Now experience your best social self. You are full of love, joy, and wisdom, and you magnetize people with the same qualities. Surround yourself with your favorite people who accept you as you are, reflect your highest self, and delight in your best efforts. See yourself at your best, bringing out the best in others. Imagine the ultimate interaction with whomever you want.

Now see yourself at your peak in your career. You are making the best use of your talents and abilities. You love what you do and are doing your best. You are the right person in the right place at the right time, making the best use of the present moment. You are achieving exactly what you want and are appropriately rewarded for your efforts.

Focus now on your greatest accomplishment. You can project as far into the future as you want. Visualize and enjoy your greatest victory. Experience every aspect of it. See yourself as all you can be. Align your thoughts, words, and behavior to match your highest vision. You are the person you most want to become. You are living your highest vision of your self. You deserve the best life has to offer!

Record your vision of your best self in your notebook right now. It will inspire you to achieve your full potential!

Marry Your Best Self

Below is an adaptation of a portion of the sacred marriage vows between husband and wife. Note your reaction as you pledge your allegiance to your best self. Are you truly committing yourself, or are you just going through the motions?

Will you permit your best self to be your internal caretaker, to live together in the estate of inner matrimony? Will you allow your best self to love you, honor you, comfort you, and keep you, in sickness and in health; and be true to you as long as you both shall live?

If your answer is yes, please proceed.

I hereby empower my best self to be my internal caretaker to have and to hold from this day forward, for better or for worse, for richer or for poorer, in sickness and in health, to love and to cherish, till death us do part.

_____   _____
Signature   Date

Below are some Optimal questions to assist you in keeping your commitment to your best self.

* *What are all the benefits I will gain and the losses I will avoid by embracing my best self?*
  To maximize your motivation to embrace your best self, jot down all the benefits you will gain and losses you will avoid by embodying your best self and allowing it to take charge. Be as specific as you can. Keep your list with you and review it whenever you have a spare moment.

- *How will I think and feel as my best self?*
  Imagine your thoughts and feelings when you totally accept yourself, become who you most want to be, and experience yourself at your best. Consider especially what ultimate self-confidence and self-respect feel like. Hold on to your vision. There is no need to wait for this experience. You can begin it now.
- *If this is what I want, why don't I have it already?*
  Now write down any possible obstacles that are in the way of your real-life experience of your best self.
- *What are the best actions I can take to overcome these obstacles?*
  Identify and note the best solutions to overcome all obstacles. Determine their priority and move into action. Place your description of your best self in the most appropriate locations, and read it every day. Look into the mirror and talk compassionately to yourself in Optimal terms every day. Remind yourself of your greatest assets and of every possible reason for accepting, liking, and loving yourself wholeheartedly.

By accepting yourself unconditionally—regardless of where you are in your journey toward becoming all you can envision—and choosing the wisest path in the present moment, you are maximizing your self-esteem!

Optimal Questions

1. What do I like most about myself?
2. Am I ready to let my best self take charge right now?
3. Can I accept myself unconditionally?
4. Which action will be most beneficial to my self-esteem?
5. How much of my activity was led by my highest self today/this week?

Optimal Action Steps

1. Think about the last time that you felt bad about yourself. What did you want from yourself? If you haven't done so already, decide upon the best actions to take to provide this for yourself.

2. Decide upon three Optimal responses to your suboptimal internal chatter. Write them down and practice them at every opportune moment. Schedule five minutes every morning to practice your Optimal responses. Initially you may feel awkward, but with practice, your Optimal responses will become second nature. Just let your best self take charge!

3. In your notebook, complete the sentence "If I were always my best self, I would . . . . . ." until you have exhausted everything that comes to mind.

CHAPTER 5

Discover Your Ultimate Direction

"The purpose of our lives is to be happy."
—The 14th Dalai Lama

The Value of a Life Purpose

For the past six years Stephen, a successful businessman, has been living with a woman he doesn't love. He can't summon the courage to end the relationship. Stephen drinks heavily at night. "It's better than the feeling of emptiness I experience when I'm sober," he rationalizes.

Rhonda enjoys her role as a devoted mother. Since her two children moved out of the house, she feels a big gap in her life. She tries to keep herself busy. Rhonda has many friends and is invited to numerous social events. "What am I doing here?" she asks herself. Most of the time she feels out of place.

John, a computer consultant, often feels tired and depressed. It is difficult for him to get out of bed in the morning. He is plagued with thoughts like: "Everything feels meaningless. I don't have a reason to live. I don't have a purpose."

Much has been written about the necessity for a meaningful purpose in life. Many people, however, are unsure of their purpose. At times they know what they want and at other times their souls yearn for direction. Some people search for a solution to their emptiness by trying to answer questions like, What's it all about?

Why am I here? What do I want to do with my life? Others do whatever they can to avoid their painful thoughts and feelings.

Your life purpose defines your most meaningful direction in life. It is your supreme reason for being and reflects your principles and what you value most in life. Your statement of purpose is the criterion or yardstick with which you evaluate everything in your life. It demonstrates your decision to live life to the fullest, regardless of your circumstances. Your purpose guides your thinking and behavior even when life deals you its toughest blows. It empowers you to make daily decisions consistent with your highest values and principles—even when you lose your spouse, your income, or your health. Your purpose does not need to be specific or measurable. Your goals provide the specific, measurable, and reachable steps to fulfill your ultimate purpose.

Do you relate to any of the following statements of purpose?

To be honest in all my dealings

To be compassionate, generous, and kind

To keep an Optimal mental attitude

To love myself unconditionally and share my love with others

To love and be loved

To be healthy, happy, and prosperous

To promote peace and goodwill in the world

To be a student of life

To be the best I can be

To inspire others to be their best

To live soulfully and make the best use of my mind

Optimal Thinkers devote their best efforts to the clarification of their life purpose. They know what they most want to achieve, what they stand for above all else, and what they are most committed to. Their purpose provides the fuel that propels them past any obstacles they encounter. These people demonstrate the highest level of personal leadership. I met two of them recently at an *Optimal Thinking for Relationships* seminar.

Cynthia had been dating Ellis, a network marketing professional, for nearly a year. Over the past year, Ellis's networking business activities had expanded throughout the world and he had many demands on his time. Cynthia understood Ellis's purpose and was comfortable with it. Above everything, Ellis was committed to doing what was "right"—regardless of the pain or inconvenience involved.

On numerous occasions, he refused to compromise his principles even when large sums of money were offered to induce him to stray from them. He consistently made decisions in alignment with his highest values on daily issues, even when it was most inconvenient. When Ellis asked Cynthia to marry him, she immediately accepted. She knew she had a top-notch man.

Identify Your Life Purpose

Jack was happily married and loved his thirteen-year-old son very much. He enjoyed the benefits of family life while accepting its obligations. He wanted to provide the best things in life for his family and worked hard to make a fine living. However, ever since he had entered the video production business, he had often misrepresented the facts to gain new accounts. He felt bad about his lack of integrity. He hated having to bend the truth to make a living. Jack desperately wanted to optimize his life, and scheduled some telephone consultations with me.

The following questions assisted Jack and will help you to identify your life purpose. Make sure you have some quiet time and your pen and notebook with you. Note Jack's responses and then write down your own. When you have many responses to a particular question, jot them all down. Then decide which one is most important to you.

- *What do I care about most deeply?*
  Being an honest person, acting with integrity
  Doing work I enjoy and am good at
  Feeling happy

- *What and who do I love?*
  My family
  My friends: Jim, Mary, Adrian, Steven, Sandra
  My dogs
  Playing golf
  Vacation home
  Going to movies

- *What am I deeply committed to?*
  Being an honest person, acting with integrity
  My family
  Doing work I enjoy

- *What do I stand for? What are my principles?*
  Honesty, doing the right thing
  Charity begins at home
  Nonviolence
  Consideration for others' feelings

- *When am I at my best?*
  When I am true to myself, and thinking Optimally
  When I am playing golf with my son
  When I relax with my family
  When I am producing videos for my favorite clients
  When I am happy
  When I don't have any financial problems

- *What has given me the greatest feelings of importance in my life? What has been most beneficial for my self-esteem?*
  Being a good family man
  Seeing the effects of my presence on my son
  Going into business for myself

- *What is it that I definitely don't want?*
  (Defining what you don't want is your most constructive intermediate step when you don't feel emotionally connected to a purpose. Once you know what you definitely don't want, then the opposite generally reveals what you do want. Compare your response to what Jack wrote.)
  To feel that my life is not worthwhile
  To feel like a phony
  To let my family down
  To be poverty-stricken
  To be unsuccessful in business
  To be confused about what I want
  To be negative and feel bad about myself, my family, and life
  To feel guilty
  To be around people I don't admire
  To be miserable
  To have no integrity
  To be intolerant and impatient
  To be without friends

- *What do I want more than anything else?*

  To make the most of my life

  To be a good family person

  To be very successful in business and financially secure

  To be clear about what I want

  To think Optimally about myself, my family, and life

  To be full of love, to love life

  To be honest about myself

  To admire the people around me

  To be happy, to spend as much time as possible doing what I enjoy

  To keep my integrity intact

  To be patient and tolerant

  To have friends I care for

  To send my son to college

  To have enough money to be able to do what I want whenever I want

- *Which activities do I enjoy most?*

  Being with my family

  Playing golf

  Going to movies

  Dancing

  Reading

  Walking along the beach

  Being with friends

  Spending money on personal whims, whatever I want

  Attending seminars on personal development

  Listening to tapes of inspirational speakers

  Finalizing large transactions

  Fine dining

- *In order of priority, what are the three things I value most in life?*

  To be an honest person, to do the right thing

  My family

  To think Optimally about myself, my family, and life

- *In order of priority, what are my three most important ambitions in life?*
For my family and me to be happy
Keep my integrity intact
Think Optimally about myself, my family, and life

- *If I had one year to live, how would I make the most of it?*
Spend a lot more time in my vacation home
Arrange my affairs so that my family will be well taken care of
List in priority all the activities I enjoy and do them
Definitely spend as much time as possible with my family

- *How would I like to be remembered?*
As an honest family man who devoted my life to providing my
family with the best life has to offer.

- *If I were given all the money I could ever need or want, how would I live my life?*
Spend much more time with my family
Concentrate on the activities I enjoy most

- *If I could experience the ultimate day, what would it be like?*
(How would you start the best day of your life? Where would you most want to be? What would you do? Who would you choose to be with? How would you feel at the end of the day?)
I'm in our vacation home with my wife and son. It is a warm summer's day. I enjoy a few hours alone with my wife. Later, we take a walk along the beach with our son, and stop off at a neighborhood restaurant for breakfast. I have a game of golf in the morning with my best friend. On the way to the golf course, I listen to my favorite cassette tape. I also listen to my favorite music. I pop into the office (near our vacation house) for a few hours and finalize the biggest transaction I have ever worked on. It is easy and enjoyable. I am in complete control. I then spend an hour with my production team, supervising the creation of the highest-budget video we've ever produced, for my favorite clients. I celebrate with my wife and son in the late afternoon. We go shopping together and buy whatever we want. We then go home, and have our favorite people over for dinner. We talk and laugh and watch

a Mr. Bean video. My wife and I go for a quiet walk after our guests leave. We go to bed happily and peacefully, knowing tomorrow will be better than today.

- *What would my ultimate environment be like?*

  My ultimate environment is our present holiday home with some modifications. We have an extra acre of land, beautifully landscaped, with the best lighting arrangements. We have an Olympic-size swimming pool. We have a view of the ocean from the living room. I have a workshop downstairs. My study is twice its present size. I have my personal gym decked out with all the latest workout equipment. My son's room is about twice as large as it is now.

- *Which one purpose would I concentrate on if I knew that there was no chance of failure?*

  Be an honest, devoted family man who provides the best of everything for my family.

- *What is my ultimate purpose? What do I most want to accomplish?*

  (After you've read Jack's response, write a one-to-three-sentence statement about the main purpose of your life. You may want to combine several responses into an overall statement.)

  To be honest and make the most of my life. To be an example of integrity, love, and Optimal Thinking for my family and provide them with the best of everything.

When Jack finally wrote out the statement that defined his main purpose in life, he felt like a new man. He was filled with joy. He knew this was exactly what he wanted. It felt completely right to him. There was nothing missing!

"He who has the why to live for can bear almost any how."
—Nietzsche

How do you feel now that you have identified your ultimate purpose in life? The next chapter will explain how to integrate your life purpose into your everyday life—through your job, business, relationships, and community. Your daily life will soon be a living reflection of your life purpose.

The Value of a Purposeful Career

*"There is no defeat except from within, no really insurmount-
able barrier save our own inherent weakness of purpose."*
—Elbert Hubbard

Now that you have determined your life purpose, you are ready to
unravel and reinforce your career purpose. Many people believe that
earning a lot of money is the path to peace and joy. Unfortunately,
some of them lose touch with their souls as they climb the ladder of
success. When they eventually achieve financial prosperity, they feel
empty, anxious, or depressed. Some talented people don't believe
that doing what they love could ever provide them with a handsome
living. Perhaps their talents, abilities, and passion were unappreciated by their parents, teachers, or peers, so they don't value them.
When they perform labors of love and receive enthusiastic feedback
from others, they are actually astonished. These people routinely
perform tasks that do not fuel their passion, and experience their
work as drudgery.

Are you pursuing a career that fuels you with boundless energy
and passion? When we lovingly contribute our talents and gifts, we
unveil our essence. By expressing our unique talents creatively
through our careers, we can experience work as a privilege rather
than an encumbrance. Work becomes a sacred activity to evolve and
fulfill our core, rather than a burden we are forced to undertake for
our sustenance. When we experience joy in sharing our greatest talents with the world and know how to optimize our financial success,
we can move forward with all cylinders.

My Career Path

Although I was often the top student in high school math classes
and solved science problems effortlessly, I had no desire to express
these natural abilities in a career. Dancing was my passion. I both
lost and found myself moving my body to the rhythm of my soul.
My parents didn't believe I could earn a living as a dancer, and I had
doubts, too, so my passion was relegated to a social activity. During
my final year of high school, my father suggested that I apply for
entrance into Pharmacy College. I followed his advice because I
couldn't think of another alternative. From the start, however, I was
more interested in playing Ping-Pong than attending classes. At the
end of each school year, I worked in a pharmacy, a curriculum
requirement. I watched the clock continually and prayed for the end

of each day. It didn't feel right and I knew I had to do something about it.

After evaluating my options and reflecting on questions similar to those below, I decided to pursue teaching. I had developed a reverence for knowledge, and it felt right. What's more, I had often dreamed of traveling the world and meeting people from different cultures. I could now fulfill this dream during the long semester breaks. Fortunately, I have never looked back—and my career has never felt like work! I taught junior high school science, then high school physics and chemistry, and ultimately chaired the high school science department. I loved challenging my students with mischievous, zany problems to solve, and they were willing participants. They entered my classroom grinning, wondering what each lesson would bring. Gratefully, I achieved my purpose at that time: to make learning synonymous with fun. My teaching career evolved to encompass a love of languages, and my deepest passion, the tuition of personal and professional optimization.

Since 1980, I have presented seminars in corporations and educational organizations and to individuals throughout the world. Initially, I adopted the "think positive" principle, but quickly recognized that this paradigm had serious shortcomings. I recall the following message from a well-known motivation expert: "Positive thinkers are the winners in this world. Negative thinkers are the losers. You wouldn't enter someone's home and dump a load of trash in his or her living room. Your behavior is equally offensive when you dump your emotional garbage on others. Fake it until you make it!" I was uncomfortable with the duplicity and lack of compassion. Although my words had not always matched my actions, I was unwilling to consciously choose hypocrisy or to sacrifice my soul to a bravado image. I responded by isolating myself from others when I felt sad or uncomfortable, because I felt guilty imposing my negative thoughts and feelings on them. I also became the quintessential optimist. I disregarded warning signals and held unrealistic expectations of people and of life. For a brief period, I disappointed and betrayed myself with wishful thinking. Ultimately, however, this was a wonderful gift—it led me to Optimal Thinking.

I began to acknowledge and challenge the deficiencies of positive thinking and formulated Optimal Thinking. Soon the media were at my doorstep. One article described me as "Australia's most successful woman in her field." One day, however, a journalist referred to me as "Australia's most successful woman." What a leap! Then came an interview with a veteran journalist who asked:

"What makes you Australia's most successful woman?" I responded: "Who am I to say who is more successful? Is Mom at home doing her best to raise decent children any less successful than the corporate executive who optimizes profits?" "With thinking like that, you have to be Australia's most successful woman!" he replied. I appeared on hundreds of shows answering questions about Optimal Thinking, and even hosted my own radio and television programs. It was fun!

When an invitation to write a book arrived unexpectedly, I agreed. For sixteen years I had researched and explored this universal, peak form of thinking and the core beliefs that prevent us from thinking Optimally. Along the way I discovered the five greatest shortcomings of positive thinking. What a joy! *Optimal Thinking* has now been translated into several languages.

Every time I deliver an Optimal Thinking seminar, I connect my best self with my audience. My consulting practice allows me the privilege of contributing Optimal Thinking in another format. I interact with all kinds of wonderful people, including students, executives and CEOs of large corporations, small-business owners, working moms, educators, and health professionals. When they gain the tools to make the most of their lives, they often say: "I feel like flying out of here!" Needless to say, I love my career. I work with a joyful heart and am blessed with endless satisfaction.

Identify Your Career Purpose

"My mom said, 'In your 20s you try it all.
In your 30s you figure out what you do best.
In your 40's you make money from what you do best.
In your 50s you just do—do what you want to do.'"

—Paul Orfalea

The following questions helped me to recognize my ultimate career purpose. By answering them, you will learn about your career calling. You will discover where you are headed and why, and where to focus your energies and best efforts. Use your notebook to access previous answers and to explore new information. For each category, list your responses and then rank them in order of priority.

Here's how Richard, the chiropractor who needed a new start, responded to these questions and discovered his career purpose. Your answers will help you in the same way.

- *What are my strengths? What are my talents and gifts? What are all the assets I bring to the table?*

  (In chapter 4, you explored your strengths and assets. There may be some unique talents and gifts you did not specify at that time. List them as they come to mind.)

  I am a skilled chiropractor.

  I'm a people person.

  I have a fun personality.

  I enjoy sharing knowledge.

  I am a great public speaker.

  I am a risk taker.

  When I set goals, I achieve them.

- *What makes me happy? What brings me joy?*

  (It may be in your best interest to put aside some quiet time for reflection. Notice what you pay attention to and what excites you most in both home and work environments.)

  Creating a trend-setting concept

  Being with people I like and care about

  Speaking to large audiences

  Being in a joyful, respectful environment

  Taking walks in nature

  Animals

- *What do I love to do?*

  "You have to find something that you love enough to be able to take risks, jump over the hurdles, and break through the brick walls that are always going to be placed I front of you. If you don't have that kind of feeling for what it is you're doing, you'll stop at the first giant hurdle."
  —George Lucas

  (You deserve to enjoy each day doing what you love. Take some time to write down what you love to do.)

  Speaking engagements to large audiences

  Make big money

  Show people how to take care of their health

  Listen to classical music

  Travel to new places

- ***What am I most interested in doing? What is my passion?***

  "Cooking is like anything in life. You have to have passion to do it right."

  —Wolfgang Puck

(If you follow your passion it will introduce you to your innate talents. John D. Rockefeller III wrote: "The road to happiness lies in two simple principles: find what it is that interests you and that you can do well, and when you find it put your whole soul into it—every bit of energy and ambition and natural ability you have." The words of the French impressionist painter Auguste Renoir are worthy of our deepest consideration. He said: "The work of art must seize upon you, wrap you up in itself and carry you away. It is the means by which the artist conveys his passion. It is the current which he puts forth which sweeps you along in his passion." Access your intuition, listen to your heart, and complete the following three sentences. Then write down what you are most passionate about.)

I secretly desire . . . . .

If there was no chance of failure, I would love to . . . . .

If my life was ending, I would regret not having completed . . . . .

Communicating, inspiring and connecting with others

Sharing meaningful health information with others

Public speaking

Having a meaningful impact on others

Being successful

Traveling to new places

Learning how to enjoy peak fitness

- ***How do I most enjoy contributing to others?***
  (You may enjoy encouraging others, entertaining them, organizing people and events, educating, or healing the sick. Trust yourself and write down how you most enjoy helping others.)

  Sharing meaningful health information with others

  Inspiring others to optimize their health and fitness

- ***Which cause do I most want to serve?***
  (Your highest calling may be to optimize the plight of senior citizens, orphans, college students, immigrants, the homeless, or those with life-threatening illnesses. Needless to say, the

cause you most want to serve must be worthy of your best efforts.)

Sharing meaningful health information to people who are physically challenged

- ***What kind of organization am I best suited to?***
  (Would you feel more comfortable in a cozy environment or in
  a large, powerful corporation?)

  Small organization

  My own business

- ***What is my career purpose?***
  (Write a one-to-three-sentence statement about the main purpose of your career. You may want to combine several responses
  into an overall statement.)

  Help the physically challenged to optimize their health and fitness by sharing meaningful, trend-setting information.

Ready to Commit?

*"Everyone has his own specific vocation in life. . . . Therein he
cannot be replaced, nor can his life be repeated. Thus, everyone's task is as unique as is his specific opportunity to implement it."*

—Victor Frankl

When you commit to your purpose, make the best use of your talents, and do what you love, you are being who you want to be, doing
what you want to do, and creating what you want! Your thoughts,
words, and actions align with your supreme reason for being. Are
you willing to do whatever is necessary to fulfill your life and career
purpose? Take some time to write down your answers to the following questions and make a life commitment to yourself.

- How much time am I willing to commit to my purpose daily?
- Is it worthy of my best efforts?
- Why?

How did you answer the questions? Are you fully committed to
your purpose or will you allow yourself to be unnecessarily distracted? You probably know that all distractions are equal! We all
become distracted, break stride with our highest ideals, and experience disappointment from time to time. Acceptance followed by the

best action provide the best strategy for staying on purpose. Simply embrace your detour as a reminder of your humanity, and answer the following Optimal questions to restore your focus:

- *Is this action in alignment with my purpose?*
- *What's the best action I can take to achieve my purpose right now?*
- *To what extent are my actions leading me toward the fulfillment of my purpose?*

Now that you have defined your life purpose and the purpose of your career, the next chapter will help you set SUPREME goals, which will provide you with the best path and Optimal action steps. For example, if your life purpose is to be the best you can be, your next step could be to volunteer at a local help line once a month, read for the blind twice a week, or volunteer at the local animal shelter every Saturday. As you read the next chapter and complete the exercises, you will determine which step is in your best interest and how you can best achieve all your dreams and goals. You are ready to create the ultimate blueprint for your life—read on!

Optimal Questions

1. What do I value/care about most deeply?
2. How can I express my best self?
3. What is my supreme reason for being?
4. What is the most meaningful direction for my life?
5. Are my thoughts, feelings, and actions in alignment with my ultimate purpose?

Optimal Action Steps

1. Before you doze off to sleep each night, take a minute or two to visualize yourself doing what is supremely important to you. See yourself on purpose!
2. Check in with yourself a few times each day and ask yourself: *Am I on purpose? What's supremely important to me?*
3. Imagine you are a pilot choosing your ultimate destination, then flying your plane. Visualize your steadfastness as you stay on course—even when the wind blows in the opposite direction and the weather is terrible.

CHAPTER 6

Plan Your Best Life

"I know the best way to achieve my most important goal."
—Optimal Thinker

Set SUPREME Goals

You can give yourself the best of life. You can choose the people you most want to associate with, the area you wish to live in, and the career you are most suited for. It is your right to choose, plan, and experience your desired reality!

SUPREME goals provide concrete checkpoints required for the achievement of your purpose. Optimal Thinkers set **S**pecific, **U**plifting, **P**aramount, **R**eachable, **E**xciting, **M**easurable, **E**njoyable **goals** to be achieved within definite time frames.

SUPREME Goals are . . .

Specific
Your goals must be stated specifically, so that uncertainty and conjecture are eliminated. Specific goals produce specific outcomes. Vague goals produce vague outcomes or no outcome at all. Goals such as "to have a large income," "to be a caring partner," and "to have peace of mind" are vague. Grossing $100,000 a year, setting aside two nights each week to be alone with your partner, or playing nine holes of golf every Tuesday morning are specific goals.

Uplifting

When your goals are uplifting, the rewards you enjoy by achieving them outweigh any price you have to pay. Achieving SUPREME goals enables you to experience the greatest satisfaction and joy.

Paramount

Paramount goals reflect your most important personal values, needs, and wants and require your best efforts to achieve them. They are not based on competition with others. These goals inspire you to be your best, do your best, and experience the best in life. They stop you from settling for second best!

Reachable

Your goals must be realistic and attainable. When you know that you can achieve your goals, you are motivated to accomplish them.

Exciting

There is no excitement in just getting by or in mediocrity. Making the car payments and paying your telephone bills will not make life exciting for you. Big goals are exciting and challenge you to do your best. When your goals are exciting, you automatically experience an intense desire to achieve them.

Measurable

Your goals are most effective when you can measure their achievement. When your SUPREME goals are scheduled within optimum time frames, you have the best checkpoints to measure your progress. You have no interest in wishful thinking, because you have verifiable evidence that your goals are attainable.

Enjoyable

Optimal Thinkers bring joy *to* their goals instead of attempting to extract joy *from* them. Enjoyable goals are the tangible results of the joy you bring to them. Most interestingly, what you enjoy doing is generally what you're best at.

Anyone can set and achieve SUPREME goals. Jim, for example, wants to enjoy more romance in his marriage. Lately he and his wife have been taking each other for granted. Jim wrote down three SUPREME goals to achieve his purpose:

1. Send Pam an Optimal e-card to express my love and appreciation today.

2. Give Pam a dozen red roses next Friday.
3. Schedule a candlelit dinner for two at our favorite restaurant to celebrate the end of every month.

Why Plan Optimally?

"Your ultimate goal in life is to become your best self. Your immediate goal is to get on the path that will lead you there."
—David Viscott, M.D.

Many people complain of lack of time and resources when lack of direction is their real problem. They don't know exactly where they want to go, and then they arrive where they don't want to be. You might chuckle at the following scenario: .

A doctor was called out one morning to deliver a baby. On his way to the hospital he noticed the grass was very dry, so he detoured toward the house to turn on the sprinklers. As he picked up the paper he noticed an ad for a play he wished to attend, so he tore it out and placed it on the dining room table, where he would be sure to notice it. On the dining room table he noticed several dirty dishes, so he went to the kitchen to wash them. There, he noticed another pile of dishes, and proceeded to wash them, too. Finally, in desperation, his wife went to the hospital and delivered the baby.

As this story shows, to make the most constructive use of your assets, resources, and time, you must take the best actions toward your SUPREME goals. SUPREME goals provide the most constructive path to achieve your purpose.

Do you ever find yourself thinking the following?

What am I doing here?

Constant interruptions prevent me from getting things done.

I have so many responsibilities, I can't manage all of them.

I don't know how to get what I want. I feel like I'm going around in circles.

There's just too much to do!

I can't rely on others, so I end up doing everything myself.

I don't feel motivated.

Such statements are based on suboptimal planning of your resources and your time. An Optimal plan provides you with the best possible map or blueprint for your success. It enables you to see how to reach your SUPREME goals, and gives you assurance that they can be achieved. When you plan Optimally, you choose to make things happen on purpose instead of relying on circumstance or chance. Once you know where you want to go and how you plan to get there, you can place your full attention on the step you are taking in the current moment.

Write Down Your SUPREME Goals

The results of a 1973 survey revealed some enlightening information about the value of written goals. In 1953, a group of graduating students at Yale University was asked a series of questions, which included, "Have you set clear, specific goals for your life? Have you written them down and have you made plans to accomplish them?" Of those interviewed, 3 percent had written down their goals and formulated specific plans to attain them. Twenty years later the surviving members of that class were again interviewed. The 3 percent who had written down their goals had achieved greater financial success than all of the other 97 percent. The participants had originally been chosen because of their similar family and socioeconomic backgrounds, intelligence, academic ability, and even physical appearance. The only visible difference between the successful 3 percent and the others was that they had written down their goals and plans.

Do you think that major corporations such as Intel or General Electric would experience the same success if their directors had the corporate goals in mind rather than written down? Writing down your SUPREME goals clarifies your thinking and purpose, providing the Optimal track for your progress. You know exactly what you must do to achieve what you want. By frequently referring to your written SUPREME goals, you can minimize distractions and interruptions. You generate more time to do what you really want to do. You also gain clear mental pictures of exactly what you want. This stimulates the visualization process, which prepares you to achieve your goals. Conflicts and inconsistencies become more apparent and you can focus on resolving them before they become serious problems. Writing down your SUPREME goals can also help you communicate clearly what you consider to be most important.

Modes of Optimal Planning

There are two modes of Optimal planning: forward planning and reverse planning. It is most important to balance their use. Remember, only when you implement your Optimal plan will you experience the ultimate success you desire.

Optimal Forward Planning

You need to know where you are if you want to use a map to help you to arrive at a chosen destination. Only when you know where you stand now do you have the basis for determining exactly where you want to go and how to get there. In the forward planning process you start from where you are. *You move forward as far as you can see, and when you arrive at that point, you look farther.* You write down your SUPREME goals in order of priority and then move into action. You continually ask yourself, *What is the most important goal I must achieve?* and *What's the best action I can take toward it right now?*

We all differ when it comes to planning ahead. Some people have no difficulty setting short-, medium-, and long-term goals. They plan years ahead. Others plan to achieve SUPREME goals several months ahead. Some can only plan a few days in advance. Some people consider short-term to be sixty days, medium-term six months, and long-term two years. Others use completely different time frames. What do you consider to be short-, medium-, and long-term? How far ahead do you plan?

Setting and achieving short-term SUPREME goals maximizes your confidence and builds the habit of taking the best path to achieve your success. Each experience of success forms the foundation for more. Let's explore how this is done.

Lisa, a thirty-nine-year-old financial planning consultant, works from home. She is very competent and professional in her business dealings. A lot of her energy goes into making her business a success. Lisa's struggle is internal. She has been divorced for seven years and has not had a serious relationship since. She feels sad, disappointed, and angry about her barren personal life. Although she has never had a strong, persistent desire to have children, she wonders whether she has missed her chance. Her business is suffering.

When Lisa told me her story, I suggested she clarify her purpose and jot down her SUPREME goals. Lisa made sure every sentence was Optimally stated when she wrote down her goals. Her list of SUPREME goals for the next two months, in order of priority, was as follows:

1. After work this evening write a list of the most important characteristics I would like in my future mate. (6:00 P.M. April 10)

2. Write a list in my diary of my ten best business prospects to contact each day. (5:35 P.M. nightly starting April 10)
3. Schedule three business meetings daily. (10 A.M., 12 noon, and 3 P.M. starting April 11)
4. Employ Optimal Thinking each morning for 20 minutes to prepare myself for an Optimal day. (Every day at 7:30 A.M. starting April 11)
5. Write in journal every morning, "I let my best self take charge!" for five minutes. (Every day at 7:50 A.M. starting April 11)
6. Schedule five hours next week to investigate the best ways to meet the most appropriate single men. (April 13, 7 to 10 P.M. and April 15, 6 to 8 P.M.)
7. Invest three evenings each week in the most uplifting singles environments or with suitable male prospects. (Tuesdays, Fridays, Saturdays)
8. Attend weekend seminar on relationships. (May 1 and 2)
9. Attend National Financial Planning conference. (May 11)

Janine, an Optimal Thinker, was committed to living a balanced life. Her main roles in life were that of wife, mother, daughter, history teacher, and masters degree student. She wrote down her roles in order of priority and then set short-term SUPREME goals to empower her to be her best in each role. Bearing in mind the priority of her roles, she then allocated prime time for the most important activities in her daily planner. Because Janine prioritized her primary areas of dedication, she was able to perform daily tasks to support her best interests.

Which SUPREME goals do you want to achieve in the short- and medium-term? Make sure they are in alignment with your ultimate purpose before writing them down. Take some time NOW to plan ahead. You deserve it!

Optimal Reverse Planning

In the reverse planning process, you break down your most compelling dreams and SUPREME goals into realistic action steps. You begin by listing your Optimal dreams and goals. Dreams are desires that do not have a clear series of steps attached to their fulfillment. Never judge or discount dreams; they are real and meaningful to you. They become goals when you can clearly define the specific actions necessary to achieve them.

Because impulsively set and casually entertained goals are often discarded at the first obstacle, reverse planning is helpful. When you reverse plan, you decide if a goal is in your best interest before involving yourself in the activities necessary for its accomplishment. Once you decide that a goal will bring out the best in you, will inspire the fulfillment of your ultimate purpose, and will triumph over the price you'll have to pay, you know that it is in your best interest to proceed. Sometimes you plan out the fulfillment of a dream only to discover that it isn't currently in your best interest. You then simply trash the information and abandon the project, or file it for later consideration. By reverse planning, you avoid wasting time through trial and error.

Below are some Optimal questions to assist you in the process of reverse planning. Take some time to write down your responses.

What Do You Most Want to Be, Do, Have, and Contribute?

"The only place where your dream becomes impossible is in your own thinking."
—Dr. Robert H. Schuller

Here it is most important to jot down whatever comes to mind. Find a quiet place where you can relax. Let go of any judgments or self-imposed limitations. Put your dreams and goals down on paper. If you could be anyone you wanted, who would you be? A politician? A leading physician? A film director? An athlete? A business magnate? An accomplished artist? A spiritual master? Remember that the greatest inventions and developments in history came from the minds of dreamers who made their dreams come true. You can do it, too.

Ted Leon did it. In 1982, he was returning from a business trip when his plane was forced to make an emergency landing. Ted was twenty-five years old at the time and didn't want to die. A week later, he wrote a list of 101 things he wanted to achieve in his life. He wanted to pay off college debts, fall in love and get married, own a beach home, go to the White House and meet the president, own a sports team, change someone's life via a charity, catch a foul ball, get a hole-in-one, own a convertible Porsche or Mercedes-Benz, go one-on-one with Michael Jordan, go to Paris, and give one million dollars to Georgetown University, among other things. The ambitious list he wrote has served as a blueprint for a life of no regrets.

Ted Leon, now middle-aged, has already achieved 70 of the 101 goals on his list. The son of a secretary and a waiter, he has become one of America's most successful executives. Ted is still enthusiastic about realizing many more of his listed goals, which include having a net worth of one billion dollars, having great-grandchildren, and going into outer space. He believes, "If you write it down, you have the road map. It seems that the steps to get there get easier. It makes it more bite-size and there's nothing more fulfilling than getting that check mark off." On a recent television show he said, "I would like at my funeral for the list to be passed around to my close friends and family members. If I can accomplish that list, no one should feel sorry that I passed on. They should go, 'Wow, he had a heck of a ride.'"

Are you ready to identify the dreams and goals that will bring out the best in you? The question "Why haven't I achieved my ultimate purpose already?" will assist you in identifying the SUPREME goals you must achieve to fulfill your ultimate purpose. What are they?

Which Goal Is Most Important?

Now look at your list. Decide which goal is of greatest importance to you. Which goal would you dare to accomplish if you knew you couldn't fail? It is usually not in your best interest to share your goal with people who may not be supportive before you have planned its accomplishment. Others can destroy your enthusiasm with comments like: "It won't work," "That's unrealistic," or "You're crazy!" Share your goal only with those who will help you achieve it.

Apply the SUPREME Test

Before you focus on the best ways to achieve your goal, it is in your best interest to determine whether it meets the SUPREME test. Check your goal against the SUPREME criteria. Is it **S**pecific, **U**plifting, **P**aramount, **R**eachable, **E**xciting, **M**easurable, **E**njoyable—and within a definite time frame?

If your goal does not pass the SUPREME test, simply restate it in Optimal terms until you are satisfied that it meets all the criteria. It's time to stop settling for second best!

List All the Benefits to Be Gained by Achieving Your SUPREME Goal

You are probably familiar with the Law of Inertia. It states: "A body at rest will remain at rest and a body in motion will continue to move in the same direction at the same speed unless acted upon by an external force." This law can be stated even more simply: "If you do what you've always done, you'll have what you've always had."

Those who achieve their goals continue achieving their goals, those who think negatively continue thinking negatively, and those who struggle with life continue to experience struggle. The benefits to be enjoyed by achieving your SUPREME goal provide the incentive to change and optimize the speed and direction of your path. These benefits will triumph over your inertia when you give your all to attain them.

To maximize your motivation, give yourself as many uplifting reasons as possible to proceed. Why do I want it? What's in it for me? What are all the benefits? How will I feel when I succeed? Why is this of utmost importance to me? Write it all down. Keep reminders close by of all the benefits you will enjoy by achieving your goal.

Where Are You Now in Relation to Your Goal?

Martha's SUPREME goal was to reduce her weight to 120 pounds within two months. To define where she was in relation to her goal, her first task was to note her current weight.

Irwin wanted to earn $2,000 a week. When he looked at last week's commission check, he knew where he stood in relation to his SUPREME goal.

Where do you stand right now in relation to your SUPREME goal? Write it down.

Obstacles: If This Is What You Want Above All Else, Why Don't You Have It Already?

> *"Obstacles don't have to stop you. If you run into a wall, don't turn around and give up. Figure out how to climb it, go through it, or work around it."*
>
> —Michael Jordan

Mary, a thirty-eight-year-old psychologist, wants to teach psychology at the university level. She needs a Ph.D. to qualify, which would require at least two years of additional study. This would cost several thousand dollars, which she doesn't have.

Jim, forty-one years of age, wants his own radio talk show. The only credit he can put on his résumé is a ten-minute interview he conducted recently with a well-known friend. He feels he lacks presentation skills, experience, and the right connections.

Catherine, a foreign-language teacher, wants to start her own online translation business, but she doesn't have enough time.

Qualifications, attitude, experience, and *money* are the most common obstacles that frustrate our success. But with determination, initiative, and Optimal Thinking, you can take the best actions to overcome these obstacles.

After Fred Astaire's first screen test in 1933, an MGM director wrote the following memo: "Can't act! Slightly bald! Can dance a little."

After several successful years as head of the science department in a highly respected high school, a young teacher was ready to take on a new challenge. She had noticed an advertisement in the daily newspaper for language sales consultants. International travel was mentioned. She enjoyed languages, communicating with people from all parts the world, and traveling.

She had four major obstacles to overcome. First, she did not have any significant educational qualifications in languages. Her prospective employer assured her that this was not necessary. Consultants were trained extensively by the company on the "how to's" of learning languages. Second, she had a negative attitude about sales. She did not like the idea of being a salesperson. She considered herself an educator and resolved to continue viewing herself as such. She knew that her complete dedication to the educational value of the language programs could only be to the advantage of all concerned. Third, she had no sales experience. She was told that the corporate training empowered consultants to discuss the programs with people at all levels. No experience was required. Finally, this was a commission-only job and offered no financial security. She had always received a salary and was uncomfortable starting out in a new venture without any financial backing. She asked her prospective employer to provide her with a salary for three months. He agreed to match her previous salary for three months and they decided to give it a go.

There were fifty consultants in the company. She asked about the best consultant: What was his background? What kind of results was he achieving? Why was he successful? She found that the top consultant was a charming man in his late fifties who suffered various physical ailments. This man had been successful in real estate prior to becoming a language consultant. He was exceptional; she was not expected to achieve his level of success. She thought, "I am young, healthy, energetic, and have a sound educational foundation. If he can do it, I can!"

Numerous obstacles crossed her path during her first month. She persisted and gave everything she had to the tasks at hand. By the end of that month, she had reached her personal goals, doubled her previous income, and was the company's top language consultant. That young woman was me!

- Obstacles are what we see when we take our eyes off our goal.

- Obstacles are what we hear when we take our ears off our goal.

- Obstacles are what we think when we take our mind off our goal.

- Obstacles are what we feel when we take our heart off our goal.

If there were no obstacles in your path, you would have already achieved your goal. Why don't you have your SUPREME goal right now? What's in the way? Take some time now to write down your obstacles. Of all the obstacles between you and your goal, decide which one is the biggest.

Risks: What Are the Possible Damages, Injuries, and Losses? What Is the Worst Possible Scenario?

"Accept that all of us can be hurt, that all of us can—and surely will at times—fail. I think we should follow a simple rule: if we can take the worst, take the risk."
—Dr. Joyce Brothers

When you focus on all the damage, injury, and loss that could occur in reaching your goal, you face your worst fears. You must decide in advance whether you can handle them. You can then minimize the possible pain by formulating a contingency plan, which shows you how to make the best of the worst possible outcome. Once you know how best to handle the worst outcome, you are free to direct all your efforts toward achieving the best outcome. Consider the following example:

John was planning to start a new business. He believed the worst thing that could happen was that it would fail and he would lose all his money. He decided that he would drive a taxi to recoup his financial losses if this worst possible outcome occurred.

Many people fear being homeless, poor, old, sick, and alone. These fears are usually irrational. You can minimize them by realizing that they are based on unreasonable negative thoughts and expectations. Take some time now to confront the worst that could happen in achieving your SUPREME goal. It's the best way to minimize your fears.

Optimal Resources: What Are Your Greatest Strengths?
Which Organizations, People, and Information Can Best
Assist You in Achieving Your SUPREME Goal?

Your highest self is your greatest resource. The most resourceful people discover and acknowledge their strengths and encourage their full expression. They incorporate their greatest strengths into their Optimal plan to achieve their ultimate purpose. Take some time now to itemize the best resources available to achieve your SUPREME goal. Make sure you list them in order of their importance to you.

Optimal Solutions: What Are the Best Actions You Can Take
to Overcome the Obstacles and Minimize the Risks? What Are
Your Optimal Action Steps, in Priority, with Target Times?

When you fight shadows or move in the dark, it's hard to forge full speed ahead. It is best to throw light on the obstacles and risks involved. Accept them and then tackle your biggest obstacle first. Ask *What's the best action I can take to overcome this and take me closest to my goal?* Acceptance, followed by the best possible action, will work in your best interest every time. For example, if your SUPREME goal requires proficiency in computer programming, you may need to take a class to optimize your skills. As you move toward your SUPREME goal, if you require additional skills it will become apparent.

Consider Esther, a saleswoman I coached, who knew that recognition was of utmost importance to her. She was ambitious and wanted to reach her full potential. She was the top producer for the company in her first year, but her employer chose not to mention her achievements at the national awards meeting. He even promoted someone else above her. She felt hurt and disillusioned. Her productivity drastically declined.

To overcome this obstacle, Esther acknowledged that this employer did not value her best efforts. She decided that her most constructive course of action was to seek another job, one where her efforts would be appreciated. She found a similar position and quickly rose to the top. In her new position, she enjoyed the respect of her colleagues. At the end of her first year she accepted an offer from her employer to head a new division.

Negative thinking, procrastination, and feelings such as fear, worry, doubt, guilt, hurt, and anger can cripple your progress. When you become conscious of negative thoughts or feelings, simply accept them, seek to understand them, and then use Optimal

Thinking to resolve them. Ask yourself the best questions, listen to your inner voice for the best answers, and then incorporate your solutions into your Optimal plan. Ask, *What has caused this? What are my options for resolving this? Which one is best? What's the best action I can take to overcome this now?* and *What's the best use of my time right now?*

Optimal action steps, such as asking the top person in your field for advice, or reading the most enlightening literature, provide the superlative path to your SUPREME goals. These are the best steps you can take to maximize your momentum. Write down your Optimal action steps, prioritize them, and then decide on the best time frames for their completion. You might like to think about each action step and ask: *What will make this most pleasurable/profitable/time efficient?* Transfer your list of Optimal action steps to your daily calendar to remind you when to take action. As you work on your Optimal plan, the best of life will unfold.

What Is the Best Time Frame for the Completion of Your SUPREME Goal?

It is now realistic to set the best time frame for completing your SUPREME goal. Optimal time frames motivate you to employ your best efforts to do what's necessary to get the job done. These time frames change the operational value of your plan from "it can be accomplished one of these days" to "it will be accomplished by the best date." Be flexible. If you do not achieve your goal within the stated time and it is still in your best interest to pursue it, simply extend the target date. Make sure that you are the master of time and that time is not your master!

What's the First Step You Must Take to Activate This Plan?

Take a look at the Optimal action steps you have identified in achieving your SUPREME goal. Select the action steps—or parts of them—that are best achieved today. Identify the first Optimal action step to achieve your goal, and DO IT NOW! The step you are taking right now is the only part of your journey that is real. It is all there is!

Are All the Benefits to Be Gained Worth the Price You'll Have to Pay? If So, Why? If Not, Why Not?

Be entirely honest with yourself as you consider whether this SUPREME goal is worthy of your complete commitment (emotional, financial, and otherwise). The answers to these questions will determine your commitment to implement your Optimal plan. Strength of desire and total commitment to your goal are paramount to success.

Which Optimal Affirmations Will Be Most Helpful in Accomplishing Your SUPREME Goal?

Optimal self-talk is an Optimal verbal application of "act as if." Many Optimal Thinkers use the following declaration: *I am now taking the best action to accomplish my most important goal.* Some prefer to mention the benefits of achieving their goal. The following affirmations will help you make the best use of your time:

- I am making the most profitable use of my time right now.
- My fastest route to success is my Optimal plan.
- I give everything I have to attain my most important goal.
- I am doing the most important task right now.
- I am making the most of every moment.
- I am making the best use of my time right now.
- I am enjoying the most pleasurable path to my goal right now.
- I obtain the best results within the least amount of time.
- I am always punctual.

Which Optimal affirmations are most appropriate for you? Take some time to write them down in your journal now. Remember that the best way to integrate them is to focus on them as often as you can, and to resolve unsupportive reactions as you become aware of them.

Which Optimal Visualizations Will Be Most Helpful in Accomplishing Your SUPREME Goal?

Colonel Harvey Johnson was an enthusiastic golfer whose score was consistently around 90. He stopped playing golf for eight years. The next time he played eighteen holes of golf, he shot a 75.

For those eight years Colonel Johnson had been a prisoner of war in Vietnam, isolated from others that whole time. Initially he feared for his sanity but after a few months he decided to take total control of his mind. He set a SUPREME goal to achieve a score of 75 when he next played eighteen holes of golf at his favorite course. Each day he mentally played his best game of golf for four hours. Through visualization he chose his favorite golf course, dressed himself in his best golfing clothes, and approached the tee every morning. He paced himself as though he were physically present on the golf course. He noted the weather as he put the ball down. He viewed—in complete detail—the green grass, the slopes, the trees, and everything else that would affect his game. He made sure that he held his club correctly and visualized himself swinging and following through on each shot. He watched the ball fly down the fairway, hit the ground, and roll to the exact spots he aimed for. Colonel Johnson played eighteen holes of golf every day for eight years. He saw himself score 75 every time. It is no wonder that when he did finally reach his favorite golf course eight years later, his score was, indeed, 75.

Are you ready to create your most vivid mental picture of exactly what you want? Make the best use of drawings, photos, pictures, and other visual aids to assist you in visualizing your SUPREME goals.

How Do You Know You're on Track? How Can You Most Effectively Monitor Your Progress?

Your confidence and desire to accomplish your SUPREME goal are optimized when you monitor your progress. Keeping records will help you gain an accurate picture of how far you've come, your best results, strengths, weaknesses, and more. You can use your daily calendar, diagrams, graphs, ledgers, flow charts, and other Optimal tracking devices. You may choose to monitor the achievement of your goals by using lists. What is the best action you can take to monitor your progress right now?

Alternative Plans of Action

It isn't always possible to see clearly into the future. Any Optimal plan you develop is the best you can do at the time. As new circumstances arise and changes occur, updating will be necessary. When you are confronted with unexpected obstacles, alternative plans are essential.

Presidential candidate Ross Perot repeatedly expressed his belief in optimization. He talked about implementing new policies by testing them in small regions until they were perfected. The policies could then be implemented nationally with minimum wastage. When he announced his candidacy, he told the American nation, "I am a great believer in fine tuning and optimizing."

Wall Street analysts adjust their earnings estimates when they receive guidance about short- and long-term visibility from corporate principals.

We all learned how to walk, talk, read, write, drive a car, and cook by the principle of *attempt, fail, adjust, attempt again.* As an Optimal

Thinker, you can, at worst, *attempt, fail, optimize, and attempt again.* If you are confronted with an unexpected obstacle or change of circumstance, reevaluate the situation to determine the best outcome. Monitor, update, and optimize your plans to take account of the new circumstances. Always take the best action to achieve your end result. Where there's a will, there's an Optimal way!

Consider Paul, a corporate CEO who has attended many of my seminars. He had planned a weekend fishing trip with his son Andrew, but on Friday, Andrew injured himself during a football match. Paul, an Optimal Thinker, asked himself how he could still make the most of the weekend. He found himself looking at his list of SUPREME goals. His number one priority was to organize a party for his son's twenty-first birthday. He immediately started visualizing the ultimate party, and wrote out the guest list. Paul wrote down an Optimal plan to accomplish his SUPREME goal and moved into action, starting with the highest priority on his list. He knew this weekend would still be an Optimal one!

Make the Best Use of a Calendar

A calendar or planner will help you achieve your SUPREME goals and fulfill your purpose. At the beginning of each year, make sure your SUPREME goals are written down. You can then break them down into time frames that suit your lifestyle and needs. Many people set quarterly, monthly, weekly, and daily SUPREME goals. Some people only set weekly goals. Others set weekly and daily goals.

To set weekly goals, for example, consider your most important activities for the coming week. At the beginning of each week, plan ahead by asking yourself these four Optimal questions:

1. What are the most important goals I must achieve this week?
2. How can I make the most of this week?
3. What are the best actions I can take to achieve my ultimate purpose this week?
4. What are the best actions I can take to achieve my company's corporate mission? (if appropriate)

You can use the same procedure on a daily basis. Every evening, simply ask the following Optimal questions:

1. What are the most important goals I must achieve tomorrow?
2. How can I make the most of my day?

3. What are the best actions I can take to achieve my ultimate purpose?
4. What are the best actions I can take to achieve my company's corporate mission? (if appropriate)

Remember to jot down all the Optimal action steps in your calendar. Prioritize the imperative tasks with an A, then the important tasks with a B. Activities that are not important but could be useful, are best noted with a C. You may find that a task rated as a B is really a less important C. Your priorities will become apparent in time. If you have many As, Bs and Cs, write subcategories in order of importance: A1, A2, A3, B1, B2, and so on alongside your planned activities. Be sure to consider how long each task will take, so that your schedule is achievable.

Many people fail to keep to their schedules or to implement their plans because they underestimate the amount of time they spend reacting to unexpected and urgent issues. Bear in mind how much reactive time is usual in your own situation. Look at your last week or a realistic time frame to discover the ratio of your "proactive," or planned, time to reactive time. Keep this in mind when organizing your daily schedule. Set yourself up for the highest possible productivity each and every day.

Jane, a freelance writer, works best in the mornings. In the afternoons, she finds it difficult to come up with new ideas. Do you find that you are more productive at certain times of the day? If so, simply schedule the activities that require your greatest productivity for those times. Save other tasks for times when you are less productive.

Be realistic. You cannot do thirty-five hours of work in fourteen hours. Consider Jack, who was in the habit of writing thirty to forty tasks on his "to do" list each day. He usually completed about ten of them. He was overwhelmed by all the work that needed to be done and felt like a failure every day. It was too much for him and he desperately needed an experience of success. When Jack attended an *Optimize Your Time—Don't Just Manage It!* seminar, he decided to take charge of his time and his life. He began by setting an achievable number of SUPREME tasks every day, and at the end of each day, he proudly checked off the tasks he had accomplished. Once he was able to achieve what he wanted on a daily basis, he began to appreciate and enjoy his life.

A journey of a thousand miles does start with a single step. An Optimal daily "to do" list will inspire you to put your best foot forward and challenge you to do your best. At the end of each day, you can answer the question *How much of my activity contributed to my ultimate purpose today?* You can check off what you've done, or if you don't complete a task on a specific day, simply reschedule and reprioritize it for the next day. You may wish to circle it or place a T next to it (to indicate its transference from day to day) until you complete it. Your calendar provides a checklist of exactly when your goals were set and completed. When you are feeling unproductive, a list of completed goals can be your greatest source of inspiration.

When you go shopping, do you use a list to remind yourself of what you want? While you are walking around, do you consider buying other items that appeal to you? You can choose to live your life in the same manner. Give yourself some unplanned time every day to enjoy and make the most of unexpected opportunities. While you're completing the actions on your "to do" list, welcome all the unexpected opportunities that encourage the fulfillment of your purpose. Schedule some free time every day to do whatever you feel like doing. You can use this time to relax, enjoy your intuition, and be creative. Balance planned time with spontaneous time.

Your calendar can also help you make the most of Optimal affirmations. When you want to integrate an affirmation—for example, "I am making the most productive use of my time right now" or "I am doing the most important task right now"—jot it down on a transferable sticker, place it on your calendar, and move it forward every day. Post-It notes are ideal. I note my Optimal affirmations on these stickers and am compelled to confront them several times a day.

Would you like to introduce a new habit into your life? Your calendar can keep you focused. Remind yourself of the desired new behavior every day by moving a transferable sticker on your calendar each day. Debbie implemented this idea when she decided to resume her program of regular exercise. She had become bored with her previous aerobics program, but hadn't found an adequate enjoyable substitute. Debbie wrote "half-hour daily enjoyable aerobic exercise" on a bright sticker on her calendar and moved it along daily. On the first day she ignored it. On the second day she felt guilty. On the third day she felt very guilty. On the fourth day she managed two minutes of a new aerobics program. Soon, Debbie was enjoying thirty minutes of aerobic exercise every day.

Make sure your calendar or planner is always accessible so that you can remind yourself of your plans every day. Rodney completes and checks his schedule at night so that his subconscious mind can prepare him for the following day while he is sleeping. During the day, he writes down various activities for the following days as they come to his attention.

Many years ago, I created the *Optimize Your Time—Don't Just Manage It!* seminar, which I have presented in many parts of the world. I am always inspired by my audiences' ideas on how to adapt planners to serve unique personalities and needs. I am sure that you are equally creative. So, how can you make the best use of your calendar right now?

Optimal Questions

1. What are my most important goals?
2. What are the rewards that will maximize my desire to achieve them?
3. What are the best time frames for completing these goals?
4. What are the best/wisest actions I can take to achieve these goals?
5. How much of my activity contributed to these goals today/this week?

Optimal Action Steps

1. Before you start each day, optimize your motivation to achieve your SUPREME goal by reminding yourself of all the benefits you will gain by accomplishing it.
2. At least twice each day, rehearse and enjoy the experience of being your best self as you accomplish your SUPREME goal. See, hear, feel, taste, and touch all of it in your mind's eye.
3. Make friends with your inner critic as you move along the path to your SUPREME goal. Embrace all criticism and optimize, by taking the best action. Check in with yourself throughout each day, and ask yourself: *What's the best action I can take toward my SUPREME goal?*

CHAPTER 7

Optimize Your Feelings

"The action is best which procures the greatest happiness of the greatest number."

—Francis Hutcheson

The Value of Emotions

Your emotional life is a natural and sacred part of you. Your feelings are direct responses to your perception. They signal whether your experiences are pleasurable or painful. When you acknowledge your feelings, you are in touch with your humanity, and when you honor them, you demonstrate self-respect. You can take the wisest actions to minimize your troublesome feelings when you take responsibility for creating them. Embracing vulnerability is your path to wholeness.

Your emotions are physical sensations within your body. These invaluable allies serve as your inner compass. They inform you whether your thoughts and actions are in harmony with your core self. Sometimes they guide you with a whisper, and if you don't heed their message, they increase their volume until you are forced to pay attention. Painful feelings alert you that your thinking or actions are not good for you, so that you can make changes in alignment with your soul's highest calling.

Your passion indicates what has meaning or importance for you and provides the motivation that propels you to accomplish your goals. The expertise of a top executive, athlete, or entertainer is gained through a focused desire for mastery. When you recognize what you feel passionate about, you can determine if it serves your best interest, and then choose the wisest response. You will experience your best feelings when your best self is in charge and your most important needs are met.

Consider Cheryl, a single mother who had worked as a producer in the film industry for nearly twenty years. Her résumé showed a variety of positions, yet her status and salary remained mediocre. Although her main priority had been raising her son, Cheryl felt bad that she had not progressed in her career. Above all else, Cheryl wanted to produce an inspirational film about motherhood. She had asked her colleagues to look for a script, but had not found any that even remotely met her needs. One day, Jim, an old friend who understood Cheryl's priorities, asked her to read a script he had just completed. The film explored a mother's unconditional love for her troubled son, and provided a superlative example for struggling mothers. Cheryl couldn't remember being so inspired by a script. "This is my opportunity to make a lasting contribution to the world. This script is the basis of a top-notch feature film. I have to produce it!" She was on top of the world. Here was an opportunity to give her best efforts to a project that ignited her passion. When she called Jim the next day, she couldn't wait to start work.

So where does Optimal Thinking fit in? You have the best chance of meeting your needs when you think, feel, and give your best. Optimal Thinking is the vehicle that enables you to call forth your highest self to best meet your needs, achieve what is most important, and make the most of your feelings.

Overpowered by Emotions?

Anita and Lionel were intensely attracted to each other some ten years ago. Anita had suffered tremendous hurt when Lionel later rejected her; now, suddenly, he was in her life again. When she heard his voice again for the first time, her heart pounded violently and she struggled to speak articulately. Within a few minutes she was mindlessly snacking even though she wasn't hungry.

Have you ever had feelings that were threatening to your sense of security? It's not the presence of emotions that can be detrimental to you, but the inability to incorporate them productively into everyday behavior. Many people actually view their feelings and thoughts as separate and incongruent parts of themselves. Some people avoid, ignore, devalue, and wallow in disturbing feelings because they don't know how to deal with them. Others use drugs, alcohol, gambling, food, or other addictions to avoid their troublesome feelings. These people gain temporary relief, but as soon as their defenses are down, the feelings return. Have you ever asked why someone was angry only to hear him or her scream, "I'm not angry!"? When we don't resolve our disturbing feelings, we carry them around as baggage and then respond disproportionately to transgressions. Denying feelings like anger and resentment may cause them to build up into rage. When there is a strong background emotion such as rage, jealousy, or guilt, your perception and thinking can be distorted. For instance, if you are seething with anger about a friend's betrayal, it is dangerous to share your vulnerability with people who are cold or hostile. The stronger your emotions, the more likely they are to overpower your ability to reason.

Are you ever too angry to be reasonable, too excited to be rational, or too depressed to think in terms of your best interest? Can you stay logical and reasonable when powerful feelings are involved? Many people fear the loss of control that can accompany the expression of strong feelings.

Consider Cathy, an attorney who was abused and rejected by her father. Ten years ago, her unresolved anger wrecked her relationship with her boyfriend. When Howard discovered that his mother had lung cancer, he was devastated. Even though he assured Cathy that his emotional turmoil had nothing to do with her, she felt angry and rejected. When Howard decided to spend a weekend on his own to sort out his feelings, Cathy wrote him a nasty letter. He was deeply hurt and ended the relationship. To this day, Cathy is terrified of rejection and does not trust herself to behave rationally in intimate relationships.

Do you ever deny what you feel, rationalize, misinterpret, or use pretense to avoid your pain? Inventing an inauthentic life—by denying your feelings—can protect you temporarily but is usually counterproductive in the long term. Unfortunately, unresolved pain often motivates behavior that has long-term negative consequences. Here is an example.

When Margaret was five years old, her brother died. Sadly, her parents focused their attention on her sister and ignored her. She received no love or attention and felt lonely and hurt. To find comfort, Margaret married the first man who showed an interest in her, and they had four children. Sean watched television religiously to avoid intimacy, and was unable to keep a job. As long as Margaret complied with his wishes, Sean was civil. However, when she disagreed with him, he would insult her, rage at the children, and then withdraw for days on end. Fearful of being alone again, Margaret refused to face the fragility of their relationship or acknowledge her ambivalent feelings toward Sean. She put on a happy face and dutifully performed the role of the obedient wife. After seven years of denying her emotions, Margaret sank into a deep, dark depression. There were many months when she could barely get out of bed. Eventually, she could not bring herself to leave their apartment. Her life with Sean had become intolerable. She had no education or job skills and now faced the burden of raising four children on her own.

Sean's childhood had been a nightmare. His father was an alcoholic who went into tirades for no apparent reason. Sean lived in constant fear. When he was seventeen, he began to use alcohol to soothe his anxiety and ultimately became an alcoholic. Sean married Margaret and had a family to escape his misery, but was emotionally unavailable and abusive to her. He repeated his father's destructive behavior because he had not resolved his own painful feelings.

Can you recall instances where you have been overwhelmed by troublesome feelings? Are you willing to deal most effectively with the feelings that disturb you? You can use Optimal Thinking to master these feelings and optimize your behavior in even the most emotionally charged situations.

How to Master Disturbing Feelings

Step 1. Accept Your Emotions

> *"Emotions are not fleeting events isolated in mental space; they are expressions of awareness, the fundamental stuff of life."*
> —Deepak Chopra, M.D.

Take five minutes now to explore your internal world. You will need to sit in a comfortable position, close your eyes, and notice what happens. Is your inner world dominated by feelings or by thoughts? Is there a balance of both? Do you feel afraid, hurt, angry, disappointed, abandoned, disrespected, betrayed, unappreciated, or ashamed? Do you feel loving, appreciated, safe, joyful, grateful, curious, confident, comfortable, powerful, or peaceful? Which emotion is dominant right now?

Stay present. When you observe your emotions, you are no longer unconsciously identified with them—or under their control. Simply witness your feelings without judging them, and ask yourself,

What emotions are involved here? What do I feel? Now focus on the bodily sensations associated with your feelings. You may feel some restriction in your chest, solar plexus, abdomen, back, shoulders, or other parts of your body. By embracing these physical sensations, you are accepting the totality of your emotional experience. When you welcome your full range of emotions, the energy you used to judge and suppress them becomes available to optimize your life. Accepting responsibility for your feelings is the basis of creating your own happiness.

Step 2. Understand and Learn from Your Disturbing Emotions

Like any other threat to your safety, unpleasant emotions are handled best when you are clear about what you are facing. When you understand your emotions, you can interpret your responses and make sense of the world around you. Your feelings provide you with knowledge and understanding about yourself and others. After you identify the origin and purpose of the beliefs that are fueling your emotional turbulence, you can access the superlative response. You have to first allow yourself to feel the emotional turmoil. Observe the pain, then validate and appreciate yourself for your willingness to accept your troublesome feelings. When you understand what you are doing to create your emotional turmoil, you can avoid unnecessary reoccurrence. Ask questions like:

- Why do I feel this way?
- What am I not listening to?
- What am I not dealing with?
- What am I afraid of?
- What did I lose?
- What am I thinking or doing that is causing these feelings?
- What are these feelings trying to teach me?
- What can I learn from these feelings?
- Have I felt like this before?
- What situation, event, or person is linked to this feeling?
- How do I behave when I feel this way?

Step 3. Determine the Best Way to Heal Disturbing Emotions

"Healing is the process of accepting all then choosing the best."
—Neale Donald Walsch

You are the source of all your feelings and are always responsible for your emotional responses, so make sure your primary focus is internal. Blaming others for your feelings is a waste of your energy. People and situations only trigger what is already inside you. When you deal with your feelings as soon as you are aware of them, you live wholly in the present moment where you can most influence your life. Of course, your perception and interpretation of current events are always colored by your past experiences. As you uncover and correct the erroneous beliefs from the past that are causing you to create pain in the present, you will heal. There are many ways to process and heal disturbing feelings. You can ask:

- What do I need and want above all else here?
- What are my options here?
- What's the best way to deal with these feelings?
- What's the best way to resolve these feelings?
- What's the most constructive action I can take to achieve what I want?
- What can I do to create the Optimal solution right now?
- What is the most loving action I can take for myself?

Sometimes recalling a previous experience where you handled the same emotion properly is all that is needed. Simply ask:

- What did I do in the past?
- What did I focus on and which actions did I take?
- How can I make the best use of this successful strategy right now?

When Feelings Are Manageable

If you are feeling slightly agitated about something, you can:

Step 1.   Look within and ascertain exactly what is provoking your feelings.
Step 2.   Explore the lesson you are being offered.
Step 3.   Decide if you want to give yourself a cooling-off period.
Step 4.   Determine the best way to handle your feelings.

Mary, a certified Optimal trainer, used this four-step procedure while she was conducting a seminar series. Her audience was enthralled with the unique content, superlative perspective, and her presentation style. Paul, an aspiring seminar leader, had attended every seminar in the series. He was thrilled with them, and shared numerous stories of the benefits he had gained with the other participants. He even called Mary's office and asked if he could provide training for the company. Mary explained gently that there were no positions currently available and advised him to submit his résumé for future consideration.

During the coffee break at the next seminar, Paul confronted Mary and told her that her seminars were the worst he had ever attended. He pointed out numerous flaws in her presentation and said she lacked professionalism. He concluded the confrontation by informing her that he was the best in this field. Mary was troubled by Paul's attack. She referred to a three-by-five-inch card on which she had written the following questions: *Why am I feeling bad? What precipitated this feeling? What am I thinking or doing to create this? What is the lesson for me here? What's the best way to resolve my feelings about this? What's the best action I can take to achieve what I want right now?* She realized that she was distressed because she felt helpless around people who behaved irrationally. Paul's irrational behavior reminded her of how helpless she had felt as a child when her mother became irrational. Mary's next step was to recognize that she was no longer a dependent child. She was then able to embrace the current situation and accept her helplessness over Paul's change of heart and his irrational behavior. She then resolved to focus on what was within her control, and to conclude the seminar series as well as she could.

Mary approached Paul and said: "I am sorry you are unhappy with the seminars. I am interested in your *most constructive* feedback. Would you like to write it down for me?" Paul agreed, the dispute was diffused, and Mary continued to put her best foot forward.

When Feelings Seem Unmanageable

When you are overloaded with disturbing feelings, and feel devastated and out of control, you can optimize your response with these consecutive steps:

Step 1. Stay present, observe your feelings, and give yourself a cooling-off period.

Step 2. Look within and ascertain exactly what is provoking your feelings.

Step 3. Explore the lesson you are being offered.

Step 4. Determine the best way to handle your feelings.

When you are overwhelmed by your feelings, you are fully identified with them. By consciously choosing to observe your feelings in the present moment, you immediately reduce their power over you. Instead of acting impulsively, you can now choose what is in your best interest.

Unfortunately, many people act destructively when they are overwhelmed by their feelings. Consider my clients Gary and Beverly, two small-business owners who loved each other but couldn't get along. Whenever Beverly annoyed Gary, he would lash out at her. When she couldn't take it anymore and ended the relationship, Gary took responsibility for his anger instead of blaming her for it. He realized that his angry reactions were protecting him from feelings of inadequacy, and his aggressive behavior had destroyed their relationship. Gary learned how to contain his turbulent feelings and explore his unmet needs instead of giving in to his old impulsive, destructive behaviors. Every time he felt distressed, he took time to observe what was happening inside him and to cool off. He practiced asking for what he needed—in the most constructive manner possible—before resuming communications with the person who triggered his reaction. After six months of committed focus, Gary trusted himself enough to approach Beverly to start afresh.

Les, an industrial property owner, measured himself by his financial worth. Sadly, a tough economy had taken its toll on Les's business affairs. Some of his tenants had gone out of business and many of his buildings were now vacant. When Les became irrational and yelled at a prospective tenant who decided against leasing one of his properties, he realized he needed a cooling-off period. Les immediately focused on activities where he could experience some "wins" to regain his equanimity and reinstate his self-confidence. He was then in the right frame of mind to confront his turbulent feelings and determine the most appropriate way to deal with the situations that provoked them.

You can use a similar procedure to minimize the negative impact of disturbing feelings. You may choose to involve yourself with something you can do by yourself for yourself where you are in complete control. Left-brain activities involving simple sequences are most beneficial at this time. You can inhale deeply, counting from one to four, then exhale, counting again from one to four, or simply count to one hundred. Continue this procedure until you regain your sense of bodily awareness and a feeling of equanimity. When overwhelmed by your feelings, you can also take a walk, go for a run, play with a pet, talk with a friend, write in your journal, play the piano, or listen to your favorite music. When you have regained your composure, you can look at what the disturbing feelings were all about. Where did they come from? What provoked them? What's the most constructive way to deal with them?

You can master essentially any emotion when you employ the three-step method for emotional mastery. To optimize your emotional life, I recommend that you jot down the three steps on three-by-five-inch cards. Keep them with you and use them as soon as you become aware of a disturbing emotion. You might feel awkward initially, but with practice and commitment, the three steps—and emotional mastery—will become second nature. If you find yourself dealing with the same emotion repeatedly, just keep choosing an Optimal response. Eventually you will accept painful emotions as sacred counselors who steer you in the right direction.

Optimization Signals

All painful feelings—including anxiety, hatred, disappointment, guilt, frustration, rage, terror, shame, discouragement, jealousy, and hopelessness—stem from a threat, loss, or wound. When you are emotionally upset, potent chemical and physiological changes occur within your body. You can employ these disturbing emotions to optimize your life. Take the best path to becoming a fully realized being. You may need to read the following section many times to remember what each emotion is teaching you. Be sure to highlight the Optimal questions, and summarize the most useful information on three-by-five cards. Carry the cards with you, put them on your refrigerator, the screen saver of your computer, and the sun visor of your car. You will then have at your fingertips the mental software to optimize your emotions, and you'll be able to figure out the best actions in the moment.

Helplessness

All of us feel helpless when we are impacted by people, incidents, or forces out of our control. Helplessness is the intense exasperation we experience when we feel powerless in meeting our needs. When a friend dies, your spouse has an affair, or a natural disaster destroys your home, it is natural to feel helpless. To allow your feelings of helplessness to point you in the right direction, ask yourself:

- What is out of my control here?
- Which needs are being unmet in this situation?
- Can I accept this?
- What is within my control here?

- What is most important to me?
- What are the best actions I can take to achieve what is most important?
- What is the best use of my time right now?

Accept what is out of your control and optimize what is within your control. When you focus all your attention on what you have control over and take actions in your best interest, you have supreme control of your life. You will have to accept that you are powerless over everything other than yourself. You only have control over your own choices and purpose. You may impress others, but you do not have control over them. Instead of trying to change people or events that do not live up to your expectations, focus on being true to yourself by reevaluating what is most important to you. Clarify your priorities, stay focused, and take the best actions to achieve what you want.

Recently Jerry, a small-business owner, came into my office feeling helpless and victimized. From a heavy heart, he said: "I'm desperate. Over the past three months, everything has gone wrong. Customers aren't paying their bills on time, my operations manager is incompetent and probably on drugs, and on top of this, my business is now being audited. I should have stayed in my last job instead of getting involved with this business." Jerry could not see an end to his burdensome situation. When I asked him what was within his control, he continued to describe events that were out of his control. I then said, "Jerry, I know you are feeling helpless and it is very painful. Are you willing to view this from an Optimal perspective? When you dwell on what is out of your control, you are not paying attention to what is within your control. By neglecting what is within your control and magnifying what is out of your control, you are choosing to be a victim and are sabotaging your life. Are you willing to focus on what is in your best interest right now?"

Jerry immediately started focusing on what was within his control. He decided to arrange a meeting with his accountant to discuss the audit; to train another employee to optimize the operations department; to instruct his office manager to call clients who were delinquent in their payments; to institute an incentive for prompt payment; and to place advertisements in the local paper to bring in more business. Jerry then resolved to focus his attention on his highest priorities. His business was on track within two weeks, and he subsequently found relief.

Discomfort

Discomfort alerts you that something is wrong. This uneasy feeling may be experienced as apathy, impatience, boredom, embarrassment, tension, or confusion. When you judge or deny aspects of your personality, you will most likely feel discomfort. Discomfort informs that you need to change your thinking and behavior and create what is right for you. Your journey to wholeness requires that you embrace all facets of your multifaceted nature without judgment. When you accept all the different aspects of your personality—particularly those that make you most uncomfortable—you are embracing your individuality and loving yourself unconditionally. You can then see the uniqueness in others, embrace them, and love them in a similar manner. You can understand your feelings of discomfort, learn from them, and take the most restorative actions, by asking:

- What exactly am I feeling?
- What isn't right for me here?
- What am I thinking or doing to create this feeling?
- What do I really want?
- What must I think and do to create what I want?
- What do I need to do to eliminate this distress or discomfort?
- What is the most constructive action I can take right now?

Here's how Shana and Stella employed these questions and used their feelings of discomfort to point them in the right direction. Shana was planning a holiday with Tracy, a new friend. While they were discussing the itinerary, Tracy picked up the phone and chatted with her daughter about an unrelated issue. As the conversation progressed, Shana felt increasingly uncomfortable. She opened her pocketbook and took out her three-by-five emotional mastery cards. Shana quickly realized that her discomfort was a reaction to being excluded, without any consideration for her feelings. She did not want to go on a holiday with Tracy and feel excluded. Shana decided to tell Tracy how she felt, explain her reasons, and observe Tracy's reaction. If she felt uncomfortable with Tracy's response, she would make other plans.

Stella was dating Joel, an A-type personality with poor social skills. Something didn't feel right, but at first she couldn't put her finger on it. When Joel yawned in social situations and made insensitive comments, Stella felt particularly uncomfortable. By exploring her feelings of discomfort, she realized that she felt embarrassed by Joel's behavior. She really wanted a man who was friendly and sociable, and knew she couldn't be proud of a man who was brusque. Stella immediately decided to stop seeing Joel and to only date men with whom she felt comfortable.

Anxiety

Fear is nature's way of protecting you from real and current danger. It prepares you to escape from harm. Anxiety is the fear of future or the remembrance of past hurt, danger, or loss. Anxiety varies in form and intensity and can be based on real or imagined situations. You can feel uncertain, edgy, apprehensive, worried, insecure, nervous, or terrified, and may experience physical symptoms such as "butterflies in your stomach." You sense that something bad is about to happen. Sadly, many people create anxiety gratuitously by dwelling on negative possibilities with "what if's." To understand how you create anxiety, you can ask questions like:

- Why do I feel anxious?
- Am I afraid that something bad is about to happen?
- What is causing me to feel threatened?
- What am I afraid of losing?
- What am I thinking or doing to create this?
- What can I learn from this?

Feelings of anxiety are best eliminated not by defensively denying or ignoring them, but by removing the threat that's causing them. By taking the best actions possible, you optimize your self-reliance and achieve the highest level of control over your environment. You can minimize your anxiety by asking questions to invite resolution and by focusing specifically on the best ways to achieve what you want. Allow your anxiety to protect you by answering these Optimal questions:

- What is the best thing I can do to remove the threat(s)?
- Which changes in my thinking are necessary to create safety/security in my life?
- How can I best prepare myself to handle this?
- What's the best action I can take to prevent the loss and minimize the pain?
- What's the most constructive action I can take to achieve what I want?
- What is the wisest action I can take under the circumstances?

Here's how a successful writer used his anxiety to optimize a nasty situation. John was in the middle of an acrimonious divorce.

He had already spent eighty thousand dollars on attorney's fees and did not see an end in sight. His days were fraught with anxiety, and his nights offered little relief. He could barely function. During an *Optimize Your Emotional Life* seminar, he learned about emotional mastery. After answering the questions on his three-by-five card, John realized he was extremely threatened by his wife's vindictiveness. He was terrified of being helpless and persecuted. The attorney's fees were escalating and out of control, and if his wife got her way, he would be wiped out financially.

John needed to find out if his wife would consider a fair settlement. He wrote down all the benefits she would gain by agreeing to his proposal and rehearsed his conversation with her until he felt confident that he could maintain his composure. He decided that if she was not willing to settle the matter, he would meet with his attorney the following day to discuss how he could best contain costs. Armed with his Optimal strategy, he was able to minimize his anxiety when he called his wife and hammer out an equitable settlement.

Hurt

As we make our journey through life, none of us escapes being hurt. These painful feelings arise when we experience loss. The greater the loss, the more profoundly we hurt. Hurt tells you what is important, and that your expectations have not been met. You are likely to feel hurt when you are betrayed, badly treated, or ignored by people you care about. It hurts when they are insensitive to your needs. You will need to acknowledge your loss, feel the pain, and recognize your role in creating it. To understand your hurt, ask:

- Why do I feel hurt?
- What am I thinking or doing to create this hurt?
- Which expectations did I have that were not met?
- How was I injured?
- What did I lose?
- Was the hurt intentional?

Accept what can't be fixed, and then decide on your best approach for optimizing what is within your control. You may need to meditate, write a letter, or talk to the person involved to resolve your loss. To release and heal the hurt, you can answer these Optimal questions:

- How can this loss best serve me?
- What is my best strategy for letting go of these feelings?

- What are the best changes I can make to release the pain?
- What's the best thing I can do under the circumstances?

If you believe that someone intentionally hurt you, you will need to decide if it is in your best interest to communicate your loss directly to him or her. When you share your vulnerability with someone who doesn't care about your feelings, you risk more pain. Sometimes hurt is best resolved when you recognize that all you lost were your illusions. When you express your hurt to those directly involved, you stand up for yourself—and expose your vulnerability. You might say something like: "When you excluded me from your plans I felt hurt, because I interpreted this to mean that I am not important to you." You can then explain how you would like to be treated in the future.

Consider my client Julia, who trusted people. As long as their shabby behavior did not have any impact on her, she believed in them. However, when she relied on people and they disappointed her, she felt betrayed and hurt. Unfortunately, Julia received a gut-wrenching lesson when her father passed away. A few weeks after his death, her sister Jane asked her to promise that she would not contest their father's will. Before Julia had even read it, Jane was pressuring her to abide by their father's wishes. Julia sensed something was wrong. When she asked to see the will, Jane threw a tantrum and stormed out of the house. Then the ugly truth came out. A few weeks before Julia's father died, he had changed his will in Jane's favor. He had been medicated at the time and probably did not have all his faculties.

Julia felt betrayed and deeply hurt. Upon reflection, she realized that her own unrealistic expectations were causing her pain. She recognized that she had always given her trust to others before they earned it—and even when they showed they were untrustworthy. She knew Jane was deceitful. However, Jane's financial greed had never been discernible. Sadly, Julia needed this wake-up call to optimize her thinking and behavior. She immediately hired a top-notch attorney to take proper care of her interests. She then resolved to let people earn her trust by remaining objective, observing their behavior in different situations, and evaluating their trustworthiness when she had gathered enough information.

Are you ready to put your unresolved hurt to rest? In your notebook, make a list of people who have hurt you. Next to each name, write down the best strategy to restore your aching heart. If you decide to speak to the person who hurt you, jot down exactly what you want to say to that person. Now make a list of all the losses that are blocking you and rigidifying your heart. Use the information and questions above to resolve your feelings and keep you on your Optimal path.

Anger

You feel angry when you take offense at being hurt or experiencing loss. Angry feelings arise when you feel helpless, threatened, deprived, or unfairly treated. Anger is a physiological sensation created by the production of adrenaline in the body, and a protective mechanism that prepares your body to fight against attack. Bodily tension and other disturbing emotions often accompany anger. You can experience frustration, irritability, annoyance, resentment, hatred, or even rage. You may choose to react with anger rather than feel hurt, because you perceive hurt as a sign of vulnerability. Anger keeps people at a distance and enables you to conceal your vulnerability. Anger is a shield to cover your underlying fear.

Anger informs you about unwelcome violations of your personal sanctum. You can minimize your vulnerability to emotional trespasses by establishing boundaries that optimize your safety and personal power. In social situations, anger will define the limits of acceptable behavior for you. You can use it to protect your dignity, identity, and self-esteem. Anger enables you to stand up for yourself and defend against violation. It is the part of you that believes, "You can't treat me that way." Whereas fear prepares you to escape from danger (the flight response), anger prepares you to attack (the fight response). When the anger is intense, it is best to take time to cool down and figure out what is causing it, so that you can determine the most appropriate response. You can answer these questions:

- What am I thinking or doing to create this anger?
- What am I afraid of?
- How have I been hurt?
- Why do I feel wounded?
- Was the injury intentional?
- Did I overlook something important that caused me to feel betrayed/hurt?
- Were my expectations realistic?
- Have I become aware of my limits and established boundaries that are important to me?
- What's the best thing I can do to make sure these boundaries are not violated in the future?
- What is my most constructive response here?

Anger can be very destructive if you express it aggressively to attack others. Sarcasm, put-downs, and verbal abuse are all aggressive behaviors where anger is externalized and used as a weapon to hurt others. Similarly, if you are unable to express anger, it festers within you, and your happiness is squandered. Self-pity, grumbling, and idle gossip are behaviors that indicate unresolved anger.

Anger is most constructive when it serves as a motivating force to optimize your life. It is best to address the issues that trigger anger in your life when you are calm. When you determine the cause of your hurt, you can explore your options and decide upon the Optimal solution. You can then take the most constructive actions to end the issue and release the anger and hurt. You might engage in vigorous exercise to cool off, write in your journal, or discuss your grievance with a trustworthy person, if you do not want to confront the person who hurt you. You may choose to resolve your anger on your own. Greg, a journalist I coached, was furious when his boss criticized his latest story. He immediately took a brisk walk around the block to cool off. He then took out a pen and paper and analyzed his anger in the following way.

Situation: Boss complained my work was inadequate.

Emotion involved: Anger

What caused the disturbing emotion? Describe loss, threat, or wound: I'm afraid my job is at risk because my work is not good enough. I think that my boss doesn't respect my professional capabilities when he complains about my work, and this stirs up my feelings of inadequacy.

What are my options for resolving this? Take time to understand how my job insecurity and other feelings of anxiety originated, and realize that I'm not in the past now. Discuss with therapist on Tuesday to gain understanding of how the fear originated. Observe my inner critic and look at the beliefs that are fueling the criticism. Acknowledge and remind myself of all my accomplishments. Assess what is in everyone's best interests before writing each new story. Talk to my boss. Tell him that I produce my best stories when he points out the flaws and the value. I will then be receptive to accepting the flaws and finding the best solutions to overcome them.

Optimal response, best strategy/actions to be taken:

- Realize that I'm not in the past now and embrace the present moment.
- Observe my inner critic. Understand its purpose.

- Assess what is in everyone's best interests before writing each new story.
- Talk to boss on Monday. Tell him that I will produce my best stories if he points out the flaws and the value in my work.

You might wish to release your anger in writing by employing the following three-step process. The three steps enable you to express your anger to all concerned. When you take full responsibility for your anger, you release yourself from feeling victimized.

Step 1.   *Express your anger, then your hurt, to the person who injured you.*

Step 2.   *Express your anger, then your hurt, to others in your life who have injured you in a similar way.*

Step 3.   *Express the anger, then your hurt, toward yourself for creating the injury.*

When you decide to resolve the issue directly with the person who hurt you, anger will best support you as an Optimal assertive response, which neither retreats or attacks, but stands firm. For example, if you feel angry because someone put you down, you can respond with: "I want to hear what you are angry about, but it is hard for me to listen when I perceive that you are insulting me. Are you ready to resolve this matter with me respectfully now, or do you need some time to cool off? What is in your best interest?" Expressing the underlying hurt is the best way of resolving your anger because it makes your wound the primary issue. You can tell the person why you feel angry, point out how his or her behavior is causing you problems, and express commitment to finding the best solution for all concerned. Say: "When you do this, I feel angry/hurt because I interpret it to mean . . . What's the best way we can resolve this?"

Weigh the risks and benefits of such a confrontation to decide what is in your best interest. Even if you end your association with an abusive person, you will need to let go of your hurt and anger, so that you are not controlled by hurtful memories. By letting go, you are not condoning hurtful behavior or absolving anyone of the consequences of his or her behavior. You are simply freeing yourself from the festering residue of your anger, so that you can optimize your life.

Disappointment

You will feel disappointed when you want something and no longer believe that you can have it. When you are disappointed you feel let down, sad, disillusioned, hopeless, and defeated. You set yourself up for disappointment when you entertain unrealistic goals, or practice wishful thinking. If you trust people and they let you down, you will naturally feel disappointed in yourself and in them. To understand and resolve these feelings, ask:

- What am I thinking or doing to create this?
- Do I have realistic expectations?
- Is it possible that I could still achieve what I want?
- Do I still have the time and resources?
- What can this situation teach me so that I can achieve what I want in the future?
- What is my most important goal right now?
- What are the most empowering actions I can take toward my SUPREME goal?
- What's the best action I can take right now?

You will need to assess whether your goal is still reachable and if you are willing to do whatever is necessary to achieve it. If the goal is no longer achievable, minimize your feelings of disappointment and helplessness by focusing your attention on optimizing what is within your control. Set and achieve a SUPREME goal. Respect yourself for doing your best!

Elaine, an attorney who was deeply disappointed with her life, consulted with me. When Elaine was growing up, women were considered defective if they did not marry and have children. Elaine's parents were devout Catholics, and from an early age, she was aware that she could only marry a Catholic man if she wanted her family's approval. When Elaine was nineteen years old, she had a relationship with Greg, a Mormon, behind her parents' backs. She knew she would never marry him. After Greg, she dated lots of Catholic men, but did not find a lasting relationship with any of them. Disappointed and depressed, she continued her search for Mr. Right. When she reached her late thirties and was still alone, she became desperate. Then she met Ian. He had just started a new business, was struggling to make ends meet, lacked social graces, and did not fit her picture of Mr. Right. At thirty-eight, Elaine had tried everything in her power to find her life partner and nothing had worked. When Ian asked her to marry him, even though she knew she was settling for second best, she accepted his proposal.

It didn't take long for Elaine to see why Ian had been divorced before. She never knew when her husband would be kind or mean-spirited. Sadly, the marriage ended when he found another woman.

After her divorce, Elaine dated many men. Initially she was optimistic that her marital experience would help her to choose a better man. However, as time went on, her disappointment with life and the belief that she would never have a family returned. Elaine met the man of her dreams two months after the following conversation. Here is some of our dialogue:

Elaine: I've tried everything. I'm worn out. What's the use of trying anymore? All I get is a big zero!

Rosalene: Elaine, do you believe that it is still possible to meet the right man?

Elaine: Yes, it's possible, but it's a very tough goal to achieve.

Rosalene: If there were no chance of failure, would you still pursue your goal?

Elaine: If I knew I couldn't fail, I would definitely keep trying.

Rosalene: So you still believe it is possible to achieve your goal. You're disappointed that you haven't achieved it yet, and that the journey is difficult, is that it?

Elaine: You got it.

Rosalene: Are you willing to give it your best shot? Are you willing to do whatever it takes?

Elaine: I guess so. The alternative of being alone forever is depressing.

Rosalene: Are you ready to focus on optimizing what is within your control? Are you ready to set a SUPREME goal?

Elaine: Yes.

Rosalene: How can you state your goal so that it passes the SUPREME test?

Elaine: I could set a goal to put myself in social situations three times a week where I can interact with singles like myself.

Rosalene: Sounds right. Which beliefs would best support you in achieving this goal?

Elaine: These: "I am true to myself and live an authentic life, I am doing all I can to attract my life mate, and I am the right person, in the right place at the right time, doing the most important activity in the best way."

Rosalene: What are the most empowering actions you can take to move toward your goal right now?

Elaine: Buy a calendar. Block out time for social interactions with single people. Figure out the activities that are in my best interest.

Guilt

Healthy guilt occurs when you have hurt or wronged another person or yourself. You regret your actions and feel undeserving, wrong, stupid, ashamed, sorry, or disappointed in yourself. It occurs when your anger is turned inward. When you lie to those who trust you, cheat on your partner, or blame someone else for something that's really your fault, you are liable to feel guilty. The remorse you experience is an expression of your conscience and guides you to act in a manner that is in alignment with the best person you can be.

When you feel disappointed because you haven't lived up to your own or others' unrealistic expectations—by insisting on perfection or believing you are good only when you follow someone else's rules—you experience unhealthy guilt. By persecuting yourself, you avoid facing your helplessness. Unhealthy guilt can give you a false sense of power and control. To help you understand your feelings of guilt, simply answer the following questions.

- Which expectations have I disappointed myself with by not living up to them?
- Which moral principles have I violated?
- Are these moral principles well founded and rational?
- Were there other factors that contributed to this?
- Am I completely to blame for this?
- Is my life based on my own or someone else's standards?
- Am I a perfectionist?
- Am I making excessive demands on myself?

When you feel guilty, begin by examining your expectations. For instance, it is unreasonable to expect that you will never get angry with your spouse, children, or friends. You are a student in this life, and you will make mistakes like all of us. Mistakes are learning opportunities that signal you to optimize. To resolve your feelings of guilt and recover your buried, untarnished essence, jot down everything you feel guilty about, then ask yourself:

- Why am I afraid to express my anger?
- Can I make up for my mistake?

- What's the best way to resolve this?
- What is the right thing to do here?
- What's the best thing I can do under the circumstances?
- How can I optimize my behavior in the future?

It may be in your best interest to share your guilt with your most trusted friend or counselor to figure out how to best substitute appropriate behaviors when you are faced with similar issues. If there is something you can do to alleviate your guilt, go ahead and do it. If not, you must accept that the past is over and that nothing can be gained by torturing yourself. Instead of holding on to guilt, resolve to learn from your mistake and do the right thing now and in the future.

Depression

When you suffer pain and loss and do not express and resolve your feelings of helplessness, hurt, anger, and grief, you will eventually experience depression. For instance, when you lose your source of income or realize that your spouse doesn't love you, you can feel gloomy, dejected, weary, miserable, hopeless, defeated, despairing, tormented, exhausted, and even suicidal.

When you are depressed, you tend to focus on losses, your inner emptiness, unfulfilled dreams, and problems. You may experience feelings of worthlessness. The thick blackness pervades your entire being and your suffering seems endless. You may lose interest in food, people, and sex, and have difficulty sleeping. When you are mildly depressed, you can manage your day-to-day activities. Mild forms of depression are considered normal depression. There are, however, two certified depressive disorders: unipolar depression and bipolar, or manic-depression. Some therapists believe that unipolar depression is a severe form of normal depression. Manic- or bipolar depression always includes manic episodes—unjustifiable euphoria, frenzied talk and behavior, grandiosity, and almost no sleep for days at a time. The mania is preceded or followed by a period of depression. It is in your best interest to seek professional help for unipolar or bipolar depression. Psychiatrists prescribe a drug called lithium carbonate to relieve the manic aspect of bipolar depression. It is effective in more that 80 percent of cases.

In *Learned Optimism*, Dr. Martin Seligman states, "A pessimistic explanatory style is at the core of all depressed thinking. A negative concept of the future, the self, and the world stems from seeing the causes of bad events as permanent, pervasive, and personal, and seeing the causes of good events in the opposite way." When you feel depressed, do you blame yourself for having no control of your life and reinforce your helplessness? You might have thoughts like, "I've tried for twenty years to make it in my career and it hasn't worked. It's hopeless." Or "I am a dork. I am short and ugly and I can't change that." You can learn about your depression and optimize your life by asking:

- What am I not dealing with in my life?
- Why am I feeling overwhelmed?
- Am I looking at life through pessimistic eyes?
- Do I believe that my situation is permanent?
- What am I thinking or doing to create these feelings?
- Am I unnecessarily taking all the blame for my life being bad?
- Am I paying attention to my feelings and taking the wisest actions to fulfill myself?
- What are the most empowering thoughts I can employ to take control of my life?
- How can I take control of optimizing my life?
- What are the best actions I can take to create what is most important to me?
- What are the most nurturing actions I can take for myself?

To overcome normal depression, begin by observing your thinking. Optimize your interpretation of the problems you are dealing with so that you no longer view them as permanent or out of your control. Put OptiSelf in charge of listening to your needs and taking the most nurturing actions on your behalf. Focus your attention on what is within your control and what is most important to you. Carry your notebook with you and record your negative thoughts and feelings. When you feel depressed, question and resolve your pessimistic thoughts with Optimal Thinking. Allow OptiSelf to embrace your negative voice, and ask the best questions to obtain the most empowering resolution. Act upon your Optimal responses and you will be your best even in the toughest circumstances. Here's how Richard, the chiropractor, did it.

Negative Voice: I ruined my last business. I'm afraid I'll do it again.

OptiRichard: It's natural for you to feel scared. If you take it one step at a time, you will restore your confidence. Which changes in your thinking would be most helpful in restoring your self-confidence? What's the best step you can take right now to achieve what you want?

Negative Voice: I have wasted so much time.

OptiRichard: I understand you are feeling bad because you have been unproductive for the last few years. You're also feeling bad because you're focusing on the past, which is no longer in your control. Are you willing to optimize what is within your control? What is the best strategy you can implement to maximize your productivity?

Grief

Grief occurs when we experience a major loss. The excruciating pain of losing a loved one can be the most severe suffering we ever endure. Feelings such as anger, hurt, dismay, emptiness, sadness, devastation, and helplessness are evoked. The pain can be all-consuming, overwhelming, and incapacitating. Although transient, grief is agonizing.

In *On Death and Dying*, Elisabeth Kübler-Ross identifies the following natural stages of the grieving process:

1. Denial (This can't be true.)
2. Anger (It's unfair. Why me, why now?)
3. Remorse (If I had not done this, maybe things would be different.)
4. Depression (Helplessness and surrender.)
5. Acceptance (This is the way it is. I will accept and make the most of it.)

When you lose a loved one, many of your hopes, dreams, expectations, and desires are shattered. Similarly, your hopes and dreams of resolution are crushed when an important troublesome relationship is terminated. When you suffer such losses, it is in your best interest to identify and complete the undelivered emotional communications that keep you feeling victimized by hurtful negative memories. Contained within the unspoken messages are multitudinous feelings including joy, sadness, love, fear, anger, relief, and compassion. Simply give yourself permission to mourn and complete your relationship to the person as well as your relationship with the pain you create when you think about the person. Allow yourself to mourn and complete your unmet hopes, dreams, and expectations in your own time. This is how you will restore your vitality and happiness. You can answer these questions:

- What am I thinking or doing that is causing me to feel pain in the present moment?

- What am I thinking or doing to feel overwhelmed by these feelings?
- Which hopes, expectations, and dreams have been shattered?
- What do I need to express to feel I have communicated everything?
- What is the best means of expressing my thoughts and feelings?
- What are other ways I can fulfill my hopes, dreams, and expectations?
- What are the most nurturing actions I can take for myself?
- How can I optimize the present moment/this hour/today?

Ricki, a dentist, came to my office three years after her husband died of congestive heart failure. She was grief-stricken. As she described her wonderful twenty-three-year marriage, I understood why it was so difficult for her to move on with her life; she had lost her soul mate. Ricki was comforting herself with food while she watched television to numb her pain. She had gained fifty pounds and could hardly work. I asked her to imagine that Ed was sitting on the opposite couch and gave her the following sentences to complete: "When I think about you, Ed, I feel . . . because . . . What would work best for me is . . ." Here is a snippet from an early consultation:

Rosalene: When I think about you, Ed, I feel . . .

Ricki: When I think about you, Ed, I feel devastated. I don't know how I can get along without you. You were the light of my life and now that you're gone, it's all darkness.

Rosalene: Ricki, can you stay with the feeling? When I think about you, Ed, I feel . . .

Ricki: (sobbing) When I think about you, Ed, I feel abandoned and hurt.

Rosalene: And . . .

Ricki: Furious and afraid.

Rosalene: Because . . .

Ricki: Because you were everything to me. You were the reason I woke up in the morning. I lived for you. I have nothing to live for without you. I can't stand life without you. I love you. You are the only person I want to be with. I hate God for taking you away. I have lost my will to live.

Rosalene: When I think about you, I feel devastated because . . .

Ricki: I don't know where to start. I am so unhappy. I miss you so much. I miss your humor, the special names you reserved for me when I showed my different faces, and you were always my greatest fan. And when we fought, you always understood my point of view. I have never had that before and I don't believe I could ever find it again.

Rosalene: When I think about you, I feel abandoned and hurt because . . .

Ricki: You left me. I know you were sick and you stayed as long as you could, but you left me. I feel so alone now. I feel I have lost what was most meaningful to me in life.

Rosalene: When I think about you, I feel furious and afraid because . . .

Ricki: I hate being alone and I am terrified of all the sharks out there. I don't have any confidence. I feel so vulnerable and alone.

Rosalene: What would work best for me is . . .

Ricki: What would work best for me is to go to places where I feel comfortable. I haven't been going to church as often as I would like.

Rosalene: What would work best for me is . . .

Ricki: What would work best for me is to find healthy ways to comfort myself. I could spend an evening in the library, go to a movie with a friend on the weekend, and do some volunteer work.

Ricki sobbed and gagged as she delivered her unspoken communications and uttered her good-byes. She then decided to place her best self in charge of her life and allocated one hour each day specifically for the "grieving widow" to express herself. As the grieving widow developed a relationship with her highest self, her feelings of loneliness and abandonment subsided. Eight months later, Ricki proudly informed me that the "grieving widow" had evolved into "the widow."

Envy

Envy results from feeling deprived—not necessarily because you don't have enough, but because someone else has more. Being around people who are happy, healthy, or wealthy when you are in pain, stricken with a debilitating illness, or deprived of an income can easily stir feelings of envy. Feeling resentful that you don't have what someone else has distracts you from your dissatisfaction with yourself and from concentrating on creating what you want. To resolve your feelings of envy, you can ask:

- Why am I distracting myself from optimizing my life?
- Why am I afraid to assume responsibility for optimizing my life?
- What am I thinking or doing to create dissatisfaction with myself?
- Which beliefs are inhibiting my Optimal well-being?
- What am I afraid of?
- What is within my control?
- What is most important to me?
- What are the best actions I can take to create what is most important to me?
- What are the best actions I can take to feel good about myself?
- What is the best thing I can do to minimize my anxiety?
- How can I take the best possible care of myself?

When Henry was growing up, his mother criticized his every move and often compared him to people who were more accomplished. Nothing Henry did was ever good enough. As an adult, Henry was miserable. He felt defective and was afraid to make any meaningful decisions on his own. When Henry was twenty-five years old, his father passed away, so he took over the family business. Henry hated the business but didn't have the courage to try anything else. He constantly measured himself against the successful people he knew and was clearly envious of their accomplishments. Henry was using envy to distract himself from taking responsibility for healing his pain and optimizing his life. Here is a portion of my consultation with Henry.

> *Henry:* I hate myself. I don't have what it takes to make it. Look at all my school friends. They have a good life. My life is a mess.

> *Rosalene:* Henry, are you willing to focus your attention on what is within your control?

> *Henry:* Yes.

Rosalene: What are you thinking or doing that is inhibiting you from feeling good about yourself and achieving what you want?

Henry: Good question. I focus on what others have, instead of how I can create it for myself.

Rosalene: Why are you distracting yourself from making the most of your life?

Henry: Good question again. I'm afraid I don't have the skills or courage to make it in life.

Rosalene: Henry, I understand how scary this must feel for you. Can you acquire the skills you need?

Henry: Yes.

Rosalene: So you need courage. Courage means that you feel the fear and take action regardless, one step at a time. You don't allow fear to paralyze you. Are you willing to do that?

Henry: Yes. I am ashamed of being so afraid of life. It is horrible to feel like a coward.

Rosalene: Will this make you feel good about yourself? Is this in your best interest?

Henry: It will definitely make me feel better about myself. I will give it a try.

Rosalene: What is the best strategy you can implement to create what is most important to you?

Henry: I will write SUPREME goals down in my notebook, figure out my priorities, and take one step at a time.

Loneliness

We all suffer the misery of loneliness at some time in our lives. You feel lonely when you experience yourself as separate and disconnected from others. You may find yourself observing the people around you, but are unable to participate. When the pain of your isolation is overwhelming, you feel heartbroken. Loneliness is an authentic sign of unfulfilled social or intimacy needs. Loneliness advises you about emotional availability—whether you or others are emotionally open or shut down. You can feel lonely when you are by yourself and have no one to connect with, or when you are with others who are emotionally unavailable. You can gain vital information and understand your loneliness by asking yourself:

- What am I thinking or doing to create these feelings of loneliness?
- Do I feel unlovable?
- Do I feel unneeded and different from others?
- Am I afraid of being evaluated and not measuring up?
- Am I blaming my loneliness on what is unchangeable?
- Am I emotionally available?
- Am I trying to connect with someone who is emotionally shut down?
- Am I expecting more from others than they are willing to give?
- Is my loneliness informing me that I need to reach out and connect with people?
- What are the best actions I can take to overcome my fear of rejection?
- What are the most constructive actions I can take?

Many irrational ideas and assumptions lead to feelings of loneliness, including: "No one likes me," "There is no one available," "I have to cater to the other person and there's no time for me," or "My partner will leave me if I show my true self." Question the validity of any self-defeating thoughts and explore what is in your best interest. Minimize your lonely feelings with statements like: *This is temporary. What's the best thing I can do?* Keep your focus on what you can and are willing to optimize. Being alone is a natural state of every living soul. If you enjoy being alone, you will most likely be able to reach out to others. Be true to yourself and understand that not everyone will love you. Loving yourself, sharing your love unconditionally, and communicating your boundaries to others are the best ways to optimize your connection with them.

How Do You Relate to Your Feelings?

Below are several statements to help you gain insight into how you relate to your feelings. In each sentence there is space allotted for you to add one of the following words: *always, usually, often, sometimes, rarely,* or *never.* In your notebook, after each statement, write the best action you can take to make the most of the awareness you have gained.

1. I _____ accept my feelings.

2. I _____ listen to both my mind and my heart.

3. I _____ resolve my feelings of discomfort.

4. I _____ resolve my feelings of hurt.

5. I _____ resolve my feelings of anxiety.

6. I _____ resolve my feelings of anger.

7. I _____ resolve my feelings of guilt.

8. I _____ resolve my feelings of depression.

9. I _____ resolve my feelings of grief.

10. I _____ resolve my feelings of envy.

11. I _____ resolve my feelings of loneliness.

12. I _____ resolve my feelings of disappointment.

13. I _____ feel confident.

14. I _____ trust myself.

15. I _____ feel joyful.

16. I _____ feel loving.

17. I _____ understand my feelings.

18. I am _____ confident that I deal with my feelings in the best possible ways.

19. When I'm angry, I _____ take time to cool down and regain my composure.

20. I _____ forgive myself and others.

21. I _____ count my blessings.

22. I _____ use Optimal Thinking to resolve my feelings.

23. I _____ experience myself at my best enjoying exactly what I want.

24. When I am distressed, I _____ resolve my feelings.

25. I _____ laugh each day.

26. I _____ share my emotions when appropriate with other Optimal Thinkers.

You can now rate your attitude and emotional skills for each statement. If your response to any statement was:

Always, your attitude and emotional skills in this area are Optimal—congratulations!

Usually or often, your attitude and emotional skills in this area are extraordinary, close to Optimal. It will be easy for you to bridge the gap.

Sometimes, your attitude and emotional skills in this area are mediocre. Are you ready to take the most constructive actions to rectify this?

Rarely or never, this is a negative area for you. Are you willing and ready to take the most constructive steps to rectify this right now? You do deserve to have exactly what you want!

How to Optimize Your Feelings

"The man who makes everything that leads to happiness depend upon himself, and not upon other men, has adopted the very best plan for living happily."

—Plato

Many people wrongly believe that their best feelings are derived from external sources. They believe that if they get love, affection, understanding, or respect from another person, they will be happy. These people do not understand that their best feelings are generated from within. Does your happiness depend on something that is out of your control? Do you believe that you need a relationship, material possessions, or an outstanding achievement to be happy? If so, you will inevitably feel unhappy. When you honor your own feelings and use Optimal Thinking to optimize them, your happiness is completely within your control. You discover that an Optimal connection with your feelings is the authentic source of your best feelings.

You can maximize your most positive feelings by exploring which needs are met when you experience them. Ask: *What are my most important needs and what's the best way I can satisfy them?* Optimal Thinking is the ultimate mental tool to create those situations, circumstances, and events where your most beneficial emotions are felt and your needs are met. Here are some Optimal strategies and techniques to assist you in optimizing your feelings.

Stream-of-Consciousness Writing

In stream-of-consciousness writing, you express whatever comes to mind. It doesn't matter what you write, how you express yourself, or how long it takes. You simply write two or three pages each and every day in your notebook. You might release a stream of anger, a stream of hurt, then suddenly, you will be aware of a current of joy. Your inner critic may rule for a while, and then without warning, love will find its way through you. As you express your authentic self on paper without judging the content, you connect with your soul. You will experience intuitive flashes of awareness as your creativity is unleashed, and your life becomes the sacred expression of your highest self.

Forgiveness

When you harbor a grudge against yourself or those who have hurt you, you nurture your anger and hurt and prevent its resolution. You are actually punishing yourself. By exercising forgiveness, you relieve yourself of the burden of carrying the hurt, anger, pain, and loneliness. You relinquish your grievance and consequently your grief—and healing occurs. This does not mean that you condone or are legitimizing the hurtful behavior, or that you have reestablished a comparable level of trust with the person who wounded you. When you forgive, you concede that your pain has passed. You let go of your resentment so you can get on with optimizing your life.

Martin Luther King Jr. believed: "We must develop and maintain the capacity to forgive. He who is devoid of the power to forgive is devoid of the power to love. There is some good in the worst of us and some evil in the best of us." Once you make compassion a higher priority than judgment, it makes sense to forgive. When you forgive, you are no longer resisting life. You are allowing life to express itself through you. You can ask yourself:

- Why do I feel this way?
- What am I thinking or doing that is causing me to hold on to the hurt and anger?
- What changes can I make to release the pain and resentment?
- What is my best strategy for letting go of these feelings?
- What is the best action I can take right now to move on with my life?

Gratitude

If you don't appreciate what you have, you may as well not have it. When you count your blessings, you can generate your most positive feelings. It is truly in your best interest to develop and maintain an Optimal attitude of gratitude. Start with what you appreciate most about the present moment. Celebrate the opportunity to create your best life by choosing to be your best self in every given moment. Think about all the people you love and the wonderful things that have happened to you. Recognize and appreciate all you can in yourself, others, and the world. Resolve to cherish each day of your life as a supreme gift. Embrace your life journey with gratitude, so that how you travel your path is more important than reaching your ultimate destination. When you appreciate and embrace it all—including the blessings from your past—you celebrate your most exquisite gift, life itself!

Self-Confidence

Do you feel confident in your day-to-day life? Do you feel that you have what it takes to create what you want? You can maximize your self-confidence by resolving your fears and focusing on what you do best. When you give yourself credit for what you do best, you will create an environment for optimizing your feelings. You can then decide how to make the most of your talents, assets, and accomplishments. Remember to always reinforce your accomplishments and triumphs by appreciating and celebrating them.

The philosopher and poet Goethe wrote, "As soon as you trust yourself, you know how to live." Trust stems from confidence in your ability to deal with your feelings and the circumstances you encounter. When you use Optimal Thinking to master your feelings, you can rely on yourself to take the best possible care of them. You are open to new experiences and all feelings.

Love, Joy, and Happiness

"No man is a failure who is enjoying life."
—William Feather

Many people spend their lives looking for love instead of recognizing that love is where they are coming from. They don't believe that giving themselves the love they need and sharing it with others are more valuable than getting love. When you give love to yourself and others without calculation or expectation of anything in return, you experience feelings of joy, love, confidence, and trust in your life. Giving is then truly the expression of love. Your highest possible feeling of love is the experience of unity with all there is. By experiencing unity with all the diversity, you feel universal love. Your highest self knows this bliss.

You experience joy when you are truly grateful for life and your well-being. Joy is a signal of Optimal functioning. Your greatest bursts of creativity, for example, will most likely occur during joyful moments when you are most willing to experiment and spread your wings. When you express yourself authentically, you experience the joy of being yourself. You joyfully express your gifts and allow them to guide you into experiences that encourage your most beneficial emotions to thrive.

Abraham Lincoln said, "Most people are about as happy as they make up their minds to be." Make up your mind to take full responsibility for your happiness right now. Surround yourself with people and things that make you laugh. Think about what makes you laugh and about all the times you have laughed. Make a list of everything that makes you laugh and brings you happiness. George Burns said, "I would rather be a failure doing something I love than be a success doing something I hate." Meditate often on the words "love," "joy," "laughter," and "happiness." Participate in joyful activities—and your life will soon be filled with them.

Optimal Affirmations

Make it your business to talk Optimally to yourself at any given moment. Give OptiSelf, your highest self, complete freedom to optimize all your suboptimal voices. By using Optimal affirmations you can create an emotional climate of supreme self-confidence, where your most positive feelings can flourish. Here are some examples:

- I trust myself completely.
- I love myself unconditionally.
- I accept all my feelings.
- I take the best actions to resolve my disturbing feelings.
- I feel my best when I do my best.
- I am completely capable of making myself happy.
- My life is now filled with pleasure.

Optimal Visualization

Optimal visualization enables you to obtain a clear picture of your most important goals and the feelings associated with their accomplishment. You can choose to view, and feel, what it's like to be your best. You can create your most pleasurable feelings by employing words and symbols with the most fulfilling emotional content. Here's how it works.

Danielle was ready to invest in her dream home. She experienced superlative feelings every day by imagining herself living happily in her favorite home on the beach. Daily she visualized herself happily strolling along the shore, feeling the warm sand under her feet. She saw her home in detail. She saw herself confidently furnishing each room. She imagined herself enjoying quiet nights as well as joyfully entertaining her favorite people. She pictured herself engaged in activities where she gave of her best. She listened to the waves pounding against the shore, watched the seagulls, and felt the serenity and joy of having done all that was necessary to attain her heart's greatest desire.

Danielle spoke with her realtor regularly, and invested every Saturday looking at suitable beachside properties. Four months later, she found and bought her dream home.

Alpha (Self-Hypnosis)

When you slow down your brain wave activity to a frequency of eight to thirteen cycles per second, you enter a hypnotic state of relaxed receptivity called the "Alpha state." Once you are in Alpha, you can access your subconscious mind and empower your highest self. You begin by imagining yourself completely calm, relaxed, and peaceful as you visualize the colors red, orange, yellow, green, blue, indigo, and violet. Next, slowly count down from twenty-one to zero, and feel the relaxation spread throughout your entire body. Then place yourself in your ultimate passive scene of nature. You may choose, for example, your favorite seaside, mountain retreat, or beautiful garden. You can then program your subconscious mind with creative visualization and Optimal affirmations. Let OptiSelf take charge. Imagine the feelings associated with being and doing your best!

When you are in the Optimal Alpha state, place the palms of your hands together. Once you have secured this conscious-subconscious connection, you can utilize this palm-to-palm connection to achieve instant relaxation and a connection with your highest self. Then whenever you use the palm-to-palm connection, you can enter the Alpha state and feel completely calm, relaxed, and in your Optimal state.

You can add other posthypnotic suggestions by including words like "peaceful" and "joyful" while you are in the Optimal alpha state. You can repeat them whenever you wish to regain access to your highest self, and reenter the hypnotic state.

Relaxation and Meditation

If you are often anxious, you need to learn to relax. To relax completely, make sure you are entirely comfortable, regulate your breathing, and do visualization exercises to eliminate muscle tension. Creative visualization specialist Marilyn Winfield suggests the following exercise:

Take three deep breaths, holding on the inhale. Now visualize a silky smooth liquid of total relaxation and sense it entering your toes. As it does, feel the toes relaxing. Sense each muscle, each fiber, and each cell relaxing. Allow this soothing, healing relaxation to flow up into your pelvic area, your abdomen, your solar plexus, and into your torso. As the feeling of relaxation reaches the torso, sense it splashing down your arms, filling up the palms of your hands, your wrists, and your fingers into the fingertips. The relaxation permeates your shoulders and neck and fills your head and face. Every muscle in your body is now bathing in silky smooth, soothing relaxation. You are now completely relaxed.

Meditation is also an Optimal form of relaxation. In *Conversations with God*, Neale Donald Walsch said: "You will gain in-sight when you look within. . . . If you do not go within, you go without." In 1977, I began the daily practice of transcendental meditation and subsequently learned advanced techniques known as the *sidhis*. I have experienced feelings of bliss in meditation, which empower me to optimize my everyday life.

You can sit comfortably, close your eyes, and meditate on an Optimal feeling such as joy, peace, serenity, love, Optimal self-esteem, compassion, strength, or laughter. Choose the feeling you most wish to embody, and continually repeat to yourself the word that best describes that feeling. Fully embrace your Optimal word. You can meditate on the meaning it holds for you and how to make the most productive use of the feeling in your life. When other thoughts cross your mind, accept them, and as soon as possible, return to embracing your Optimal word. When you experience another feeling or bodily sensation, simply accept it, then refocus your attention on your Optimal word. It is best to schedule twenty minutes a day, before meals, to enjoy this most relaxing and fulfilling process.

Recall Optimal Emotional Experiences

Can you recall a place, time, or circumstance where you felt your very best? Optimal Thinkers often remind themselves of their most empowering experiences. They can recall numerous experiences when they assessed situations accurately and made Optimal choices in life-changing situations. Each time you recall your most pleasurable experiences, you reinforce your highest emotional state. Be sure to maximize the light, color, sound, and action of your peak emotional experiences!

Jim, a race-car driver, uses this technique. Whenever he wants to feel fully focused, exhilarated, skillful, and totally confident, he mentally places himself on the track and imagines himself speeding around the corners. He also jots down his victories in his Optimal journal. On occasions where he doubts himself or faces a frightening experience, he uses his journal to remind him of his numerous accomplishments. He optimizes his self-confidence!

Verbalize Your Emotions to Other Optimal Thinkers

Talking rationally about, for example, your fear or anger (instead of displaying it) tends to demonstrate self-confidence and self-control. You put your highest self in charge when you say: *This is how I feel about the problem. I believe this is the best way to resolve it. What's your input on how to most effectively deal with it?* When you honor your feelings, apply Optimal Thinking to make the best of them, and assess what is in your best interest before taking action, you demonstrate the most constructive rational behavior.

Do Your Best

W. H. Sheldon said, "Happiness is essentially a state of going somewhere wholeheartedly." Even when life deals you its hardest blows and it rains on your parade, don't deny your feelings! Embrace them as sacred messengers, and let your highest self take care of them. Let OptiSelf make the most of every situation! Attempt, as much as possible, to do your best in what you most want to do. When you do your best in every circumstance, you inevitably feel your best. Your body, mind, and soul are in the right place!

Optimal Questions

1. Am I observing my feelings or am I fully identified with them?
2. What is my greatest emotional weakness? What is the best thing I can do to overcome it?
3. Which emotion(s) is/are inhibiting me from enjoying life to the fullest? What is the best thing I can do to resolve this/these emotion(s)?

4. How can I maximize my enjoyment of life right now?

5. Which emotions empower me to live life to the fullest? What is the best thing I can do to maximize these feelings?

Optimal Action Steps

1. Take some time now to think back to your last emotionally disturbing experience. With pencil and paper, start examining it, using Greg's list (in the section about anger). Make a few extra lists and keep them handy. The next time you face an emotionally disturbing situation, take out a list and use it to examine the situation. Eventually you will form the habit of making the most of each emotionally upsetting situation—by accepting the feelings, analyzing the causes, and responding most intelligently.

2. For the next month, start every day by writing ten expressions of gratitude for your life. Optimize your emotional wealth!

3. Complete the following sentence until you have exhausted everything that comes to mind. "I am maximizing my happiness by _____."

PART THREE

Optimize Others

"My best friend is the one who brings out the best in me."
—Henry Ford

Rate Your Communications and Work

The following questionnaire will enable you to identify your dominant level of thinking at work and in your relationships. Simply circle the number that best describes your thoughts about your current situation. Then add your score.

3 = *Always*   1 = *Reasonably or sometimes*
2 = *Usually or often*   0 = *Rarely or never*

1. My intimate relationships are in my best
   interest.   0   1   2   3

2. I openly share my feelings and needs with
   my family and friends.   0   1   2   3

3. I treat others respectfully.   0   1   2   3

4. I listen carefully when people speak to me.   0   1   2   3

5. I discover what is in the best interest
   of others.   0   1   2   3

6. I am a dedicated leader/manager/colleague/
   employee.   0   1   2   3

7. I communicate my boundaries effectively
   to others.   0   1   2   3

8. I am appreciated for the work I do.   0   1   2   3

9. I express my talents through my work.   0   1   2   3

10. My coworkers respect me.   0   1   2   3

11. I am passionate about my work.   0   1   2   3

12. I express my creativity in my work.   0   1   2   3

13. I look forward to going to work.   0   1   2   3

14. I am an optimizer.   0   1   2   3

15. I respect the dignity and rights of others.   0   1   2   3

16. I respect myself in all my communications
    with others.   0   1   2   3

17. I lose track of time when I am working.   0   1   2   3

18. I praise and reprimand others appropriately.   0   1   2   3

19. I am comfortable when I am alone and with
    others.   0   1   2   3

20. I am emotionally available in my relationships.   0   1   2   3

21. I cooperate with others to create the
    best results.   0 1 2 3

22. I motivate others to do their best.   0 1 2 3

23. I am moving toward my highest vision.   0 1 2 3

24. People can rely on me.   0 1 2 3

25. I am the right person doing the right job. 0 1 2 3

If your score is 70–75, you are a consistent Optimal Thinker. This section of *Optimal Thinking* will support your thinking, choices, and actions. You will also acquire additional strategies to optimize your work skills, and communications with family, friends, and coworkers.

If your score is 46–70, your communication skills and work expertise are extraordinary. You are achieving more than the average person, but you are not optimizing your work or communications with others. This section of *Optimal Thinking* will give you specific tools to assert your best self, minimize unwanted behaviors, resolve conflicts, and more. You will gain the thinking and skills necessary to optimize your communications at home and at work.

If your score is 16–45, your communication skills and work life are mediocre. You are making moderate use of your talents and abilities, but you are functioning well below your peak. In this section of *Optimal Thinking*, you will gain the "mental software" to empower your best self to take charge in your relationships with others. You will learn how to assert your most important needs, minimize unwanted behaviors, resolve conflicts, bring out the best in others, and much more. In short, you will learn how to optimize your personal communications and work situation.

If your score is 0–15, your people and work skills are negative. You are probably feeling disillusioned, and may be wondering if it is still possible to get your personal communications and work life on track. Let me assure you that you do not need to be a rocket scientist to acquire the right skills. This section of *Optimal Thinking* will provide you with the "mental software" to overcome the obstacles that are inhibiting your success. You will learn how to instantly assert your most important needs, make the best use of your talents, resolve unwanted behaviors, deal with conflicts most effectively, bring out the best in others, and more. You will formulate a simple strategy to optimize your people skills and work life. Where there's a will, there's an Optimal way!

CHAPTER 8

Maximize Your Communications

"What's best for you?"
"What's best for you?"
"So what's best for us is . . ."

—Two Optimal Communicators

Suboptimal Communication

All of us have experienced the frustration of ineffective communication. You have, I'm sure, participated in conversations where one party gained at another's expense. You have felt manipulated in some of your communications. You may have manipulated others. You have shared your heart, only to discover that the other person didn't care. Divorces, broken hearts, disappointing careers, and broken dreams can all result from ineffective attempts to relate to others.

During the past two decades, much has been written about a form of effective communication that some experts have called "win-win communication." In win-win communication, people take each other's goals into account and negotiate for mutual gain. Win-win communication results in benefit for everyone involved but is often suboptimal. When the parties merely improve their circumstances—instead of optimizing them—the communication is incomplete. The parties often ponder the unexplored options well after the win-win communication has taken place.

Obstacles to Optimal Communication

All of us bump into barriers in our communications with others. A large barrier to Optimal communication is lack of awareness of our own limits, feelings, beliefs, and expectations. It is difficult to understand others if we don't understand ourselves. When we deny undesirable traits within ourselves, we are easily upset by these negative qualities in others. If we haven't delineated personal boundaries to protect our emotional domain, we feel unsafe in the world. When our inner sanctum is violated, even if the transgression is unintentional, we muster defense mechanisms such as denial, accusations, withdrawal, and threats to establish a sense of control. We endure irritating small talk, rudeness, and tantrums because we don't know how to set appropriate limits and are afraid of rejection.

Some people are inhibited by a limited vocabulary and have difficulty conveying their ideas. Others are handicapped by physiological impediments such as poor eyesight or deficient hearing. Many are overwhelmed with psychological challenges. Emotional burnout or a stress-related disease can distort your perception and interpretation of events. Most people have difficulty dealing with mixed messages of a verbal nature. They are even more baffled by incongruous nonverbal and verbal messages. When we exhibit nonverbal messages such as slumping, preoccupation with something else, or refraining from eye contact, we erect barriers to Optimal communication. Our actions speak louder than our words.

If we are only interested in what we can get out of a relationship, our communications will reflect our self-serving intention. Whenever we use praise to manipulate people, make them feel guilty, or withhold relevant information to get what we want, we obstruct Optimal communication. Attempting to dominate others by using criticism, orders, and threats eradicates trust and respect. Imposing our own solutions on others is a form of control that doesn't respect others' ability to find their own Optimal solutions. When we avoid other people's concerns by ignoring their feelings or diverting the conversation, we inhibit Optimal communication.

Many famous people have overcome enormous barriers in order to deliver their message to others. Franklin D. Roosevelt inspired strength and heroism to an entire nation from his wheelchair. Winston Churchill suffered from a severe speech impediment into early adulthood. Helen Keller inspired courage and hope in others, even though she was blind and deaf. You can do it, too!

Optimal Communication

Some time ago, I was listening to a cassette tape in my car. A well-known author and teacher was expounding her views on how we are all essentially connected. At that very moment, I glanced at the license plate on the car directly in front of me. It read: ROSINME. As my family and friends call me Ros, I got the message. By our very existence in this universe we are connected, and in relationship with all there is! Have you had experiences like this? Keep them with you as you read on.

Your purpose in relationships is simply to be your best self, regardless of the circumstances. You can then make the highest choice in response to any situation. When you relate to others, your suboptimal selves will invariably reveal themselves. You will notice the judge, victim, tyrant, coward, loser, hypocrite, and other characters within you. As you become aware of their existence, you can place your best self in charge to heal them. Answering the questions *What is most loving action I can take right now?* or *What is my wisest course of action?* will lead you in the right direction. The actions of others are not as important as your reactions to them. Suboptimal reactions signal you to optimize. The gap between your reaction and your response is your opportunity to make your highest choice.

Do you accept others as they are? Do you bring out the best in them? An Optimal relationship provides a safe environment for all thoughts and feelings to be shared. Optimal communication involves an acceptance of all the messages exchanged. The dignity, rights, vulnerability, and best interests of all parties must be respected at all times. Here is an example.

Mary and Annette hit if off when they met at college. They have shared a mutually rewarding friendship for nearly eighteen years. They confide their deepest concerns and share their joys on a daily basis. Annette is married and devotes herself to postgraduate studies. Mary is a public figure and is still single. Their relationship blossoms despite their changed circumstances because they continue to trust, respect, and communicate openly with each other. Mary says, "No matter what I share with Annette, she is always on my side. She always accepts me." Annette says: "I trust Mary with my life. She always cares about my best interests."

It is natural to want the best for those we love. Do you consider the best interests of others when you communicate with them? When a mutual purpose is shared and the best ways to achieve it are sought, communicated, and applied, all involved are inspired to be, do, and feel their best—and Optimal communication flourishes. The best means of satisfying the best interests of all concerned must be employed for Optimal communication to succeed. Only when we understand each other can we determine the best ways to give one another what we need and want. By honoring feelings, thoughts, and motives, we establish our most rewarding connections.

Consider my client Brian, who lives life to the fullest and does his best to please his wife, Lynn. He listens carefully to her needs and does whatever he can to meet them. He sets aside time to pursue fun activities with her, surprises her with thoughtful gifts, remembers important occasions, and organizes romantic getaways. Recently, Lynn had mentioned taking a year's leave from work to write a book. Even though their income and lifestyle would be dramatically compromised, Brian remained open and supportive of her best interests. He asked Optimal questions to ascertain Lynn's most important priorities, embraced her ambivalent thoughts and feelings, and listened attentively to make sure they understood each other. Their open communication enabled them to determine the best means of obtaining the best outcome for both of them. Here is a portion of their conversation.

Brian: I know you're concerned about losing your income, so let's figure out what is in your best interest here.

Lynn: Brian, I really need to write this book. If I don't, I'll regret it. On the other hand, I feel guilty. I don't want to leave you with the burden of taking care of both of us financially.

Brian: Lynn, I make enough money to support both of us, and you really don't need to worry. I want to support you in achieving this goal. You have to write this book, so let's figure out the best way of accomplishing it. What can you do to get rid of your guilt?

Lynn: If I eliminate unnecessary expenses, I will feel better. I also need to let my boss know about my plans. He will have to train someone to do my job.

Brian: Okay. Is there anything else that is preventing you from feeling that it is the right thing to do?

Lynn: I need to update my files at work so that everything is in place for the next person. I also need to be sure that this doesn't damage our relationship in any way. Are you certain that this is in the best interest of our relationship?

Brian: Lynn, I am one hundred percent behind you. If I wasn't happy about it, I would tell you. Just go for it! Give it your best shot! It will make me happy to see you happy!

Lynn: You're the best!

Optimal communication enables us to make the most of our relationships. Getting along with people as well as we can is the key to maximizing our success at home, with friends, and in other relationships.

Ask Four Optimal Questions

When you relate to others, do you employ Optimal communication skills? Imagine you are conversing with someone who is important to you. Take a few moments to respond to the four questions below, and note your answers. It might be in your best interest to jot down these four questions and any relevant information on a three-by-five card and carry it with you.

Am I Giving My Undivided Attention?

By giving your complete and undivided attention, you show respect for the other person.

Am I Showing Total Interest in the Other Person?

The psychologist William James observed, "The minute anything becomes personal with anyone, it becomes the most interesting thing in the world." Be sure to show genuine interest in other people's favorite subject: themselves.

Am I Seeking Mutual Understanding?

Mutual understanding requires complete openness of expression. You've heard it said, "Don't judge others until you have walked a mile in their moccasins." No matter how painful the message, accept other people's right to communicate their reality. Be aware of the main purpose of your communication and look for common ground. Focus on what unites you and welcome ambiguity as an Optimization signal. Discover what is most important to others and what motivates them to do their best. Think and talk in terms of their best interests.

Am I Inspiring Optimal Action/Resolution?

Encourage other people to make full use of their strengths and determine the Optimal action steps necessary to obtain the best outcome. Be sure to ask the best questions and listen for the best answers.

Listen for Optimal Communication

Shakespeare said, "Give every man thine ear but few thy voice." When you listen with not only the ear and the mind, but also with the eye and the heart, you gain the understanding necessary to motivate the most appropriate actions. You demonstrate to other people that regardless of their message, they are worthy of your full attention. Did you know that the average person speaks at a speed of approximately 125 words per minute? And you probably think at a rate of 400 to 600 words a minute. You have listener's "leisure" time at your disposal during every conversation. You can learn how to make the best use of it. Here are some suggestions.

Give Your Undivided Attention

The most respectful attitude you can offer someone is your unconditional interest. Create an environment free of distractions or reduce them to a minimum. You may need to close the door, allow voice mail to pick up your calls, or even take your phone off the hook. It is best to lean forward, face the other person, and maintain eye contact. Smile and nod when appropriate, withhold judgment, be open and empathic. Show the other person you care by making sure you understand him or her. Respect the other person's views and feelings, particularly when they differ from yours.

Tune in Completely to the Other Person's Needs and Wants

You can help the other person open up by saying, "You seem worried about something. What's bothering you?" Open-ended questions encourage the other person to talk. Avoid questions that encourage only yes or no answers. Questions like: Who?, What?, When?, Where?, How?, and Why? stimulate open communication.

When you pause before responding, you can give full consideration to the other person's input. The pause indicates to the speaker that you are truly listening, and encourages the expression of his or her needs and wants. This will enable you to discover how the person perceives his or her reality before you respond. You will foster more expression with the most sensitive use of comments like: "What's on your mind?," "Oh?," "Tell me about that," "Right," "Really?," "Yes," "And," "Go on," "So?," "Sure."

Most important, never interrupt! A parent who interrupts a child won't find out what the child really needs. The wife who listens to her husband can identify his needs and discover the most constructive ways to meet them. The most gracious gift you can offer anyone is the space to be.

Respond With Optimal Reflection

When you employ reflective listening, you restate the feeling or the meaning of the communication (or both) in a way that demonstrates understanding and nonjudgment. By rephrasing the message and restating it to the other person, you verify that the message has been received without distortion. You can encourage other people to discover their own best solutions using Optimal questions like: *What's the best thing you can do about that?*, *What's your best option?* Here are some examples.

Suzanne was married to Simon, a man who had great difficulty acknowledging and verbalizing his feelings. Suzanne consulted with me during the third month of their marriage, because she was afraid they might lose their emotional connection. She learned how to serve as an Optimal mirror for Simon. During the first few years of the marriage, she helped him to identify his negative feelings by verbalizing them for him without judgment. In time, Simon began to acknowledge his feelings. He even learned to respect them. Suzanne nurtured emotional intimacy with him by responding with Optimal reflection. Here's an example of how she did it.

> *Simon* (embarrassed and disappointed): I told everyone that I'd win the trophy this year, and I didn't.
>
> *Suzanne:* Are you disappointed and embarrassed?
>
> *Simon:* I sure am.
>
> *Suzanne:* I understand. What's the best thing you can do about it?

Anne and John had dated for two months. He was attracted to her, but when she shared her problems with him, he pushed her away. When John consulted with me, he was bewildered by his own behavior and concerned that Anne felt hurt and rejected. After a two-week break, they agreed to meet for lunch at a restaurant near Anne's office. The chemistry between them was strong. Anne asserted herself and John responded with Optimal reflection. Here's a key portion of their conversation.

> *Anne:* John, I have a lot of feelings about you. Would it be all right if we talked about them?
>
> *John:* You want to discuss your feelings about me. Go ahead.

Anne: John, I feel very hurt when I try to talk to you about something that's bothering me and you ignore my feelings. I feel you're not accepting me for who I really am.

John: Oh. You feel hurt and rejected because I haven't been sensitive to your feelings.

Anne: Yes, and talking about it is hard because I don't want to feel hurt again.

John: So it's difficult for you to talk about it. You're afraid I won't be sensitive to your feelings because I haven't been in the past.

Anne: Yes. I need emotional support in a relationship through good and bad times.

John: I understand. You want your man to be there for you emotionally.

Anne: Yes, I do.

John: I want to be there for you whenever you need me. What's the best thing I can do to be more sensitive to your feelings?

This mirroring process is most beneficial when you are angry and need to express your feelings to the person who provoked them. You simply tell that person that you are angry and need to have your feelings understood. You then ask them to paraphrase your feelings as you share them. Share one or two statements at a time and when your partner responds correctly, confirm that your message has been understood. This process minimizes defensive responses from the other person.

Remember Craig, who squandered two marriages because he couldn't control his temper? During one of our consultations, I mistakenly thought he had finished what he was saying and asked him a question. Craig asked me if I would mirror his feelings. Here is a portion of our conversation:

Craig: I can't handle being interrupted. It reminds me of my last marriage. When my wife interrupted me, it drove me nuts!

Rosalene: So when you feel unheard, you get really angry. Is that right?

Craig: Yes. When I am interrupted, I just want to leave.

Rosalene: So when you feel unheard, it is intolerable for you. Do I understand you correctly?

Craig: Yes. It reminds me of my childhood. My father never listened to me.

Rosalene: So it reminds you of the pain you experienced with your father.

Craig: Yes. My father only paid attention to me when he wanted me to do something for him, or when he could criticize me. If I wanted to speak to him, he would cut me off.

Rosalene: You felt hurt because your father made you feel that you were unworthy of his attention. Is that how it was for you?

Craig: Yes. It really hurt. And then when my last wife did the same thing, it nearly killed me. In retrospect, I know my last wife loved me, but I just couldn't handle the pain when she did anything that reminded me of my father. When she interrupted me, I felt she didn't love me.

Rosalene: It really hurts when you feel unheard because you feel unloved or unlovable. Is that it?

Craig: Exactly. I felt like dirt when I was around my father. I sure didn't feel loved or lovable.

Rosalene: You feel hurt because you took your father's behavior personally. Is that what you're saying?

Craig: Yes. I was really a good kid but he refused to see it. I'm still basically a good guy.

Rosalene: So you know that you are valuable. It sounds like your father was too wounded to recognize your intrinsic value. Is that it?

Craig: Yes.

Rosalene: You seem to be in a different place emotionally. How do you feel right now?

Craig: I feel vulnerable.

Rosalene: What's the best thing you can do for yourself right now?

Do you listen reflectively without judgment to gain complete understanding? It is often best to reflect on the meaning of the message being delivered. It may be necessary to recap significant parts of a lengthy conversation to ensure that you have understood the other person correctly. To promote accurate feedback, you can say: "Is that what you mean?" or "Did I understand you correctly?" You can then ask Optimal questions to help them discover their own best solutions.

Nonverbal Communication

Approximately 85 percent of our communication is nonverbal. According to the communication experts, nonverbal messages are the most reliable means of communicating emotions. Nonverbal messages not only reveal feelings, but also show how the person is relating to the feelings. When verbal and nonverbal messages contradict each other, it is best to rely on the nonverbal message.

Remember Jack, who wanted to provide his family with the best of everything? His wife, Lindy, was organizing a vacation for the family and discussed it with him. With a troubled look on his face, Jack told Lindy he was pleased with her plans. Lindy noticed the discrepancy between Jack's verbal and nonverbal response. Let's tune in on the rest of their conversation.

Lindy: Jack, you mentioned you're pleased with my plans, but you don't look very happy. How do you really feel about it?

Jack: Lindy, you've done a first-rate job of organizing everything, but I'm worried that this might be over our budget.

Lindy: Yes, I know we need to watch our expenses. What is the best way to organize this so that we can afford it?

Here's another instance where nonverbal messages provided the information necessary to produce the best outcome. Bill wanted to buy a classic car but didn't know how to go about getting the best deal. Frank, a car mechanic and friend, was happy to help. They decided that Bill would get the best buy through a private owner. The first car they saw had everything. It looked terrific, the color was perfect, the price was right, and it drove like a dream. Frank asked the owner if the car had been properly serviced. The owner defensively folded his arms across his chest, and said yes. Frank then asked if the car had been in an accident. The owner, displaying the same defensive posture, declared that it had not been in an accident. He did not look Frank in the eye. Frank had attended an *Optimal Thinking for Communicators* seminar, and knew how to read nonverbal messages. He suspected from the owner's responses that the car had been in an accident. Noticing the incongruent nonverbal messages, Frank asked if he could see the service records. The owner said he had misplaced them. Frank and Bill left without the car.

The next car they saw looked great and was in the right price range. The owner talked enthusiastically about how well he had maintained it, and proudly showed Bill and Frank the service manual. The service record couldn't have been better. As the owner discussed the car, he displayed completely open body language. He looked Bill and Frank straight in the eye throughout the conversation. Frank and Bill drove the car around the block, Frank checked it over mechanically, and after a short discussion, Bill told the owner he had a deal.

Body Language

Body language experts Julius Fast and Alan Pease have discovered that certain gestures signal distinct messages. These messages vary from culture to culture. See if you recognize the messages that these gestures can often signal in American culture.

Facial Expressions, Postures, and Gestures

Lifting one eyebrow	disbelief
Rubbing nose	doubt, rejection, negation
Rubbing eye	don't want to see
Winking	intimacy
Hand across mouth when talking	lying
Head to side	interested
Head erect	not so interested
Head in palm of hand	boredom
Stroking chin	evaluating
Open hands	friendliness, honesty, sincerity
Arms folded across chest with closed fists	defensive
Leaning closer to someone	more interested
Leaning away from someone	less interested
Legs crossed, swinging foot back and forward	impatience
Tapping fingers	impatience
Sitting with one leg over chair	lack of cooperation
Hands on hips	aggressive

Cleaning glasses	delaying procedure
Rounded shoulders, looking down	pessimistic, lacking confidence
Standing straight, looking ahead	confident
Leaning back with both hands supporting head	superiority
Hand rubbing	excitement

The Mirroring of Nonverbal Messages

Have you ever observed that people who like each other often mirror each other's gestures? The unconscious message of "this person likes me" is relayed through duplication of their nonverbal behavior. When you want to maximize rapport with someone, start by subtly imitating the person's nonverbal messages. You may be able to lead nonverbally. If the other person follows, you have been given permission to lead. If not, simply return to mirroring the other person's message.

Remember Gary, who tongue-lashed his girlfriend Beverly when she did something that annoyed him? They actually resumed their relationship after a six-month break. However, during many of their interactions Beverly folded her arms defensively across her chest. Gary felt uncomfortable when he sensed the mistrust between them. He desperately wanted to earn Beverly's trust and optimize his rapport with her. When I explained to him the value of mirroring Beverly's internal experience—including her breathing, postures, gestures, and tone of voice—he decided to give it his best shot. When Beverly crossed her arms and moved into different postures, he gently duplicated her gestures. He began to feel her discomfort and ambivalence. For the first time, he understood what it was like to be in her shoes. During this period, Beverly sensed his empathy, and relaxed her guard. After five months, Gary earned Beverly's trust and she opened her heart to him.

Eye Movements

"Once you have flown, you will walk the earth with your eyes turned skyward; for there you have been, there you long to return."

—Leonardo da Vinci

Much has been said about interpreting eye movements. Neurolinguistic programming experts study how verbal and nonverbal communications affect our nervous system and behavior. These experts tell us that when our eyes move upward, we are visualizing—creating pictures in our mind. When we look straight ahead, to the left or right, or downward to the left, we are in the audio or listening state—creating sounds or listening to them. When we look downward to the right, we are in the kinesthetic state, which means that our focus is on bodily sensations, feelings, and emotions.

When we are visualizing the future, we generally look to our dominant side, that is, the side of our dominant hand. When we are accessing our memory, we look to our nondominant side. For most right-handed people, looking to the left indicates an emphasis on past recall; looking to the right indicates an emphasis on the future. Right-handed people who have difficulty picturing things from the past may look up to the left to jog their memory. When rehearsing a speech, they will look across to their right ear to hear how it will sound. For those who are left-handed, looking to the right indicates an emphasis on the past, looking to the left an emphasis on the future.

By watching a person's eye movements, you can discover which mode (visual, audio, or kinesthetic) they predominantly use to relate to the world around them—and adjust your communication to suit.

Optimal Verbal Communication

"Man's supreme achievement in the world is communication from personality to personality."

—Karl Jaspers

When you express your thoughts as words, you transmit your creative energy into the universe. By compassionately employing Optimal words such as best, favorite, greatest, highest, top, and paramount, along with those that express your primary mode of thinking (visual, auditory, or kinesthetic), you are communicating at your peak and encouraging others to be their best. You experience the enjoyment of being your best together.

You can use different words for different people depending on the nature of their dominant thought processes. When speaking with those who function primarily in the visual mode, such as decorators, fashion designers, and artists, it is best to use visual language. For example: "Let me show you the best way to do this," "I see exactly what you mean," "Can you picture the best outcome?" Paint your most vivid and specific pictures with Optimal words.

When talking to those who function primarily in the audio

mode, such as sound engineers, musicians, or singers, it is best to use audio terminology. Some examples are: "Does that sound right to you?," "It rings true to me," and "Tell me about your greatest achievement."

You will communicate most effectively with those who perceive their reality primarily through their feelings using kinesthetic or feeling words such as: "How do you feel about this?," "I have a gut feeling this is going to be the most rewarding job I've ever had," or "Are you completely comfortable with that?"

Here's what happened when my client Jack was excited about his new boat. He asked his friends Ralph, Nancy, and Carla if they were interested in sailing. When Ralph looked up in response to his question, Jack responded with, "Let me show you my new boat." Nancy looked sideways so Jack said, "Let me tell you about my new boat." When Carla looked down to the right, Jack said, "You'll love my new boat!" He communicated with them on their particular wavelengths!

Optimal Verbal Assertion

You have, I'm sure, met passive people who respect the rights of others but often violate their own. You have also encountered aggressive people who take care of their own needs but violate the rights of others. With Optimal verbal assertion, you take care of your own needs while respecting others' rights. You share how you feel, what you think, and what you want and don't want, in a nonthreatening way.

The passage below describes a person who approaches life with Optimal assertion. Create a two-column list in your notebook to differentiate the aspects you identify with from those you would like to adopt. Or, you can underline the parts that represent where you stand now and circle those you would like to embrace. This will make you acutely aware of where you are in relation to where you want to be. You can then use this information to optimize your communication with others.

> I take complete responsibility for my thoughts, feelings, and life. I accept and respect myself. I respect my right to live my life as I choose and to do the best I can. I do what I can to fulfill my personal needs, and experience appropriate amounts of fear, anger, trust, joy, and love. My values are worthy of my own appreciation.

I communicate openly and honestly. I communicate my feelings and thoughts when it is in my best interest. I know the best way to assert my needs and I am comfortable with the use of "I" statements, such as "I feel," "I interpret," and "I want." I seek the cooperation of others with statements like "Let's do this" or "When can I have your undivided attention?" I ask the best questions to obtain the best answers. I respect the dignity and rights of others, and support their best interests as much as possible. I am empathic and use such statements as: "How do you feel about this?," "What do you see in this?," "Does this sound right to you?" I confront others honestly and directly, stating all that occurs as it occurs. I don't allow others to violate my rights or take advantage of me.

Minimize Unwanted Behaviors

"It is funny about life: if you refuse to accept anything but the very best you will very often get it."
—W. Somerset Maugham

How do you react when you feel threatened? Setting boundaries to provide the safety you need and responding appropriately to transgressions are essential to your well-being. Communicating your response with Optimal assertion will create understanding when you feel threatened or your rights are violated. People are often unaware that they are violating your rights until you let them know. When you verbalize the problem specifically to them, as it occurs, and immediately negotiate the best solution, you are free to get on with your SUPREME goals without suppressing feelings of anger and hurt.

The goal of Optimal verbal assertion in confronting unwanted behavior is to provide the best verbal stimulus to stop the intrusive behavior and, if possible, negotiate the best solution. This is done using a three-part statement consisting of a nonjudgmental description of the undesirable behavior, the feelings you have experienced, and the effects of the behavior. The three-part statement is immediately followed by a statement expressing your Optimal solution and then an Optimal question to evoke the other person's Optimal solution. You may want to begin the conversation by sharing your appreciation of the other person's most valuable character traits. It might also be helpful to share your concerns about the consequences of your communication. Here is a summary of the steps involved:

Step 1.   Verbalize and show appreciation of the other person's most valuable character traits (when appropriate).

Step 2.   Express your fears about the consequences of your communication (when appropriate).

Step 3.   Offer a nonjudgmental description of the behavior.

Step 4.   Describe the feelings you experienced.

Step 5.   Describe your interpretation of the effects of the behavior.

Step 6.   State what will work best for you.

Step 7.   Ask the other person, "What do you think is the best solution?"

Now let's look at how this technique was used in a number of everyday situations.

Robert was annoyed because he was continually cleaning up after his wife, Betty. He asserted: "When I see your papers and clothes on the living room floor (a nonjudgmental description of unwanted behavior), I feel annoyed (feelings), because it makes more work for me to keep the room tidy (effects of behavior). What would work best for me is for you to clean up after yourself before you leave the room (Optimal solution). What do you think is the best way to resolve this problem?" (Optimal question to elicit the other person's best solution).

Ellen had been married to Ivan, an alcoholic, for fifteen years. She was terrified of verbal confrontation and avoided it at all costs. Her emotional needs were not being met in the relationship, but she couldn't bring herself to tell him that his drinking bothered her. He was very sensitive and she was afraid of hurting his feelings. After attending an *Optimal Thinking for Communicators* seminar, she decided to tell him the truth and give the relationship her best shot. She shared her appreciation of his three most positive character traits before confronting the issue. She said, "Ivan, you're a decent, caring, and generous man and I love you. This is very hard for me to say because I'm afraid of hurting your feelings. But, when I come home in the evening and find you drunk, I feel lonely and miserable because I don't have a partner to share my life with. What would work best for me is if you accept that alcohol is destroying our relationship and get some help to overcome your problem with it. What do you think is the best solution for both of us?"

Regina felt disappointed and angry when her friend called to cancel their meeting at the last minute. Regina responded with Optimal assertion when she said: "When you cancel our meetings at the last minute, I feel frustrated because it affects my plans for the rest of the day. I think we should make sure we give each other plenty of notice from now on. What do you feel is the best way of dealing with this?"

Allan, a stockbroker, used sarcasm to belittle people. After consulting with me, his sister-in-law Nanette asked Allan if she could speak with him privately. She employed Optimal verbal assertion when she said: "Allan, when you belittle people in my presence, I feel uncomfortable, because I don't feel respected. I would be most appreciative if you could discuss your grievances privately with those involved. What do you think is the best solution?" Allan was quiet for a moment and then responded: "You're right, Nanette. I'll do that in the future."

Do you currently feel annoyed by someone's behavior? The next time the person displays that behavior, tell them how you feel without judging them. Offer your best solution and request the other person's input in finding the best solution.

When time is short, you can respond quickly to put-downs with statements like: "Why is that so important to you?," "What do you mean by that?," or "Was that a put-down?" Always follow up with an Optimal question such as: *What's the best way to resolve this?*, *What is your most constructive feedback?*, or *In your opinion, what's the best solution for all concerned?*

Conflict Is a Part of Life

"If two men agree on everything, you may be sure that one of them is doing the thinking."

—Lyndon Baines Johnson

Do you avoid conflict because you fear the unpleasantness involved in facing it? Sometimes the presence of conflict is destructive and impedes progress; at other times, it doesn't. When there is complete absence of conflict, often the need for change is denied, hidden resentments accumulate, problems aren't dealt with, and creativity is stifled.

All relationships have areas of conflict. Unfortunately, many people marry without having acquired conflict-resolution skills. They are wonderful playmates but do not have the skills to be life mates. When conflict occurs, they deny the truth, withdraw, comply, blame, shame, and rage. Their relationship disintegrates as the unresolved conflicts build up.

A parent who handles conflict poorly will not bond deeply with his or her children. Consider a conflict between a father and son where the son's needs are not being met or even considered. The father reminds the son who is boss by imposing his solutions on the son. The fearful, resentful son submits to his father's domination. This is a win-lose resolution. On the occasions when the son proposes a solution to the father, the father's needs aren't met. The father fears that he has allowed his son to get "one up" on him. He believes that he has lost his son's respect. Again win-lose conflict resolution occurs.

Some ways of imposing a win-lose form of conflict resolution are:

Ordering, Directing: "Do it this way."

Judging: "You're wrong."

Distracting: "You think you've got worries, let me tell you about mine."

Reassuring by Negation: "Don't worry, it will work out fine in the end."

Warning: "If you do that again, I'll fire you."

Praising to Manipulate: "You're so good at organizing details, will you check these figures for me?"

These approaches inhibit communication, and as a result, impede conflict resolution.

Optimal Conflict Resolution

When you acknowledge and resolve conflict correctly, you minimize differences and optimize mutual understanding. You make the most constructive decisions and reduce drama and crises in your life. To resolve any conflict, willingness by those involved is essential. The objective of the two-way Optimal conflict resolution process is to find the best solution for all concerned. When you resolve conflicts with Optimal communication, the best interests of all are considered and the best solution negotiated. In the real world, however, sometimes negotiations do not result in agreement. Prior to negotiation, it is in your best interest to determine your Optimal contingency plan in case you are unable to reach agreement. This will maximize your leverage.

When discussions begin, only those directly involved in the conflict should partake in its resolution. In these conflict resolution discussions, it is supremely important that respect for others' self-esteem is always displayed. Concentrate fully on the issue, listen with Optimal reflection, and organize the best follow-up date.

The following seven-step formula can be used whenever you seek the best solution to your problems and conflicts.

Step 1. Clearly define the conflict.
This should take no more than 20 percent of your time.

Step 2. Define the main purpose of the solution.
Why do I need the solution? Why does the other party need the solution?

Step 3. Decide on all the information needed.
Identify the cause of the conflict, the major needs, interests, concerns, and common ground of all involved. You may need to gather additional information.

Step 4. Collaborate to generate possible options.
Brainstorm. Do not judge solutions at this stage.

Step 5. Evaluate the options in light of the information collected.
Examine the fairness and practicality of each option.
Consider the advantages and disadvantages and evaluate the consequences for all concerned.

Step 6. Negotiate. Decide upon, verify, and implement the best solution.
What can they give me? What can we/I give them? What is easiest for me to give? What is most valuable for them? Is it in my best interest to reveal my Optimal contingency plan? Ensure clear agreement. For the tasks involved, ask What?, Who?, Where?, Why?, How?, When's the best time? Establish the best possible checking procedure.

Step 7. Choose the best follow-up date.
Evaluate the effectiveness of the solution in light of additional experience and relevant information.

How Well Do You Communicate?

Below are several statements to help you gain understanding about your current communication skills.

Each sentence allots space to add one of the following words: *always, usually, often, sometimes, rarely,* or *never.* Choose the word that best describes your communication skills. Then, after each statement, write the most constructive action you can take to maximize your communication with others.

1. I _____ give my complete attention to others when they talk to me.

2. I _____ maintain eye contact throughout a conversation.

3. I _____ show empathy.

4. I _____ encourage others to talk.

5. I _____ ask Optimal questions to help others discover their own Optimal solutions.

6. I _____ do all I can to gain complete understanding of the other person's most important needs, wants, and expectations.

7. I _____ ask for clarification of whatever I don't fully understand.

8. I _____ paraphrase the other person's message to make sure that I have understood it correctly.

9. I _____ experience pleasant exchanges in my personal life (with spouse, children, friends).

10. I _____ experience pleasant encounters with my family and friends.

11. I _____ experience at least one satisfying communication every day.

12. When I communicate with people, I _____ accept them. I do not judge them.

13. When communicating with others, I _____ read their nonverbal language.

14. I am _____ able to deal with conflicts and differences appropriately.

15. I _____ bring out the best in others.

Now rate your attitude and communication skills for each statement. If your response to any statement was:

Always, your attitude and communication skills in this area are Optimal. Congratulations!

Usually or *often*, your attitude and communication skills in this area are extraordinary, close to Optimal. It will be easy for you to bridge the gap.

Sometimes, your attitude and communication skills in this area are mediocre. Are you ready to take action to rectify this?

Rarely or *never,* this is a negative area for you. Are you willing and ready to take steps to rectify this right now? You do deserve to have exactly what you want!

Now that you know where you stand, set a SUPREME goal, formulate your Optimal plan, and take action. You can do it NOW!

Optimal Questions

1. What is my vision of the Optimal communication?
2. How can I maximize my communication skills?
3. How can I minimize my weaknesses?
4. How can I be my best and bring out the best in others?
5. How can I minimize/resolve conflict with others?

Optimal Action Steps

1. Arrange to meet with the person who is most important to you for an hour. Mirror his or her nonverbal behavior during this time to optimize your rapport. Write down your findings in your notebook.
2. Think about the specific behavior of a person who impacts you negatively. Set aside some time to use the seven-step procedure for minimizing unwanted behaviors with this person.
3. Think about a conflict you currently have with a person who is important to you. Set aside a specific time to use the seven-step procedure to resolve the conflict.

CHAPTER 9

Optimal Thinking
at Work

*"I do the very best I know how, the very best I can and I mean
to keep on doing so until the end."*

—Abraham Lincoln

Do you long for work that fulfills your body, mind, and soul? Does your career merely satisfy your need for financial security? Because we spend almost one-third of our lives on the job, it is in our best interest to optimize our work situation. Some people have followed their innermost yearnings to their chosen careers. They discover, explore, and express their innate talents, and offer service to others in harmony with their highest calling. Initially, they may have accepted unpaid opportunities to develop their talents and optimize their craft. By valuing their capabilities and contributing them to others, they experience ultimate satisfaction in their daily work and meaningful remuneration for expressing their souls.

When you discover and embrace your career purpose, it feels right. You find yourself completely absorbed with the task at hand and may even lose track of time when you are at work. You feel that you are born to express your unique talents and that the universe supports your best endeavors. Your energy flows naturally when you do what fulfills you and benefits others. Here is an example:

In 1982, I became friendly with my neighbor, Elizabeth, a woman who was well regarded in the political arena. Elizabeth did not enjoy the world of politics, and often complained that her creativity was stifled. I can still recall the first time I entered her home.

I couldn't help but marvel at her flair for interior design. Her home was cozy, yet supremely elegant. Apparently, I was not the only one who admired her talent. In 1983, a friend asked her if she would decorate his home for a modest fee. She agreed and did a first-rate job. After that, many others paid for her services. Elizabeth has since made millions of dollars expressing her talent and doing what she loves. Last week, I asked her how she did it. She responded: "It comes naturally. I only wish I had done it twenty years earlier."

A New Optimal Paradigm

Most organizations consist of management and employees. Managers usually demonstrate good people skills and are expected to manage the job functions of their employees. Extraordinary managers base their decisions and directives on extraordinary positive thinking, whereas moderately competent managers primarily employ mediocre positive thinking. Good employees simply employ their managers' directives effectively. The dominant thinking and work environment are usually suboptimal.

Are you willing to contribute your best efforts in a superior work environment? Imagine your workplace is OptiBiz. Every individual at OptiBiz is educated in the simple art of Optimal Thinking, and his or her career purpose is in alignment with the company's mission. The leader of OptiBiz is the chief executive optimizer, and the personnel are known as optimizers. At OptiBiz, those who optimize frequently and skillfully are the senior optimizers. For example, the sales force consists of senior sales optimizers and sales optimizers—instead of sales managers and salespeople.

The organizational culture respects negative thinking and all other forms of suboptimal thinking as authentic expressions of reality and a legitimate prelude to optimization. At OptiBiz, the optimizers embrace their own suboptimal thoughts, then ask the best questions to optimize their own behavior. They invite the best actions from themselves and others with questions like: *Is this the best I/you can do? What is our best option here? What is the best action I/you can take under the circumstances?* They do not settle for second best. When an optimizer is experiencing difficulties, other optimizers assist in resolving the situation whenever possible. Optimizers progress toward seniority when their peers, superiors, and clients acknowledge their superlative attitude and skills. Can you envision the vitality of OptiBiz?

AnyBiz versus OptiBiz

You have probably been part of a typical organization, AnyBiz, which has a mixture of thinkers, most of whom are suboptimal and on different wavelengths. Let's compare life at AnyBiz and OptiBiz. Where would you rather work?

Negativity

At AnyBiz, the corporate motto is "Think positive!" Positive thinking is revered. Negative thinking is considered inferior—and may even be scorned. A positive thinker may feel miserable about the progress of an important project, but puts on a happy face at the office. Burdened with unresolved thoughts and feelings, he or she compromises morale and productivity. Such a positive thinker typically discounts input from those who are labeled negative thinkers. Negative comments are suppressed with: "That's negative!" or "You need to change your attitude. We only listen to positive comments around here." At AnyBiz, flaws in products, systems, and projects can escape necessary scrutiny when positive thinkers are unwilling to look at what's wrong. Here is an unfortunate scenario:

Consider Harvey, who chose to suppress information about an irregularity in the bookkeeping system. As a result, his bookkeeper Gloria misappropriated fifty thousand dollars from his company. An employee had alerted Harvey that Gloria's signature was on the back of a check that had been made out to a vendor, which implied she had cashed it. When the employee asked Gloria about it, she offered a lame excuse. Harvey chose to ignore the incident because he wanted to avoid an ugly confrontation and a possible lawsuit. He didn't initiate any precautionary measures in his bookkeeping system. He didn't even bother to examine his checks when they returned from the bank. A year later, however, his accountant discovered several anomalous items, and a full audit was ordered.

The audit revealed that Gloria had been selectively skimming company funds for almost three years. She had substituted her name as the payee on some of Harvey's checks to vendors, increased the size of the payments, paid the various vendors in cash, and pocketed the difference. She had marked these checks "void" in the company ledger to avoid scrutiny. Gloria also made sure that none of Harvey's accounts were overdrawn and all his vendors were paid, as she systematically misappropriated relatively small amounts from four different accounts.

Emotional bonding, loyalty, and teamwork are impaired at Any-

Biz, because individual vulnerability is not valuable at AnyBiz. Some employees who appear dedicated are actually using work to avoid their authentic feelings and intimacy. Sadly, the work environment can be impersonal, and is often a rat race. Here is a scenario you might have encountered.

Frustrated Fred: My computer is down. I'm not going to make this deadline!

Brutal Bob: Are you mouthing off again, Fred? You are so negative.

Selfish Sandra: Fred, can you keep your problems to yourself? I have enough of my own.

Optimistic Oliver: Just stick with it. You'll figure it out!

At OptiBiz, individual vulnerability is sacred in the workplace. The optimizers *embrace* negative thinking, emotions, and situations and work together to resolve issues that are raised. At OptiBiz, the personnel have been trained in Optimal Thinking and do their best to use it consistently. Optimal Thinking empowers all members of the organization to focus on the most desirable outcomes and to contribute their best. Let's observe the difference at OptiBiz:

Jim: My computer is down. I'm not going to make this deadline! I guess I'd better cool off and figure out my best option for resolving this.

Bob: Hey, Jim, can I help you solve your problem?

Jim: Thanks.

Bob: Any idea what's causing it?

Jim: Ever since I installed the latest version of my graphics program, the computer freezes.

Bob: It sounds as if the graphics program is causing the problem. What choices do you have here?

Jim: I can delete the graphics program from the hard drive and reinstall it, add some additional memory, or delete programs I don't need.

Bob: So what's your best option?

Jim: I'll delete the graphics program from the hard drive and reinstall it. If that doesn't work, I'll get rid of the programs I don't need. Thanks for helping me get back on track!

Many leading companies view negative information as a perfect opportunity to discover the Optimal solution. Do you remember the days when we walked around with handkerchiefs in our pockets to handle the common sneeze? It was certainly no fun pulling out a used handkerchief—and no greater joy laundering them. By acknowledging the inherent weaknesses of handkerchiefs, Kleenex Corporation recognized a bountiful market niche and manufactured an alternative that made the company billions of dollars. Your company can make the most of negative information, too!

Wishful Thinking versus Optimal Realism

Does wishful thinking impact you in the workplace? Brian, a property management and real estate investment business owner, knew that the industrial market was softening. An industrial tenant who was leasing space at market rate was complaining that he had too much space. Brian knew that if they lost the tenant, the space would remain vacant for some time. He estimated a cost of seventy thousand dollars to the company if this occurred. He wanted to make an interim deal below market rate with the tenant to keep him on board. Unfortunately, Brian's business partners were unduly optimistic. They believed that they should insist on market rate when the lease came up for renewal. Their wishful thinking has already cost the partnership forty thousand dollars. The space has now been vacant for six months.

Unfortunately, many employees at AnyBiz rely on optimism to solve their problems. Some of them are simply naïve and unaware of the dangers of wishful thinking. Here is a conversation overheard at a company where positive thinking had become wishful thinking.

> *Walter:* I'm not sure that I'll finish this project on time.
>
> *Wishful Wendy:* Have faith. Just be positive and everything will fall into place.
>
> *Walter:* I guess you're right.

Let's experience the difference when two Optimal Thinkers seek the best solution to the same situation at OptiBiz.

> *Jack:* I'm not sure that I'll finish this project on time. What is the best thing I can do?
>
> *Oliver:* Which resources do you need to meet your deadline?
>
> *Jack:* I have all the resources I need. I don't think the deadline is realistic.

Oliver: Jack, what's the worst thing that could happen if you don't meet the deadline?

Jack: I could lose the client and it would be a significant loss. The client invests over two hundred thousand dollars with us each year.

Oliver: What do you think is your best strategy to avoid or minimize the impact of your worst case scenario?

Jack: I need to explain my concerns about the deadline to the client and provide him with a realistic time frame as soon as possible.

Oliver: What are the most constructive actions you can take now?

Jack: I need to give the client a realistic schedule. I will also provide weekly updates to show him that this project is my highest priority.

Oliver: Sounds right to me!

Let's look at how Tom, a client I coached, uses Optimal realism to optimize his property management and real estate investment business. He has a system in place to deal with emergencies and is rarely overwhelmed or traumatized. He doesn't know when specific problems will arise, but is ready to deal with them when they do. Every morning, he prioritizes the issues that require his attention. First and foremost, he attends to situations that require an immediate response and would have the most negative consequences if neglected. For example, when storms cause floods and pumps do not operate properly, the consequences can be traumatic. Tom always has three people he can call on who clean drains. If the best person is unavailable, there are two others ready to take on the task. The second person may be more expensive, but when Tom needs the help, he has someone to do the job. He anticipates other problems, which include electrical shorts, car damage to a building, plumbing problems, a derelict sleeping in a carport, or an oil spill in a driveway. By anticipating these undesirable scenarios and being prepared to deal with them, he minimizes damage to his properties and avoids overreaction and trauma. He also lowers tenant turnover because they know he does everything in his power to service their needs.

John Chambers, CEO of computer networking giant Cisco Systems, offers the following advice: "When in doubt, we would encourage our investors to make their decisions based on the most conservative estimates." He is an Optimal realist.

Mental Wavelengths

No doubt you have experienced different levels of thinking in your work situation. At AnyBiz, the employees are on different mental wavelengths. Let's listen in on a conversation between two line managers at AnyBiz who are selecting a candidate for promotion. If you were top management, which candidate would you choose?

Mediocre Mary: We need a new manager. John is a good person and could become a good manager.

Extraordinary Ed: John is a good worker, but I think Steven would be an outstanding manager. He's great at motivating people to surpass their targets in spectacular ways.

Mediocre Mary: I hear what you say, but I think John will do a pretty good job. He's a regular guy. The average person can relate to him.

Actually, Mary wants to promote John because she feels he will be less demanding than Steven. Ed wants to promote Steven because he believes that Steven will do an outstanding job and will inspire others in his division. The line managers lack purpose, teamwork, and focus.

Now note the difference when the same issue is discussed by senior line optimizers at OptiBiz:

Cheryl: We need a new senior optimizer. Who's the best person for the job?

Ralph: Billy has been in the company for a while and has the right attitude, but he still hasn't mastered his job function. Gregory is very ambitious and he's able to optimize his own job performance, but he isn't enthusiastic about helping his peers optimize theirs. In my opinion, Sandy is the right person. She hasn't been here as long as Billy, but she invariably finds ways to optimize her responsibilities. When others ask her for help, she is always happy to resolve their challenges and steer them in the right direction.

Cheryl: I agree. Let's choose Sandy. She has the best track record for the job, and will inspire her team to achieve their full potential.

Ralph: Yes. She's definitely got the best leadership skills. What's the most constructive way to approach her about it?

Performance

Shelley, a receptionist who works at AnyBiz, does only what's necessary to keep her job. Her suboptimal attitude is clearly reflected in her performance. Because Shelley doesn't feel loyal toward AnyBiz, she makes most of her personal calls on company time. She places telephone callers on hold, forgets to check back with them, and rarely screens customers before connecting them with corporate representatives. Unfortunately, Shelley works solely for the money. Because her salary is not affected when she is sweet or surly, efficient or inefficient, there is no reason for her to optimize her performance.

Let's listen to some suboptimal conversation between employees at AnyBiz.

Suboptimal Steve: These customers get on my nerves.

Suboptimal Mary: You'll have to put up with them if you want to keep your job.

Do you work with people like Shelley, Steve, or Mary? Their suboptimal thinking is producing suboptimal customer service!

Now let's listen to some Optimal Thinkers at OptiBiz.

Optimal Cheryl: These customers get on my nerves. What am I thinking or doing to create this? What's the best strategy for dealing with this?

Optimal Lynn: You're asking the right questions! What do you think is most important to these customers? What is the best way to relate to them, bearing this in mind?

If you were a customer, would you take your business to AnyBiz or OptiBiz?

Here is another example of how a scenario was optimized immediately after company personnel attended an *Optimal Thinking for Communicators* seminar. The financial controller, Carol, had just completed an internal audit, discovering many problems in the process. She discussed her findings with her superior, James, who was always careful not to hurt others' feelings. Wearing a worried facial expression, James told Carol he was pleased with the audit. Carol was aware of the discrepancy between James's verbal and nonverbal responses and decided to discuss her observation with him. Let's tune in on the rest of their conversation.

> *Carol:* James, you mentioned you're pleased with the audit, but you don't look particularly happy. How do you really feel about it?

> *James:* Carol, I think you did a first-rate job with the audit, but I am a little worried about the unnecessary duplication of invoices. What is the best system we can implement to prevent it from happening?

> *Carol:* James, I recognize that the invoice duplication is a problem. If we note the date we receive payments into our accounting software, we can eliminate unnecessary duplication.

> *James:* Right! What is the Optimal time frame to get this organized?

> *Carol:* I'll get it done by the end of the week.

Do you always have your customers' best interests at heart? Larry, an insurance broker I coached, did everything in his power to satisfy his clients. He always chose the best insurance products and provided superior service. When Janice bought a new home, Larry keenly evaluated the most suitable policy for her. He asked numerous Optimal questions to ascertain her most important priorities. When Larry selected the policy best suited to Janice's needs, he explained why it was better than all the others. He encouraged her feedback, listening attentively to make sure they understood each other completely. Because Larry had her best interests at heart, Janice was comfortable with their communication. Mutual understanding came from an open exchange of information. When her friend Bruce bought a new home, Janice enthusiastically referred him to Larry.

Improvements versus Optimization

During the past two decades, many corporations have adopted the philosophy of "continuous improvement." They want better solutions, better quality, and higher profits. This philosophy does not produce peak performance, because it is suboptimal. Whenever corporate employees think suboptimally and seek to improve—rather than *maximize*—the status quo, the company's sales and profits are compromised. Here is an example.

Mediocre Manager: We need to improve sales figures this month.

Extraordinary Ed: Okay, I'll put in some extra time. Our figures will be better than last month's effort and we'll be in great shape.

Mediocre Manager: Smart thinking.

At OptiBiz, they choose the best, then put it to rest. Let's take a look:

Senior Sales Optimizer: We need to optimize sales figures this month. What are the best actions we can take?

Sales Optimizer: I can hire a temp to prequalify our customers so that we can make more presentations to the most suitable customers. I'll then have more time available to call my clients and offer them additional services.

Senior Sales Optimizer: Yes. What else can we do to optimize sales?

Sales Optimizer: We could work on Saturday morning instead of having our usual sales optimization meeting. Would that be in our best interest?

Senior Sales Optimizer: Yes. What else can we do to optimize sales this month?

Sales Optimizer: We can ask for referrals from our existing customers.

Senior Sales Optimizer: Definitely. Is there anything else we can do to optimize sales this month? Is this the best we can do?

Sales Optimizer: I think we have an Optimal plan here.

Senior Sales Optimizer: Okay, let's give it our best shot!

Let's look at how this simple concept empowers employees in large organizations to optimize any situation. Consider the research and development division of a large, highly respected corporation that had been studying its competitors' operations for over a year. The key decision makers had been informed of the results and agreed that although the cost of implementing its top competitor's system was considerable, doing so would improve the company's operations in the long run.

Charles, the director of research and development, told me how he used Optimal Thinking to save his company $12 million during a directors' meeting. He simply posed the question: "Is this our best solution?" The executives were obliged to reconsider their options within an Optimal context. They discussed how to minimize costs and gain maximum benefit from their existing system, and concluded that although the company would improve operations by installing the competitor's system, it wasn't in the company's best interests at the time.

Would you prefer to invest your working hours at AnyBiz or OptiBiz? Do you have the courage and commitment to do whatever it takes?

Optimal Leaders and Optimal Visions

"The very essence of leadership is that you have to have vision. You can't blow an uncertain trumpet."
—Theodore M. Hesburgh

Do you attract the right people to help you achieve what you want? Do you help others find the best ways to obtain what they want? Do others do their best, and achieve what they want, by helping you realize your purpose? The best leaders are Optimal Thinkers who are wholeheartedly committed to their purpose. Their vision or purpose is an expression of what they most deeply care about. They dedicate their lives to what is most meaningful to them. Sometimes their vision can take years or even a lifetime to manifest. In their vision, they sweep past the ordinary and extraordinary, into the world of the Optimal.

Martin Luther King Jr. shared his vision of equal opportunity for all races. His vision expressed his deep personal commitment to acknowledging God's presence within every human being. For him, God's presence unified all of humankind. This knowledge inspired him to share his vision of racial equality. The founder of IBM, Tom Watson, visualized what his company stood for regardless of the services and products it would offer in the future. In optimized corporations, the mission statement articulates the company's most desirable direction, and what the company must care about most to achieve this objective. The mission statement is the yardstick with which the company can evaluate its performance. The most empowering corporate mission statements usually include SUPREME objectives, ethical standards, approaches to customer needs, and optimization philosophy. Financial goals and employee commitment are often mentioned. Here is part of an Optimal corporate mission statement:

> Our fully committed team of optimizers
> provide the highest quality service,
> the most competitive fees,
> and best leadership
> in our industry,
> worldwide.
> Satisfying our customers' needs
> is our most valuable opportunity.

Are you demonstrating complete commitment to your mission? Superior leaders love and treasure their vision enough to do all they can to manifest it in reality. They see its implementation as an opportunity to make the most of their own talents, abilities, and energies. They are true to themselves and others. These people point the best way forward. It has been said that the first test of a leader is that he leaves behind in others the conviction and will to carry on. Optimal leaders galvanize others to involve themselves wholeheartedly because it is in their best interests to do so.

These leaders often describe their vision with compelling stories. Henry Ford inspired the full cooperation of his people through his stories. He'd never say, "I want this done!" He'd say, "I wonder if we can do it." Optimal leaders encourage input from their people. The collective aim is one to which leaders and their people can fully commit their best efforts.

Think carefully about your current work environment. What is its ultimate purpose? Which of the following methods were used to clarify its purpose?

Leader shared the purpose, which the people accepted.

Leader shared the purpose to gain acceptance.

Leader presented the purpose and responded to questions.

Leader presented a tentative purpose, subject to changes, after input from everyone else.

Leader presented a direction, obtained input, then formulated the ultimate purpose.

Leader defined the parameters within which the team formulated the purpose.

Leader and team jointly created the ultimate purpose.

After Harvey, an Optimal leader in the hospitality industry, attended an *Optimal Thinking for Leaders* conference, he presented his Optimal vision to his optimizers, asked for their input, and responded to their questions. After much discussion, they were all convinced their mission was simply to do their utmost to provide the highest quality service in their industry.

Studies have shown that the most successful leaders focus on both the task and their people. They include their people in the planning and decision-making processes. Japanese leaders, for example, involve numerous people from many different levels of their organizations in decision making. At Findhorn, a decentralized and democratic organization in Scotland, "focalizers" assist in the decision-making process with their group. The focalizers serve to focus, rather than direct, the individuals within the group. When a new innovation is explored, a team member opens up the conversation, inviting the others to share their viewpoints. Agreement is finally obtained through the alignment of individual input with the group purpose.

Optimal Leaders and Reality

"Leadership is the capacity to translate vision into reality."
—Warren G. Bennis

Are you interacting with the right people to bring your Optimal vision into reality? The most effective leaders are not lone rangers. They do not lead as "saviors," encouraging passive following. Optimal leaders do not seek to usurp others' power and responsibility. Chief executive optimizers act in the best interests of their stockholders and personnel. Speaking for and acting in the best interests of others requires cohesiveness and is most effectively done when leaders see themselves as members of their group. A young dyslexic woman recently acted as a spokeswoman for the dyslexic community on a national television show. Her sensitive disclosure of their needs and difficulties moved a record number of viewers to purchase a new reading program.

Do you accurately assess your current reality? Optimal leaders plan the best use of available resources and evaluate their greatest strengths, weaknesses, opportunities, and threats. They determine what is most relevant to the achievement of their mission and launch their vision with their feet on the ground. Reachable goals and Optimal conditions are established to motivate their people to do their best. Methods of operation are arranged so that their personnel can achieve their own goals by directing their best efforts toward the organizational objectives. Performance is monitored and measured against the highest achievable standards.

Optimal leaders enlist the best efforts of all their people to fulfill their mission. They seek wholehearted commitment from those whose skills and expertise are most suited for the various tasks. Authority, responsibilities, and structures are clearly defined so that collective effort is maximized. Everyone is involved in the optimization process. Superior leaders discover what motivates each person to do his or her best, and work with these motivations to achieve the highest standards and objectives.

Geraldine, a former business consultant I coached, joined a well-known insurance company after passing their entrance tests. The exam showed that her most important goals were compatible with the corporate mission, a prerequisite for her acceptance into the corporation. Walter, an Optimal leader, structured a schedule that inspired Geraldine's total commitment. Together they decided upon an achievable sales target to ensure her best efforts during her first year. They also worked out what she had to do on a daily and weekly basis to attain her SUPREME goal.

Geraldine was happy with the conditions of her employment. The office environment encouraged her to concentrate fully on her work. Every morning she attended mandatory sales meetings where she learned the most important ingredients for peak performance from the top achievers. She had to complete SUPREME assignments on a daily basis, such as calling ten new people or meeting with three prospective clients. Geraldine measured her progress by filling out weekly reports that enabled Walter to keep track of her performance. His feedback motivated her to do her best work. When she achieved the targets, he acknowledged her success, both personally and publicly. When she surpassed her previous best efforts, they celebrated!

Assess Your Company

You are now ready to assess the current reality and direction of your company. In your notebook, answer the following questions:

- Why does your company or team exist?
- What is its ultimate purpose?
- What are the most important objectives of your company/team this year?

- What is the best way to achieve them within specific time frames?
- What are the company/team's greatest strengths?
- What are its major weaknesses?
- What are you doing to maximize the strengths of your company/team?
- What are you doing to minimize its weaknesses?
- What are the major opportunities available to your company/team this year?
- How will you make the most of these opportunities?
- What are the major threats to your company/team this year?
- What is the best way to minimize these threats?
- What are the best actions you can take to maximize profits?
- What are the best actions you can take to minimize costs?
- What are the greatest strengths of the individuals in your company/team?
- Do their task/job profiles fully utilize their strengths?
- How is your company/team's mission helping you to achieve your purpose?
- What are the best actions you can take to be fully satisfied with your position?

Motivating Others to Do Their Best

"The best way to inspire people to superior performance is to convince them by everything you do and by your everyday attitude that you are wholeheartedly supporting them."
—Harold S. Geneen

Do you show appreciation for others as they are, and assist them in making the most of themselves? The most respected leaders begin by understanding their people's needs and desires as well as their innate limitations. These leaders discover what their people value most and the beliefs and causes they are committed to. They help them decide what they want above all else and support them in taking the best steps to achieve it. They also encourage their people to make the most of their strengths and accomplishments to reach their targeted goals. *Optimal leaders believe there is no better occupation than to inspire others to be their best.*

The most empowering leaders share stories that inspire peak performance. When their people experience a slump, they remind them of their greatest successes. They talk about others' struggles, conflicts, persistence, and eventual triumphs. American financial analyst Charles Schwab tells us: "I consider my ability to arouse enthusiasm among men the greatest asset I possess. The way to develop the best that is in a man is by appreciation and encouragement."

Tom, the real estate developer I coached, was devastated when he lost all his money during a recession. He borrowed enough money to start again and eventually became one of the largest developers in the country. Tom was a compassionate man who cared about his people. He took time to get to know and understand them and always acknowledged their best efforts. Graham, his construction superintendent of seven years, had been irritable lately and had made some serious mistakes. When Tom asked Graham what was bothering him, Graham told him that he had recently lost all of his savings in the stock market. He didn't have enough money to pay for his children's school fees and there were other bills he couldn't cover. Tom immediately advanced Graham the money he needed, and organized additional work for him on the weekends. He shared what it was like for him when he had lost his money, the knowledge he had gained, and what it had taken to bounce back. He talked about others who had triumphed over even more difficult circumstances. He then reminded Graham of all his accomplishments over the past seven years. He showed full confidence in him. Graham dedicated his best efforts to the organization and, in time, recouped his financial losses.

Optimal leaders relate to others solely in terms of their own best interests. They do not try to persuade them to do what is not in their best interests. A prime example is my client Michael, the president of our local yachting club, who had counted on Henry's administrative assistance for almost ten years. Henry was now studying to complete his M.B.A. and was often up until the early hours of the morning. He felt guilty because he hardly spent any time with his family. Michael was concerned that Henry had overcommitted himself and encouraged him to evaluate his priorities. Henry admitted that the club's administrative activities had become a burden and asked Michael to find someone else to handle some of the responsibilities. Michael agreed and immediately secured the best available administrative assistance.

The most respected leaders are top-notch communicators. They are skilled at convincing others of the value of their ideas. They communicate with people in their own language. These leaders understand nonverbal communication and make the most of it. They listen carefully to their people and then employ Optimal verbal assertion. The most beloved leaders encourage their people to express themselves fully. Many leaders believe, "If I say it, they can doubt me; if they say it, it's true." They are sensitive to the needs and expectations of their people and seek regular, honest feedback from them. They always encourage respect and understanding within their team.

Recently I conducted an *Optimal Thinking for Leaders* seminar for the senior optimizers in a rapidly expanding organization. I was delighted when the chief executive optimizer declared that regardless of position or length of service, everyone was to be treated with equal respect. He repeatedly said, "Treat others as you would like to be treated."

During his presidency, Ronald Reagan displayed a plaque that read: "You can go everywhere in life when you give others the credit." The most effective leaders acknowledge their people for their contributions. They are specific with praise. They say, "You've done a first-class job with this report" or "I am grateful that I can count on you to be punctual." They value their people for being themselves. They also recognize and applaud achievement, and celebrate accomplishments as they occur. They acknowledge and celebrate the performance of their people with letters of appreciation, weekend getaways, dinners, flowers, award ceremonies, plaques, gifts, cash awards, or simply a handshake and a smile. Many superior leaders believe they have the finest jobs in the world, because they invest much of their time honoring people.

Are you skilled in the art of reprimanding others? Do you confirm facts and identify undesirable behavior specifically? The most successful leaders act immediately to correct unwanted behavior. They do not criticize others' motives, but direct their comments to the behavior, not the person. When these leaders have to criticize, they do it privately and sometimes it is in the form of a question. This is always followed by another Optimal question, to obtain the best solution.

Consider Valerie, a senior optimizer at a large law firm, who was annoyed because Ron, an optimizer, had come late to two meetings. I suggested that she employ Optimal verbal assertion to resolve the undesirable behavior. She confronted Ron privately with, "When you come late to meetings, I feel annoyed because it disturbs the rest of us. I understand you must have good reasons for coming late.

Would you be willing to share them with me?" When Ron explained that his son had just had surgery and was still in the hospital, Valerie expressed concern about his son's health, then asked: "What's the best thing we can do to make sure our communication lines are open from now on?" Superior leaders accept their own and others' humanity, and are in touch with their feelings of anger, annoyance, and frustration. They embrace and resolve negative emotions rather than deny them, and express them to the most appropriate person.

Optimal leaders discover what "the best" means to their people, appeal to their best interests, stimulate in them the desire to be their best, and then acknowledge them for doing their best.

When Jackie, a superior network marketing professional, discovered Optimal Thinking several years ago, she decided to share it with everyone in her organization. Recently she said: "My people understand that they can't do any better than their best. They set SUPREME goals and then approach their business activities with Optimal realism. They expect some rejection and when faced with it, they place their highest self in charge. They do it by themselves!" Superior leaders are easily recognized because their people usually achieve the best results. When the Optimal leader's work is complete, their people often say, "We did it ourselves!"

Characteristics of Optimal Leaders

"The supreme quality for leadership is unquestionably integrity. Without it, no real success is possible, no matter whether it is on a section gang, a football field, in an army, or in an office."

—Dwight David Eisenhower

Aristotle said, "Character is the most effective agent of persuasion." The most powerful leaders display character in their voices, manners, postures, actions, mannerisms, and facial expressions. They follow through on what they say they will do. They honor agreements and demonstrate consistency and commitment. They act with integrity and inspire trust. German writer Johann Wolfgang von Goethe understood: "Talent develops in tranquillity, character in the full current of human life." Superlative leaders look for the best ways things can be done and use humor when appropriate.

Do you accept mistakes, take the best actions to correct them, learn from them, and move on? The most successful leaders understand that both failure and risk-taking are part of achieving their ultimate success. Theodore Roosevelt said, "The only man who never makes a mistake is the man who never does anything."

Bill Clinton became governor of Arkansas in his early thirties, a rare and noteworthy achievement. Two years later, he lost his re-election bid. Turned out of office, Clinton analyzed the reasons for his failure. He realized that he had lost focus on the most important issues facing the citizens of Arkansas. In the ensuing period, Bill Clinton ran again and was elected. He was subsequently reelected three times as governor of Arkansas before he ran for and won the U.S. presidency. President Clinton made grave mistakes during his two-term presidency. He was impeached as a result of his affair with Monica Lewinsky and was widely condemned when he pardoned fugitive Marc Rich prior to leaving office. Although most people believe Bill Clinton exercised poor judgment in these situations, most agree that he has the courage to fail amid his successes.

How do you react to change? The strongest leaders accept it, learn from it, and make the most of it. In the early 1950s, tobacco giant Philip Morris, Inc., began the "Marlboro Man" advertising campaign, which resulted in Marlboro becoming the world's most successful brand name. During the 1970s and early 1980s, the company experienced astounding growth, generating billions of dollars of profit and a cash flow that few other industrial giants could match. As evidence of the negative medical effects of smoking mounted, leadership realized that adverse change in the tobacco industry was inevitable. They clearly understood the implications and sought to diversify their business activities. After analyzing the company's strengths and opportunities, leadership decided to enter the most compatible industry with long-term growth prospects. Philip Morris then purchased some of the most highly regarded companies in the consumer food industry. Today, companies such as General Foods and Kraft are subsidiaries of Philip Morris, now known as the Altria Group.

The most successful leaders promote initiative, the generation of ideas, prudent risk-taking, and autonomy. Dr. Edward de Bono, author of *Lateral Thinking*, explains: "Creativity involves breaking out of established patterns in order to look at things in a different way." Superior leaders encourage their people to be creative and to use their best efforts to solve problems. One chief executive optimizer tells his staff: "Do everything in your power to bring me the best solutions. If you have a problem you can't solve, I'm here for you."

The most celebrated leaders encourage innovative action, flexibility, and honest feedback. They also support the collaborative efforts of their personnel. Some years ago, 3M Corporation gave scientists in their research laboratory free rein to come up with new products. Their research resulted in the invention of the temporary adhesive Post-It stickers. Although the scientists at 3M Corporation did not appreciate the commercial value of their invention, their business leaders most emphatically did. Today these stickers are a "fixture" in the business world.

Optimal leaders are also skilled at decision making, knowing that the worst decision, generally, is no decision. They keep their composure, choose the best times to make decisions, and then take the best actions. Bill Gates, CEO of Microsoft Corporation, understands the value of timely decisions. In the mid-1980s, Apple Computer succeeded in gaining a significant market share because its Macintosh computers were more intuitive and user friendly than the IBM DOS systems. Bill Gates recognized a major opportunity for the IBM market. He decided to develop an icon-based operating environment for DOS-based computer systems, similar to that used in the Macintosh. This product, Windows, resulted in billions of dollars in revenue for his company.

When resolving conflict, Optimal leaders consider which alternatives will help those involved meet their needs in ways that move the organization closest to its SUPREME goals. They consider which alternatives are most likely to minimize conflict and opposition to these objectives. They also examine what must be sacrificed to achieve the best resolution.

Do you acknowledge your intuition? According to Dr. Jonas Salk, discoverer of polio vaccine: "Intuition will tell the thinking mind where to look next." A study by Professor Weston Agor, done in 1984, showed that intuitive leaders are most likely to be found at the top of organizations. The most powerful leaders allow their intuition and Optimal Thinking to work hand in hand.

Is something holding you back? The best leaders often lack the resources we take for granted. Paul Orfalea, founder of Kinko's, the largest business services firm in America, is dyslexic. He has difficulty with reading and writing and sometimes relies on others to help him. Blind and deaf, Helen Keller inspired the world with her thinking and accomplishments. She demonstrated that a full life is possible for every one of us. When she received her honorary law degree at the University of Glasgow, she responded with, "It is a sign, Sir, that silence and darkness need not block progress of the immortal human spirit."

Your Optimal voice is available in darkness, silence, sunshine, and song. Where is it leading you?

Optimal Questions

1. What is my vision of the Optimal workplace?
2. How can I best express my talents in the workplace?
3. How can I make the most of my work situation today/this week?
4. How can I minimize the weaknesses of my work situation today/this week?
5. What can I do to bring out the best in my colleagues?

Optimal Action Steps

1. Take three actions this week to make the best use of your talents and abilities in the workplace.
2. What are the three best actions you can take to optimize your work environment this week?
3. Think about three people who are open to optimization in your work environment. How can you inspire them to do their best?
4. Share the most beneficial concepts in this chapter with three people you work with. Note their response. Ask the best questions to invite the best answers!

Epilogue

Although we may not have met face to face, the process of expressing my thoughts and feelings in words makes me feel as though I already know you. By investing your time and energy in this book, you have offered me the supreme opportunity to share my life's work and to connect my best self with yours. As you set forth on your Optimal journey, I am with you in spirit. Each time you use Optimal Thinking, I will share the joy of your success.

In the late 1980s, when I first began to formulate Optimal Thinking, I dreamed of a global community of Optimal Thinkers. Because Optimal Thinking is timeless, universal, and superlative, I wrote my first book with this vision in mind. When the Internet exploded, my dream became a reality. Every day members of the global community of Optimal Thinkers, like you, discuss personal and career issues that begin or result in optimization. They point, click, and type their communications at OptimalThinking.com. *Optimal Thinking* is now available in several languages, and we are training and certifying Optimal consultants to optimize personal and professional performance throughout the world.

Around the globe, however, times are tough. Good people are replaced by technology in the workplace, families disintegrate, terrorism is a large-scale threat, and mediocrity is everywhere. Merely being good, getting better, or even becoming great is no longer enough. It is time to be our best. Let's optimize ourselves, then optimize others, and together—let's optimize the world.

Optimal Exercises

This section provides you with some of the exercises in the book. The exercises have been arranged so that you always have easy reference, and the writing space you need. You deserve the best in life!

What Optimal Means to You

My favorite color is _____.

My most attractive physical feature is _____.

I look my best when _____.

My favorite artist is _____.

The sounds of nature I appreciate most are _____.

My favorite music is _____.

The funniest comedian I have heard is _____.

The singer who has the most pleasing voice is _____.

The most cheerful person I know is _____.

The most comfortable chair in my home is _____.

I feel my best when _____.

The most enjoyable vacation I can recall is _____.

My favorite food is _____
_____.

When it comes to friendship, my most positive attribute is _____
_____.

What I like most about my best friend is _____.

I can maximize my relationship with my partner by _____
_____.

My greatest fantasy is _____

I can maximize my income this year by _____.

The best career move for me this year is _____.

The best action I can take today toward my most important goal is

_____.

Start Each Day with Five Optimal Questions

1. _____

2. _____

3. _____

4. _____

5. _____

How Do You Value and Rate Yourself?

Assets

1. Bodily assets
2. Mental and spiritual strengths
3. Personality strengths
4. Social strengths
5. Career and/or daily task strengths
6. Personal achievements
7. What I like most about myself

Liabilities

1. Bodily liabilities
2. Mental and spiritual liabilities
3. Personality weaknesses
4. Social weaknesses
5. Career and/or daily task weaknesses
6. Personal disappointments
7. What I dislike most about myself

Optimize Your Assets

1. Bodily assets
2. Mental and spiritual assets
3. Personality strengths
4. Social strengths
5. Career and/or daily task strengths
6. Personal achievements
7. What I like most about myself

Minimize Your Liabilities

1. Bodily liabilities
2. Mental and spiritual liabilities
3. Personality weaknesses
4. Social weaknesses
5. Career and/or daily task weaknesses
6. Personal disappointments
7. What I dislike most about myself

Identify Your Life Purpose

1. What do I care about most deeply?
2. What and who do I love?
3. What am I deeply committed to?
4. What do I stand for? What are my principles?
5. When am I at my best?
6. What has given me the greatest feelings of importance in my life? What has been most beneficial for my self-esteem?
7. What is it that I definitely don't want?
8. What do I want more than anything else?
9. Which activities do I enjoy most?
10. In order of priority, what are the three things I value most in life?
11. In order of priority, what are my three most important ambitions in life?
12. If I had one year to live, how would I make the most of it?
13. How would I like to be remembered?
14. If I were given all the money I could ever need or want, how would I live my life?

15. If I could experience the ultimate day, what would it be like?

16. What would my ultimate environment be like?

17. Which one purpose would I concentrate on if I knew that there was no chance of failure?

18. What is my ultimate purpose? What do I most want to accomplish?

Identify Your Career Purpose

1. What are my strengths? What are my talents and gifts? What are all the assets I bring to the table?

2. What makes me happy? What brings me joy?

3. What do I love to do?

4. What am I most interested in doing? What is my passion?

5. How do I most enjoy contributing to others?

6. Which cause do I most want to serve?

7. What kind of organization am I best suited to?

8. What is my career purpose?

Supreme Goals for the Short and Medium Term

The Process of Reverse Planning

1. List of Optimal dreams and SUPREME goals. What do you most want to be, do, have, and contribute?

2. Which goal is most important?

3. Apply the SUPREME test.

Is it . . .

Specific, **U**plifting, **P**aramount, **R**eachable, **E**xciting, **M**easurable, **E**njoyable, and within a definite time frame?

4. List all the benefits to be gained by achieving your SUPREME goal.

5. Where are you now in relation to your goal.

6. Obstacles: If this is what you want above all else, why don't you have it already?

7. Risks: What are the possible damages, injuries, and losses? What is the worst possible scenario?

8. Optimal resources: What are your greatest strengths? Which organizations, people, and information can best assist you in achieving your SUPREME goal?

9. Optimal solutions: What are the best actions you can take to overcome the obstacles and minimize the risks? What are your Optimal action steps, in priority, with target times?

10. What is the best time frame for the completion of your SUPREME goal?

11. What's the first step you must take to activate this plan?

12. Are all the benefits to be gained worth the price you'll have to pay? Is this SUPREME goal worthy of your complete commitment (emotionally, financially, and otherwise)? If so, why? If not, why not?

13. Which Optimal affirmations will be most helpful in accomplishing your SUPREME goal?

14. Which Optimal visualizations will be most helpful in accomplishing your SUPREME goal?

15. How do you know you're on track? How can you most effectively monitor your progress?

Optimal Affirmations

I am an Optimal Thinker.

I focus on the most constructive thought at any given moment.

I accept what is out of my control and optimize what is within my control.

I'm the right person in the best place at the best time, engaged in the most important activity in the best way.

Optimal Affirmations for Core Beliefs

I deserve the best in life.

I deserve to have exactly what I want.

I am now creating what I need and want.

I can have exactly what I want.

I have everything I need to have everything I want.

I get my most important needs met.

I give myself what I really want and feel I deserve it.

I focus on what I want and all the reasons I can have it.

Life is easiest when I create what I want.

I am giving life my best shot.

I am responsible for making the most of my life.

I take full responsibility for optimizing my thoughts, actions, feelings, and life.

Optimal Affirmations for Self-Esteem

I accept myself completely.

I am doing my best.

Right now, I am the best I can be.

I am making the most of my assets.

Optimal Affirmations for Body

I enjoy the best of health. It's my birthright.

I accept my body completely. I am making the most of it.

Everything I eat produces my Optimal health, beauty, and weight.

My body is in peak condition.

I am looking my best.

Optimal Affirmations for Mind

I am an Optimal Thinker. I place my best self in charge.

I now resolve to be the best I can be.

I always do my best.

I can rely on myself to make the wisest decisions.

I am now enjoying the best life has to offer.

I am making the most of this situation.

I am one with all of nature.

Optimal Social Affirmations

I attract the right people.

I bring out the best in others.

I have all the friends I need.

I ask for what I want.

I choose to accept and love others as they are.

Optimal Affirmations for Purpose

What I want above all else is clear to me now.

I am now taking the best action to fulfill my ultimate purpose.

I am making the best use of my greatest skills.

I concentrate on what I most want to do and what I do best.

I invest my time, talents, abilities, and life in those activities
that fulfill my ultimate purpose and deserve my best efforts.

Optimal Affirmations for Planning

My fastest route to success is my Optimal plan.

I know the best way to achieve my most important goal.

I give everything I have to attain my most important goal.

I am doing the most important task right now.

I make the most of every moment.

I am making the best use of my time right now.

I am making the most profitable use of my time right now.

I am enjoying the most pleasurable path to my goal right now.

I obtain the best results within the least amount of time.

I am always punctual.

Optimal Affirmations for Feelings

I accept all my feelings.

I understand my feelings.

I deal with my feelings in the best possible way.

I am completely capable of making myself happy.

My life is now filled with pleasure.

I am now in my Optimal state.

I trust myself completely.

I love myself unconditionally.

This is the best day of my life.

I feel my best when I do my best.

Optimal Affirmations for Communicators

When I ask the best questions I invite the best answers.

I ask for what I want.

I mirror others' nonverbal gestures to enjoy the best rapport with them.

When others speak to me I give them my full attention.

I communicate the best means of satisfying the best interests of all concerned.

I communicate with Optimal assertion.

I listen reflectively without judgment to gain complete understanding.

I restate another person's message to make sure that I have understood it correctly.

I always respect the dignity, rights, and feelings of others.

Optimal Affirmations for Work

I express my greatest talents and abilities in my work.

I attract the best people.

I bring out the best in others.

What I do brings out the best in you.

I think of what is best for everyone.

I help others recognize their ability to create what's best for them.

The greatest gift I can give others is the example of making the most of my life.

People do the best they can under the circumstances.

My organization is full of optimizers.

Everyone and everything is of utmost benefit to our Optimal mission.

Optimal Questions

Optimal WHO Questions

Who is most important to me in my life?

Who do I trust more than anyone else?

Who is the most reliable person in my life?

Who do I admire most?

Who do I have the most fun with?

Who do I respect most of all?

Who promotes the greatest amount of personal and professional growth?

Optimal WHAT Questions

What is my greatest source of inspiration?

What is supremely important to me?

What is supremely important to those who are most important to me?

What are the benefits I will gain by taking the best actions to achieve what is supremely important to me?

What are the benefits I will gain by taking the best actions to support those who are most important to me to achieve what is supremely important to them?

What is in the best interest of all concerned?

Optimal HOW Questions

How can I make the most of this moment?

How can I be my best?

How can I make the most of my life?

How can I best support those who are most important to me?

How can I live life to the fullest?

How can I use Optimal Thinking as often as possible?

Optimal WHEN Questions

When am I full of gratitude?

When am I most inspired?

When am I most loving?

When am I joyful?

When am I being my best?

Optimal WHY Questions

Why is it in my best interest to accept the present moment?

Why is it in my best interest to accept my feelings?

Why is it in my best interest to be compassionate toward my shortcomings?

Why is it in my best interest to love myself and life?

Why is it in my best interest to be happy?

Why is this the best solution?

Optimal Questions for Self

Do I deserve the best in life?

Am I giving life my best shot or am I settling for second best?

Do I give myself what I truly want and feel I deserve it?

Do I get my most important needs met?

Do I use Optimal Thinking consistently to make the most of my life?

What do I like/admire most about myself?

What is my most valuable skill?

What is my greatest strength/asset?

What is my most productive habit?

What am I most grateful for in my life?

Optimal Questions for the Present Moment

What is going on inside me right now?

Am I choosing to accept "what is" in present moment, or am I resisting it (and life itself)?

What do I want from an external source that I am not giving myself?

How can I make the most of this moment?

What is the most empowering use of my time right now?

What is the wisest use of my time right now?

What am I thinking or doing that is preventing me from being my most loving self?

How can I maximize my enjoyment of the present moment?

How can I best share my love with others?

What is the most loving action I can take right now?

Optimal Questions for This Week

What are my highest priorities this week?

What are the best actions I can take to achieve them?

How can I make each day most pleasurable?

What is the best thing I can do to be happy?

How can I be my best?

How can I make the most of my life?

How can I make my life most enjoyable?

How can I empower others to be their best?

Bibliography

Adams, John D. *Transforming Leadership: From Vision to Results*. Alexandria, Va.: Miles River Press, 1986.

Badaracco, Joseph L., and Richard R. Ellsworth. *Leadership and the Quest for Integrity*. Boston: Harvard Business School Press, 1989.

Ban Breathnach, Sarah. *The Simple Abundance Companion: Following Your Authentic Path to Something More*. New York: Warner Books, 2000.

Bandler, Richard, and John Grinder. *Frogs into Princes*. New York: People Press, 1979.

Bilodeau, Lorraine. *The Anger Workbook*. New York: MJF Books, 1992.

Blanchard, Kenneth, and Spencer Johnson. *The One Minute Manager*. London: Willow Books, 1983.

Bloomfield, Harold H., and Leonard Felder. *Making Peace with Yourself*. New York: Ballantine Books, 1985.

Bloomfield, Harold H., and Robert B. Kory. *Inner Joy: New Strategies for Adding More Pleasure to Your Life*. New York: Wyden, 1980.

Boyd, Ty. *Visions: From the Leaders of Today for the Leaders of Tomorrow*. Charlotte, NC: Alexa Press, 1991.

Boyett, Joseph H., and Henry P. Conn. *Workplace 2000: The Revolution Reshaping American Business*. New York: Plume, 1992.

Bradshaw, John. *Homecoming: Reclaiming and Championing Your Inner Child*. New York: Bantam Books, 1990.

Branden, Nathaniel. *The Psychology of Self-Esteem*. New York: Nash, 1969.

———. *How to Raise Your Self-Esteem*. New York: Bantam Books, 1987.

———. *The Power of Self-Esteem*. Deerfield Beech, Fla.: Health Communications, Inc., 1992.

Briggs, Dorothy Corkille. *Celebrate Yourself*. Garden City, N.Y.: Doubleday, 1977.

Burns, David D., M.D. *Feeling Good: The New Mood Therapy*. New York: William Morrow, 1980.

Buscaglia, Leo F. *Born for Love*. Thorofare, N.J.: Slack, Inc., 1992.

Buzan, Tony. *Making The Most of Your Mind*. New York: Simon & Schuster, 1984.

Cameron, Julia. *The Artist's Way: A Spiritual Path to Higher Creativity*. New York: G. P. Putnam's Sons, 1992.

Chopra, Deepak. *The Seven Spiritual Laws of Success*. Amber-Allen Publishing and The California New World Library, 1993.

Cole-Whittaker, Terry. *Love & Power in a World without Limits*. San Francisco: Harper & Row, 1989.

Cornelius, Helena, and Shoshana Faire. *Everyone Can Win: How to Resolve Conflict*. Brookvale, Austral.: Simon & Schuster, 1989.

Covey, Stephen R. *The 7 Habits of Highly Effective People*. New York: Fireside, 1990.

De Bono, Edward. *Lateral Thinking*. London: Penguin Books, 1970.

———. *The Happiness Purpose*. Middlesex, Eng.: Penguin Books, 1977.

———. *Atlas of Management Thinking*. London: Penguin Books, 1980.

———. *Six Thinking Hats*. London: Penguin Books, 1985.

———. *Serious Creativity*. New York: Harper Business, 1992.

The Diagram Group Staff. *The Brain: A Users Manual*. New York: Putnam Publishing Group, 1987.

Dryden, Gordon, and Jeannette Vos. *The Learning Revolution*. Los Angeles: Jalmar Press, 1993.

Dyer, Wayne W. *Your Erroneous Zones*. New York: Harper & Row, 1976.

———. *You'll See It When You Believe It*. New York: Avon Books, 1990.

———. *Real Magic: Creating Miracles in Your Life*. New York: Harper Collins, 1992.

Ehrenberg, Miriam, and Otto Ehrenberg. *Optimum Brain Power: A Total Program for Increasing Your Intelligence*. New York: Gamut Books, 1987.

Evans, Patricia. *The Verbally Abusive Relationship*. Holbrook, Mass.: Adams Media, 1996.

Fast, Julius. *Body Language*. Philadelphia: M. Evans, 1970.

Fisher, Roger, William Ury, and Bruce Patton. *Getting to Yes*. New York: Penguin Books, 1983.

Ford, Debbie. *The Dark Side of the Light Chasers*. New York: Riverhead Books, 1998.

Garfield, Charles A., and Hal Zina Bennett. *Peak Performance*. Los Angeles: Jeremy P. Tarcher, Inc., 1984.

Gawain, Shakti. *Creative Visualization*. Mill Valley, Calif.: Whatever Publishing, 1978.

Glass, Lillian. *He Says, She Says: Closing the Communication Gap between the Sexes*. New York: Perigee Books, 1993.

Goleman, Daniel. *Emotional Intelligenc*. New York: Bantam Books, 1995.

Gray, John. *Men Are from Mars, Women Are from Venus*. New York: HarperCollins, 1992.

Grundermeyer, David, Rebecca Grundermeyer, and Lerissa Nancy Patrick. *Sensible Self-Help*. Del Mar, Calif.: Willingness Works Press, 1995.

Hammer, Michael, and James Champy. *Reengineering the Corporation*. New York: Harper Business, 1993.

Hankins, Gary, and Carol Hankins. *Prescription for Anger: Coping with Angry Feelings and Angry People*. New York: Warner Books, 1988.

Harrison, Allen F., and Robert M. Bramson. *The Art of Thinking*. New York: Berkely Publishing Group, 1982.

Hay, Louise. *You Can Heal Your Life*. Farmingdale, N.Y.: Coleman Publishing, 1984.

———. *Love Yourself, Heal Your Life Workbook*. Los Angeles: Hay House, 1990.

Hendrix, Gay, and Kathlyn T. Hendrix. *Centering & the Art of Intimacy*. New York: Fireside, 1985.

Hendrix, Harville. *Getting the Love You Want: A Guide for Couples*. New York: Henry Holt, 1988.

———. *Keeping the Love You Find: A Guide for Singles*. New York: Pocket Books, 1992.

Hersey, Paul. *The Situational Leader*. New York: Warner Books, 1984.

Hill, Napoleon. *Think and Grow Rich*. New York: Elsevier-Dutton, 1965.

Hill, Napoleon, and W. Clement Stone. *Success Through a Positive Mental Attitude*. New York: Pocket Books, 1960.

Hopkins, Tom. *The Official Guide to Success Vol. 1*. Scottsdale, Ariz.: Tom Hopkins International, 1983.

Jampolsky, Gerald. *Love Is Letting Go of Fear*. Millbrae, Calif.: Celestial Arts, 1979.

Jeffers, Susan. *Feel the Fear and Do It Anyway*. Orlando, Fla.: Harcourt Brace Jovanovich, 1987.

Kassorla, Irene C. *Go for It!*. London: Futura Publications, 1984.

Keyes, Ken. *Handbook to Higher Consciousness*. Marina Del Rey, Calif.: Living Love Publications, 1980.

Kübler-Ross, Elisabeth. *On Death and Dying*. New York: Collier Books, 1997.

LeCron, Leslie M. *Self Hypnotism*. Englewood Cliffs, N.J.: Prentice-Hall, 1964.

Levinson, Harry, and Stuart Rosenthal. *Corporate Leadership in Action*. New York: Basic Books, 1984.

Levy, SuSu. *Recipes for Optimal Living*. Venice, Calif.: Ad Mates, 1984.

Malone, Paul B. III. *Love 'Em and Lead 'Em*. Annandale, Va.: Synergy Press, 1986.

Maltz, Maxwell. *Psycho-Cybernetics*. Englewood Cliffs, N.J.: Prentice-Hall, 1960.

Mandino, Og. *Og Mandino's University of Success*. New York: Bantam Books, 1982.

Maslow, A. H. *Motivation and Personality*. New York: Harper & Brothers. 1954.

McGinnis, Alan Loy. *Bringing Out the Best in People*. Minneapolis: Lutheran Publishing House, 1985.

McKay, Matthew, Martha Davis, and Patrick Fanning. *Thoughts and Feelings: The Art of Cognitive Stress Intervention*. Oakland: New Harbinger Publications, 1981.

McKay, Matthew, and Patrick Fanning. *Self-Esteem*. Oakland: New Harbinger Publications, 1987.

Meister Vitale, Barbara. *Free Flight: Celebrating Your Right Brain*. Los Angeles: Jalmar Press, 1986.

Meyer, Paul J. *The Dynamics of Personal Leadership*. Waco, Tex.: Success Motivation, Inc., 1969.

———. *Executive Time Management*. Waco, Tex.: Success Motivation, Inc., 1979.

Murphy, Joseph. *The Power of Your Subconscious Mind*. New York: Bantam Books, 1963.

Myss, Caroline. *Anatomy of the Spirit*. New York: Crown, 1996.

Nirenberg, Gerald I. *The Art of Negotiating*. New York: Hawthorn, 1968.

Nirenberg, Gerald I., and Henry H. Calero. *How to Read a Person Like a Book*. New York: Pocket Books, 1971.

Peale, Norman Vincent. *The Power of Positive Thinking*. Eaglewood Cliffs, N.J.: Prentice-Hall, 1952.

Peck, M. Scott, *The Road Less Traveled*. New York: Touchstone Books, 1978.

———. *Further Along the Road Less Traveled*. New York: Simon & Schuster, 1993.

Peter, J. Laurence, and Bill Dana. *The Laughter Prescription*. New York: Ballantine Books, 1982.

Peters, Thomas J., and Robert H. Waterman Jr. *In Search of Excellence*. New York: Harper & Row, 1982.

Peters, Tom, and Nancy Austin. *A Passion for Excellence*. New York: Random House, 1985.

Postle, Denis. *The Mind Gymnasium: How to Use Your Mind for Personal Growth*. Sydney: Simon & Schuster, 1989.

Reck, Ross R., and Brian G. Long. *The Win-Win Negotiator*. Escondido, Calif.: Blanchard Training and Development, Inc., 1985.

Restack, Richard M. *The Brain, the Last Frontier*. New York: Warner Books, 1979.

———. *The Mind*. New York: Bantam Books, 1988.

Robbins, Anthony. *Unlimited Power*. London: Simon & Schuster, 1986.

———. *Awaken the Giant Within*. New York: Summit Books, 1991.

Samples, Bob. *Open Mind/Whole Mind*. Los Angeles: Jalmar Press, 1987.

Seligman, Martin. *Learned Optimism*. New York: Pocket Books, 1990.

———. *What You Can Change and What You Can't.* New York: Alfred A. Knopf, 1994.

Sheehy, Gail. *Passages*. New York: Bantam Books, 1976.

Sher, Barbara, and Annie Gottlieb. *Wishcraft: How to Get What You Really Want*. New York: Viking, 1979.

Silva, Jose, and Philip Miele. *The Silva Mind Control Method*. New York: Simon & Schuster, 1977.

Silver, Susan. *Organized to Be the Best!* Los Angeles: Adams-Hall Publishing, 1989.

Simon, David. *Vital Energy*. New York: John Wiley & Sons, 2000.

Stearn, Jess. *The Power of Alpha Thinking*. New York: William Morrow, 1976.

Stone, Hal, and Sidra Winkelman. *Embracing Each Other*. San Rafael, Calif.: New World Library, 1989.

————. *Embracing Our Selves*. Marina Del Rey, Calif.: De Vorss & Co., 1989.

Telushkin, Joseph. *Words That Hurt, Words That Heal*. New York: William Morrow, 1996.

Townsend, Robert. *Up the Organization*. New York: Alfred A. Knopf, 1970.

Tracy, Brian. *Maximum Achievement*. New York: Simon & Schuster, 1993.

Trump, Donald J., and Tony Schwartz. *The Art of the Deal*. New York: Warner Books, 1989.

Ury, William. *Getting Past No*. New York: Bantam Books, 1991.

Vanzant, Iyanla. *In the Meantime*. New York: Fireside, 1999.

Viscott, David. *Emotionally Free: Letting Go of the Past to Live in the Moment*. Chicago: Contemporary Books, 1992.

Wade, Carole, and Carol Tavris. *Critical & Creative Thinking*. New York: HarperCollins, 1993.

Waitley, Denis. *Being the Best*. New York: Pocket Books, 1987.

Walsch, Neale Donald. *Conversations with God*. New York: G. P. Putnam's Sons, 1996.

Williamson, Marianne. *A Return to Love*. New York: HarperCollins, 1992.

Wolpe, J. *Practice of Behavior Therapy*, 4th ed. New York: Pergamon, 1990.

Ziglar, Zig. *See You at the Top*. Gretna, La.: Pelican, 1984.

Zukav, Gary. *The Seat of the Soul*. New York: Simon & Schuster, 1990.

Zunin, Leonard, and Natalie Zunin. *Contact: The First Four Minutes*. New York: Ballantine, 1973.

Zweig, Connie, and Steve Wolf. *Romancing the Shadow*. New York: Ballantine Wellspring, 1997.

Optimal Thinking Seminars, Programs, and Products

The experiences of thousands of people who have attended Optimal Thinking seminars have provided the inspiration for this book. These seminars are available for individuals and businesses. Seminar topics include:

Optimal Thinking: The Mental Basis of Peak Performance

Optimal Thinking for Leaders: Being Good or Great Is No Longer Enough

Optimal Thinking for Communicators: It's Not What's Good for You or Me. It's What's Best for Us!

Optimize Your Time: Don't Just Manage It!

Optimize Your Team

Optimal Writing Skills for Business

Optimal Thinking for Business Success

Optimal Thinking for Sales Success

Optimal Thinking for Self-Esteem

Optimize Your Emotional Life

How to Eliminate Self-Sabotage

How to Make the Most of Your Relationships

How to Maximize your Personal and Professional Life with Minimal Effort

Optimal Thinking for Turbulent Times

Optimal Thinking programs and products provide a wide range of resources for individuals, families, business, government, and educational organizations.

For more information on Optimal Thinking cassette tapes, videos, and software, please contact us online (**www.optimalthinking.com**). To contact Dr. Rosalene Glickman, please write or call:

The World Academy of Personal Development, Inc.
449 S. Beverly Drive, Suite 214
Beverly Hills, CA 90212, USA
Tel.: (310) 557-2761 Fax: (310) 557-2762
E-mail: *info@optimalthinking.com*

Index